IMAGES
of America

UVALDE

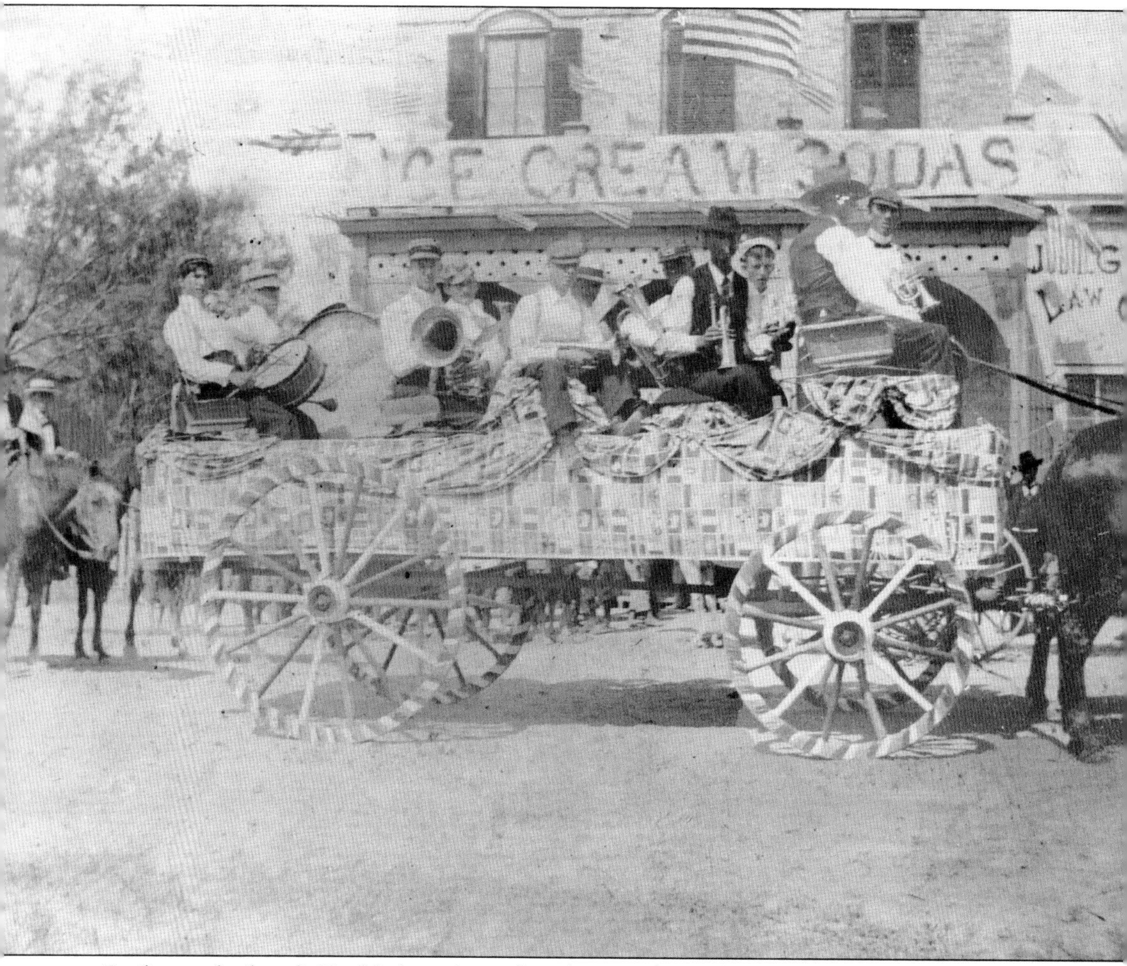

Strike up the band! Uvalde has always loved a parade, and this Fourth of July in 1897 was no exception. In the background on the right is John Garner's law office. This parade band is ready to roll down the Uvalde streets much in the same way our current marching bands do. (*Uvalde Leader News* archives.)

On the Cover: Uvalde has always taken pride in its ability to grow and change with the times. From the initial freight wagon trains of Reading Wood Black, Uvalde's founder, that ferried goods south to Piedras Negras and Old Mexico and those heading west to the frontier beyond Del Rio, growth has been a driving force in Uvalde's success. With the coming of the iron horse and Southern Pacific Railroad, Uvalde embraced a more efficient way to get goods and fresh produce to the larger towns to the east. The lead vehicle in this photograph was the first bus that ran between Uvalde and Crystal City around 1910. This group of businessmen was a committee of concerned citizens who raised $5,000 for Uvalde's transportation needs. (*Uvalde Leader News* archives.)

IMAGES
of America

UVALDE

Beverly Hadley

ARCADIA
PUBLISHING

ISBN 978-0-7385-8531-4

Published by Arcadia Publishing
Charleston, South Carolina

Printed in the United States of America

Library of Congress Control Number: 2011934986

For all general information, please contact Arcadia Publishing:
Telephone 843-853-2070
Fax 843-853-0044
E-mail sales@arcadiapublishing.com
For customer service and orders:
Toll-Free 1-888-313-2665

Visit us on the Internet at www.arcadiapublishing.com

This book is dedicated to the Friends of John Garner Museum.

Contents

FOREWORD

Uvalde, Texas, located in Uvalde County, with its hidden springs, pure water, and juniper-and-oak-covered hills, has drawn people for generations. The community evolved from the hunting grounds of the Apache and Comanche warriors to the home of modern day farmers, artists, financiers, and educators. Spanish explorers and missionaries, westward-bound immigrants from the United States, soldiers, traders, land speculators, and explorers traversed the largely unexplored area west of San Antonio in the years of the mid-19th century, before the Civil War. Reading Black, an enterprising New Jersey merchant, founded Encina (now Uvalde) on the Sabinal River in 1853. Since those early days, Uvalde witnessed growth, a changing environment, and many people who provided significant contributions to the region, the state, and the nation.

Uvalde has seen its share of history. Thanks to the efforts of Beverly Hadley, we now have a rewarding new history that captures for the first time many new and poignant scenes of Uvalde. Prominent citizens have lived, worked, and visited Uvalde since the days when Reading Black and the first hardy settlers moved into the region. This includes Vice Pres. John Nance Garner, Gov. Dolph Briscoe Jr., actress Dale Evans, and a host of community leaders and citizens who shaped the community in prosperous and difficult times. Through hard work and research, the author uncovered a significant amount of new information and outstanding photographs to document Uvalde's history. This includes photographs from the *Uvalde Leader News* archives that have not been seen for years and many that were never published. In addition, photographs from private collections are now being published thanks to the generosity of friends and the work of the author.

Local histories play an important role in telling the story of the people who inhabit the region as they relate to greater historic events and trends. The story of Uvalde and how it changes over generations is told in both words and photographs. The people and the land are the essence of this history. Uvalde, Texas has a tremendous history and Beverly Hadley has captured some of its greater and more interesting moments in word and in image.

—Patrick Cox, Ph.D.

ACKNOWLEDGMENTS

The author would like to acknowledge and extend her warmest appreciation to editor/publisher Craig Garnet and managing editor Carol Kothmann of the *Uvalde Leader News*. Their gracious generosity and access to the *Uvalde Leader News* photo archive has allowed many photographs that would have remained hidden for years to be shared.

Thanks also go to the Dolph Briscoe Center for American History at the University of Texas at Austin for access to their vast archives. Several private individuals provided photographs, and their additions were unique. Diane Dooley contributed photographs taken by her great aunt in the late 1890s. Jody Williford and the Bludworth family contributed the 1950s hunting photographs.

Thanks to Patrick Cox for his encouragement in taking on this assignment, confidence and support while writing the manuscript, and for the wonderful foreword. I will forever be in debt to Maria Lara, my coworker at the John Nance Garner Museum—her proofreading skills and willingness to say "this does not make sense" were invaluable.

Lastly, acknowledgment must be given to the Friends of John Garner Museum and their president, John S. Blades. The work they have done over the last six years as they have raised funds, given freely of their time, and helped bring community awareness to the John Nance Garner Museum has been critical to its success. They set their goals to provide supporting funds for an elevator and the museum's second floor renovation, and they met those goals with commitment and dedication. They have been great partners to work with.

Unless otherwise noted, all images appear courtesy of the *Uvalde Leader News* archives.

Introduction

Approximately 13,000 years ago, a band of nomadic people found a shelter under the limestone bluffs, up on the Sabinal River on the way to Utopia, not far from present-day Uvalde. The shelter offered protection from the north winter winds and from the wild animals. The rich, fertile lands of Uvalde and her surrounds have offered food, shelter, fuel, and the materials necessary to sustain life long before the Spanish explorers visited the area.

Diverse is an apt description of the area around Uvalde. The southeastern part of the county consists of fertile plains thick with mesquite and many other plants with thorns. These plains were the breadbasket of Uvalde and produced products from small grains such as oat and wheat to vegetables. As one travels west, the slightly rolling ground gives way to a more semi-arid scrub brush desert. To the north, the elevation rises to 2,000 feet and meets the blue hills of Edward's Plateau, which covers the northern third of the county. Three crystal-clear spring-fed rivers divide the county, with the Sabinal River in the eastern third and the Nueces River in the western third. The smaller Frio River lies between the two. Because of this diversity, the area prospered with the city of Uvalde at its heart.

In 1836, when Texas won her independence from Mexico, Uvalde was an unsettled area in a region west of San Antonio de Béxar. The area was home to Indian tribes that would not welcome the settlers who would arrive 20 years later. The land was rich in natural resources with fertile soil, bubbling springs, and rich artesian water just waiting to be brought to the surface. The grass was thick and lush and was home to the maverick cattle descendants of those that had escaped from the Mexican and Spanish explorers years before. It would be these cattle that would be caught and branded in the 1860s and then driven north to Kansas on the great trail drives. Wild game was plentiful, as were mountain lions, bears, and wolves.

It was not until hunters, prospectors, explorers, and the Mexican army traversed the area around Uvalde that it became the main road between San Antonio and the Rio Grande. Fort Inge, one of the many frontier forts, was established just south of Uvalde. The frontier fort's mission was to protect the borderlands from the Indians and disputes on the international border with Mexico.

Reading Wood Black was one of the earliest permanent settlers in what is present-day Uvalde. He was born in New Jersey on September 23, 1830. Encouraged by the stories his cousin told of Texas, he moved there in early 1852. He purchased a half-league and labor of land (2,391 acres) with his friend Nathan L. Stratton (also from New Jersey) near the headwaters of the Leona River and present-day Uvalde. He understood the importance of being located near the Leona, as it was the last permanent water source before the Rio Grande. A hard worker, Black quickly acquired 1,000 head of sheep, built a home, and planted a garden. He then mapped and laid out the town he called Encina (present-day Uvalde). During this time, he also opened a store, operated a limekiln and rock quarry, built a gristmill, and established Uvalde's first school. An astute businessman, Black established a wagon train that handled freight between San Antonio and Piedras Negras. Black, with his Unionist leanings and repulsed by the actions of the Confederate home guards, moved to Mexico in 1862 and remained there through the Civil War. On October 3, 1867, at the age of 37, Black was gunned down and killed while tending his store in Uvalde. His early death was a tragic loss for Uvalde. While the city continued to flourish, it only did so due to the foundation that Black established.

From the beginning with Black's store, trade was key to Uvalde's success. With the freight wagon trains traveling west from San Antonio, Uvalde had a steady flow of fresh supplies coming into town. When these same wagons made the return trip to San Antonio they were full of Uvalde goods. Uvalde's design, with the four plazas at the center of town, made for a thriving business center. With time and use, the road from San Antonio to Del Rio improved.

The settlements of Utopia, Concan, and Montell were in the northern part of the county and a two-day horse ride from town. Uvalde is where they traded. They would make the journey to Uvalde by wagon or on horseback to sell their goods and buy more supplies for the rest of the season. Many settlers would only make it to town once or twice a year due to the distance. There was a need for wagon yards in Uvalde as a safe place for wagons to be parked until produce could be sold and supplies repurchased. The wagon yard at Market Plaza was just one of several, as many general stores had a wagon yard for their customers' convenience.

The coming of the railway in 1883 increased Uvalde's importance as a major commercial center. With the railroad came cattle by the thousands to the holding pens at the railway siding. However, to get to the siding, the cattle had to be driven through town and up Getty Street. With only dirt roads, the dust would have been suffocating. The Uvalde railhead was two miles north of downtown and the contract with the railroad prohibited any town development at the new railhead. The introduction of a light railway company with small rail cars to ferry heavy freight to and from the railhead to the plaza area was an important addition to the local economy. This arrangement also guaranteed that the trading center for the area would stay in downtown Uvalde and not be moved to the railhead.

Even with the early growth, life was hard for the new settlers not only from the constant threat of Indians and wildlife but also natural disasters. One of the worst floods of the area was the 1894 flood. The floodwaters reached Getty Street and many citizens had to be plucked off roofs or out of trees. The community of Leona Ditch, eight miles south of the town square, was wiped off the map. The water rose so fast that most only escaped with the clothes they had on and whatever they could grab: a child, a bible, or a kitten. Sadly, many did not survive the flood. Afterwards, the remaining residents sold out and moved to Uvalde.

Agriculture, both farming and ranching, has been Uvalde's lifeblood since her founding. The rich fertile soil has grown everything from cabbage and onions to spinach and sesame. Cotton also grew well here, especially with irrigation. Corn, wheat, and oats have been vital to the livestock industry. Uvalde is great cattle country because of the area's strong, fertile soil that grows thick, nutritious grasses. To this day agriculture is just as important to Uvalde as it was in the late 1800s.

The cattle industry grew with Uvalde. The flat brush country with the mild climate was made for raising cattle. With the advent of the automobile, the trail drives through town came to an end. They were replaced with trucks hauling cattle to the sale barn and then on to the railcars for shipment east. However, the railroad came to an end in 1966 and no longer stops in Uvalde.

The Angora goat became the cash animal for Uvalde from the late 1880s to the 1980s. The area was excellent for raising goats and they flourished. Due to the Angora, Uvalde became one of the top counties in mohair production in the state.

Hunting has always been a form of recreation for Uvalde. The early settlers had to fight bears, mountain lions, and wolves for their survival. Predation by these animals also took a toll on the livestock, which affected financial survival. It was only the cooperative effort of every landowner against these predators that allowed livestock to become a viable commodity. The countryside was rich with wild game, and they offered a free food source for the settler. The white tail deer that roamed the area were to become an additional source of income to the landowners after

World War II, when Uvalde became one of the hunting capitals of Texas. It offered the rancher additional income by way of deer leases to hunters from the big cities of Dallas and Houston.

John Nance Garner came to Uvalde in his early 20s. He hung out his shingle as a lawyer and then traveled the area as a circuit-riding judge either by horseback or buggy. In doing so, he learned what was important to the people. When he was elected to the US Congress in 1902, he represented the area he used to visit on horseback. His congressional district covered an area from Uvalde to Del Rio, down to Brownsville, and up to Corpus Christi. Garner went on to represent this area for 30 years, with two of those as the powerful speaker of the House of Representatives. Then Garner "took the only demotion he ever had," and was elected vice president during the first two terms of Pres. Franklin Roosevelt. Uvalde loved Garner, the little stocky man with a cigar and bushy white eyebrows, and in turn, he took care of Uvalde the best he could.

Dolph Briscoe was destined to be a cowboy. He was born and raised in Uvalde and loved working cattle on the family ranch. After graduating from the University of Texas, he served in the army. On his return to Uvalde, he and his wife, Janey, took up ranching at the Dry Rio Frio, and he served in the Texas legislature. Upon the death of his father, the younger Briscoe took up the reins of the family ranching business. Briscoe was responsible for the eradication of the screwworm, a parasitic worm that would feast on open wounds and kill the livestock at alarming rates. He also understood the difficulties remote ranchers and farmers faced when getting their produce or stock to market. One of the biggest changes to the rural fabric of Texas was the introduction of the farm-to-market roads that Briscoe initiated. After serving from 1973 to 1979 as governor of Texas, Briscoe returned to the town he loved, ranched, and was chairman of the board of First State Bank of Uvalde, the bank Garner used to own.

As you view the photographs in this book, enjoy the trip back in time, but remember, it is important that stories be recorded with photographs. Therefore, I encourage all readers to take the time to record their own family's history along with their pictures. It only takes a generation for the stories to be lost forever.

One

On the Banks of the Leona River

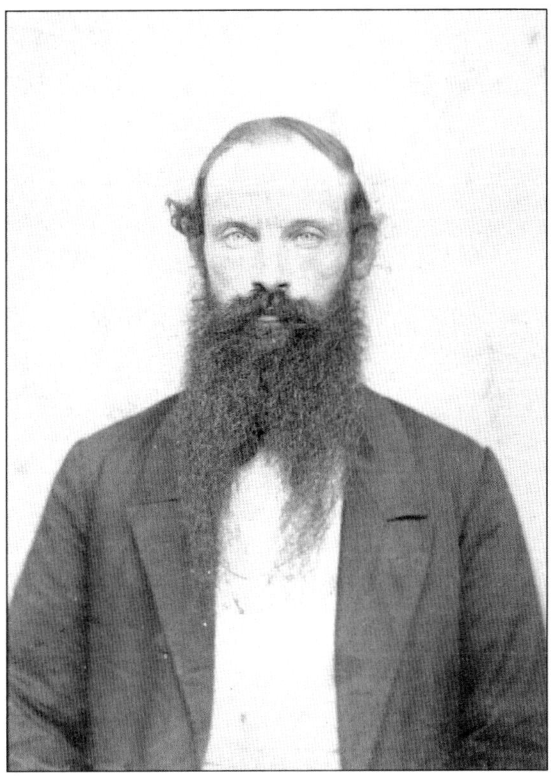

When Reading Wood Black laid out the town, it was known as Encina because of the live oaks that covered the area. It was changed to Uvalde when the county was finally organized a year later, in 1856. One of the biggest problems the area faced was the constant threat by Indians. Black was a Quaker, and kindness and tolerance were his strengths. (Briscoe Center for American History.)

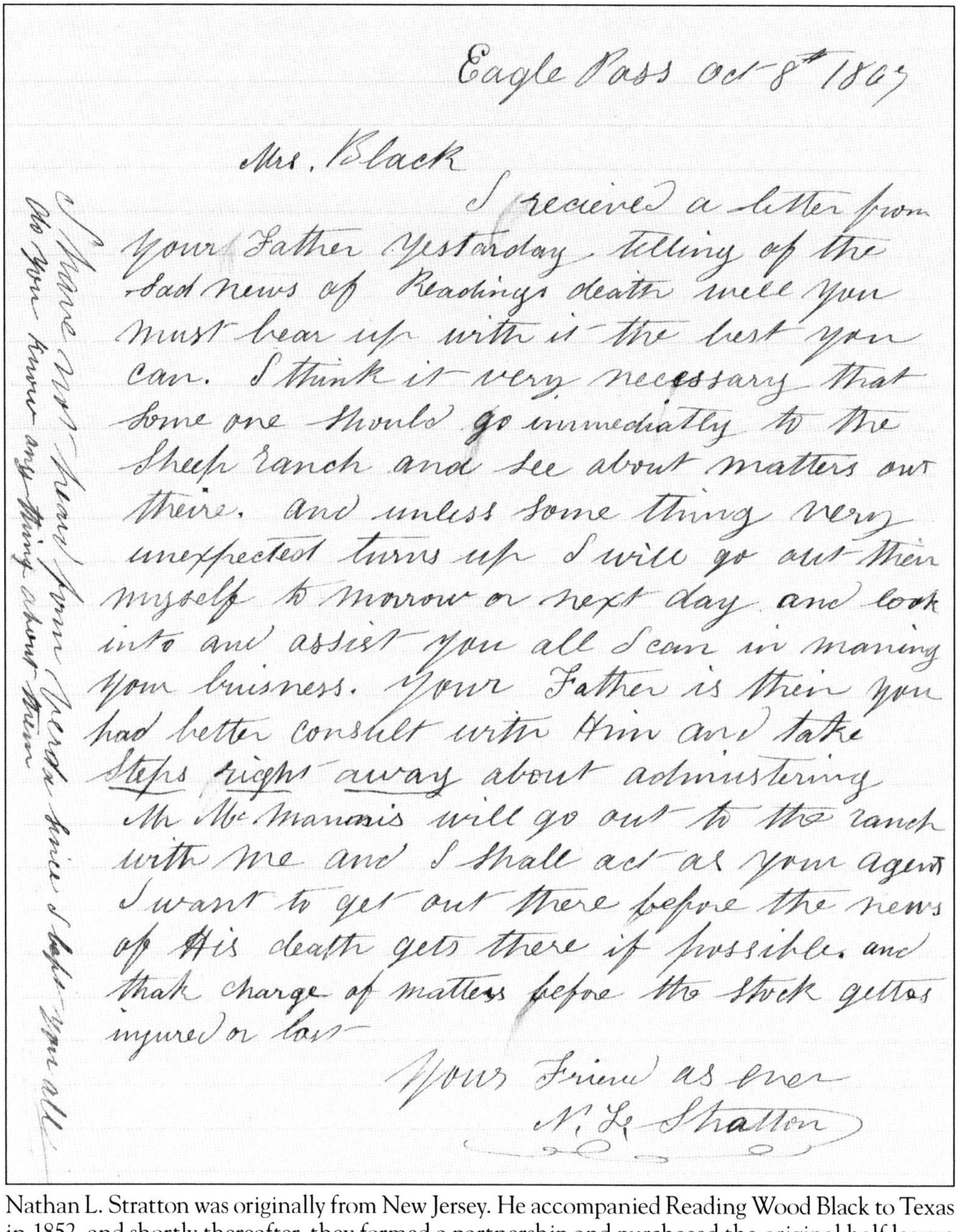

Eagle Pass Oct 8th 1867

Mrs. Black

I recieved a letter from your Father yestarday. telling of the sad news of Readings death well you must bear up with it the best you can. I think it very necessary that some one should go immediatly to the Sheep ranch and see about matters out there. and unless some thing very unexpected turns up I will go out then myself to morrow or next day and look into and assist you all I can in maning your buisness. Your Father is their you had better consult with Him and take Steps right away about administering Mr McMannis will go out to the ranch with me and I shall act as your agent I want to get out there before the news of His death gets there if possible. and thak charge of matters before the stock getts injured or loss

Your Friend as ever

N. L. Stratton

I have not heard from Uvalde since I left you all do you know any thing about them

Nathan L. Stratton was originally from New Jersey. He accompanied Reading Wood Black to Texas in 1852, and shortly thereafter, they formed a partnership and purchased the original half league and labor of land (2,391 acres) that is the site of present-day Uvalde. This partnership remained strong throughout the life of the men. In this letter, dated October 8, 1867, five days after the fatal shooting of Reading Wood Black, Stratton offers his condolences to Permilla Black "of the sad news of Readings [sic] death." Stratton then offers his assistance at the sheep ranch and shows concern with the need to oversee its day-to-day administration. His concern was so great that he wrote, "Mr. McMannis will go out to the ranch with me and I shall act as your agent. I want to get out there before the news of His death gets there if possible. And thak [sic] charge of matters before the stock gets injured or loss." (Briscoe Center for American History.)

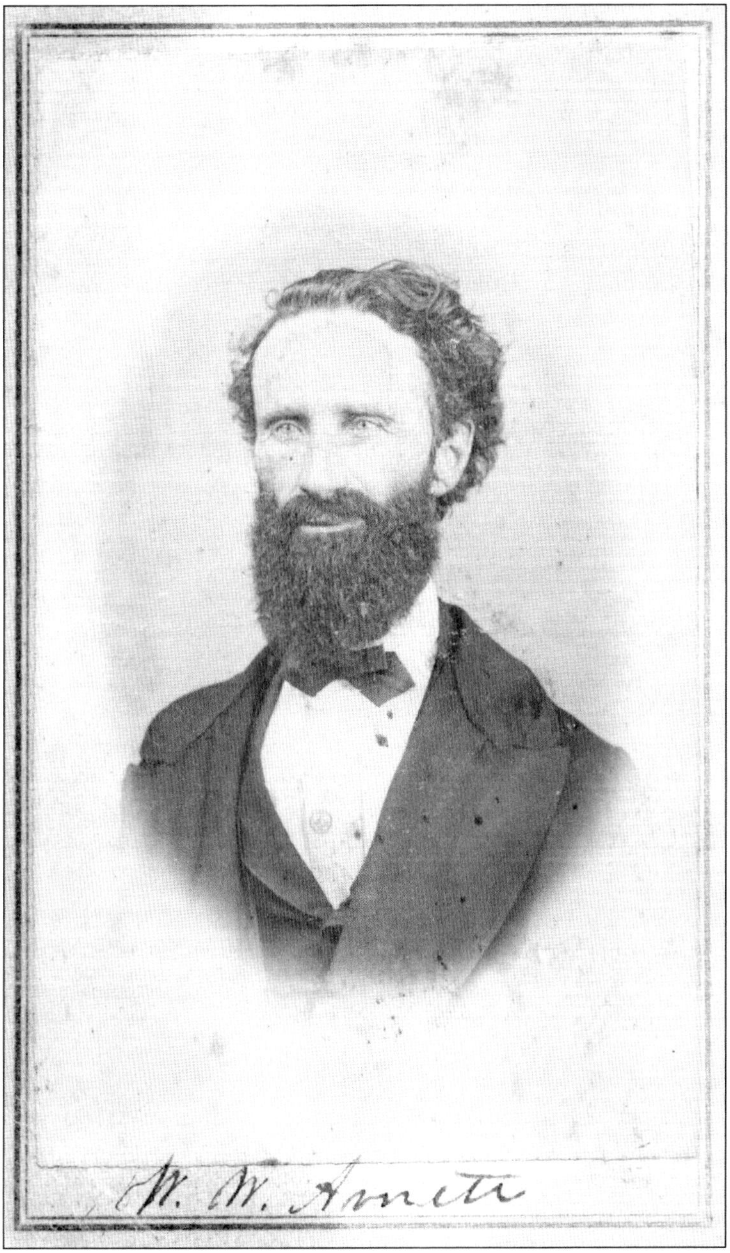

William Washington Arnett was born in Franklin County, Alabama, on January 5, 1823. He moved to Texas from Mississippi in 1845, after his marriage proposal to a local heiress was rejected. He resided with family in Tyler County, married, and eventually served in the Mexican War as a private until 1848. In 1852, Arnett, with his wife and children, moved to the present site of Uvalde. One of his closest neighbors was Reading Wood Black. Life was difficult; the Arnetts' land and home were remote and the area dangerous. He chronicled that the threat from wild animals, especially wolves and lions, were as constant as that from the hostile Indian tribes. From his home on the banks of the Leona River, Arnett delivered hay to the Army at Fort Inge. During 1856, he served in Capt. Reading Wood Black's company of minutemen. (Briscoe Center for American History.)

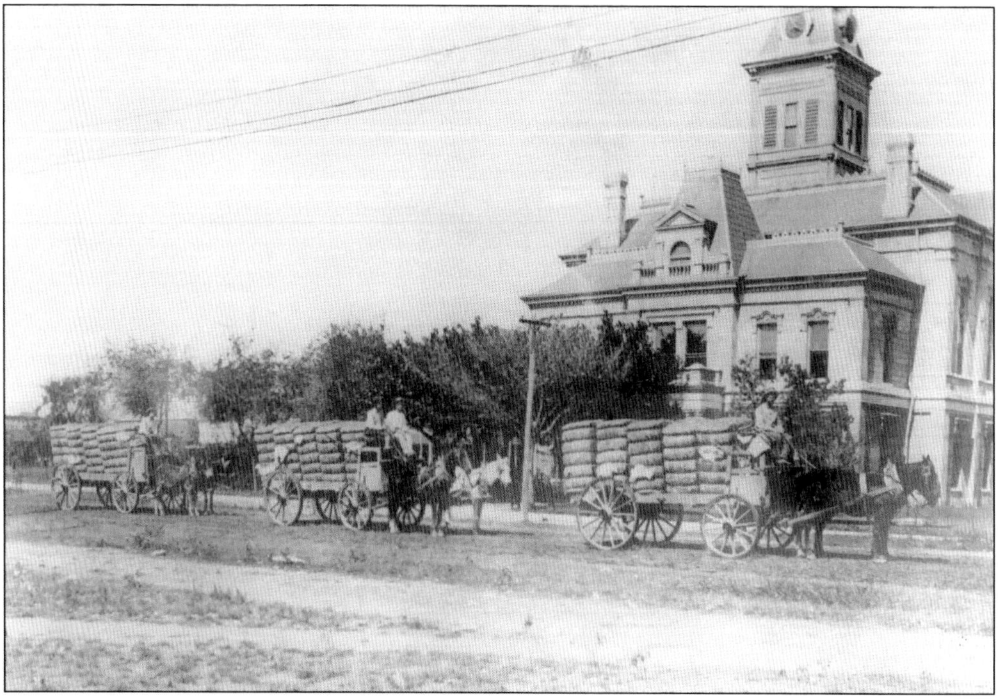

Uvalde's beautiful square and wide streets should most likely be credited to German surveyor and lithographer William Thielepape, who Reading Wood Black hired to survey and plat out the town. As the many street scenes of early Uvalde in this book are viewed, the planning that went into this beautiful town should be remembered. Above, the 1890s courthouse is framed by freight wagons carrying cotton and pulled by mules. The April 25, 1910, photograph below was taken looking north on Getty Street. The ever-popular Uvalde Grand Opera House is on the left. For a Monday, the town appears very busy.

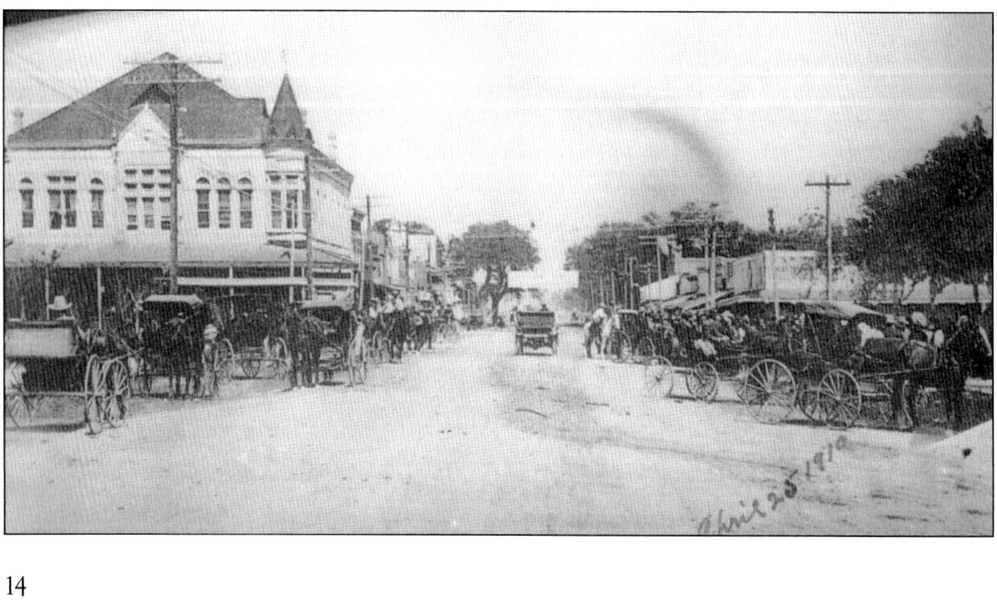

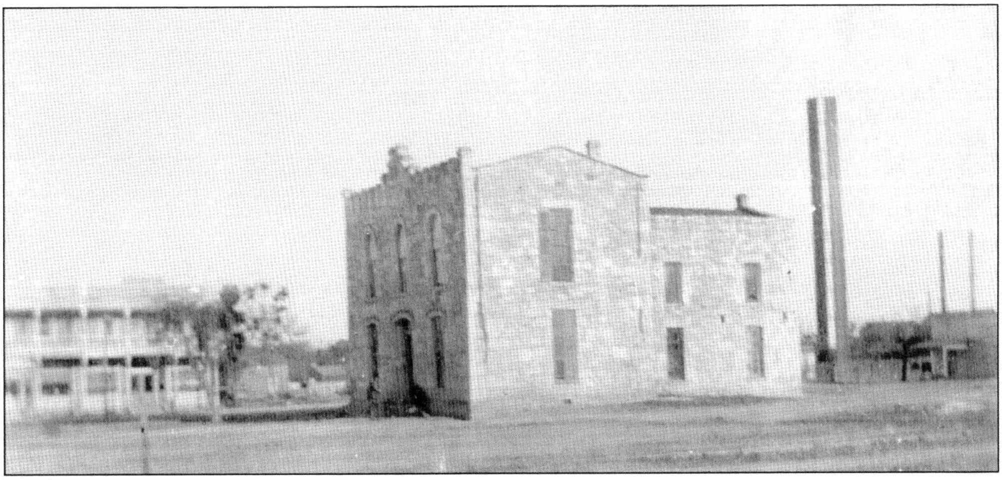

In Reading Wood Black's plan for the town he established on the banks of the Leona River, the town hall square was in the southeast part. One of the first structures on this square was the County Jail, constructed of native stone. Eventually, the city government took over the location. As hard financial times hit in 1900, the city hall was rented to the law firm of Ellis and Garner. Later, to make way for a larger facility, the building was torn down and the rocks were used for construction of the bandstand at Memorial Park. (Diane Dooley and *Uvalde Leader News* archives.)

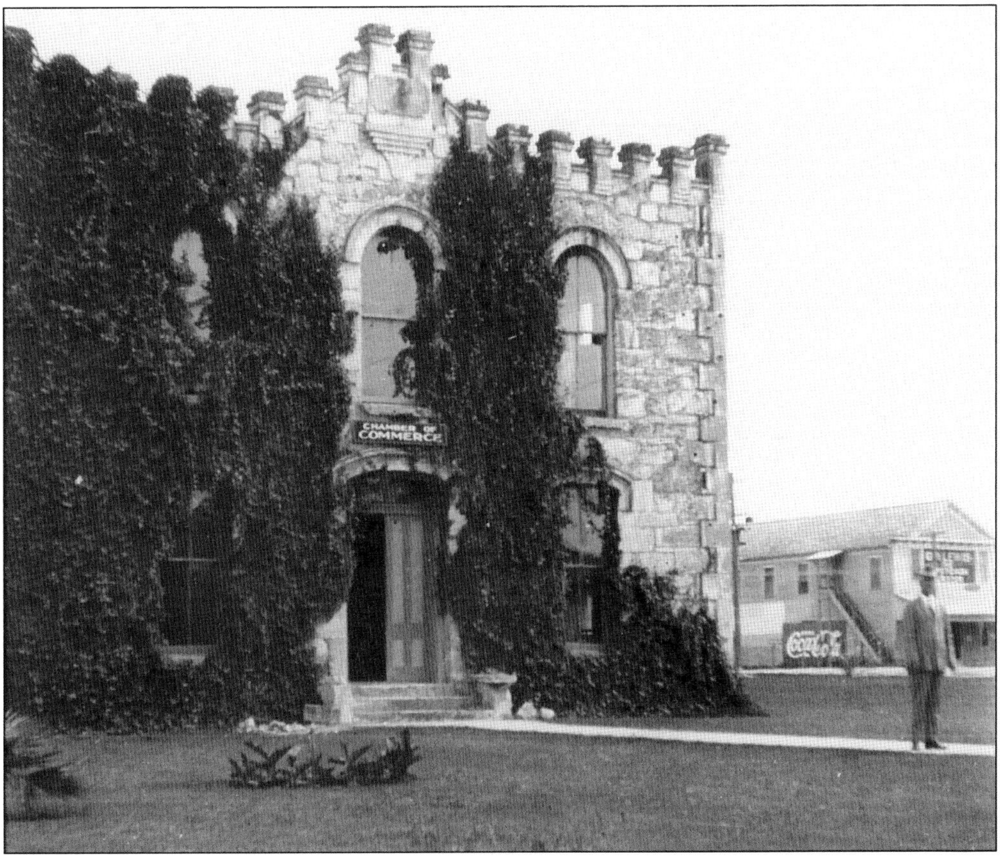

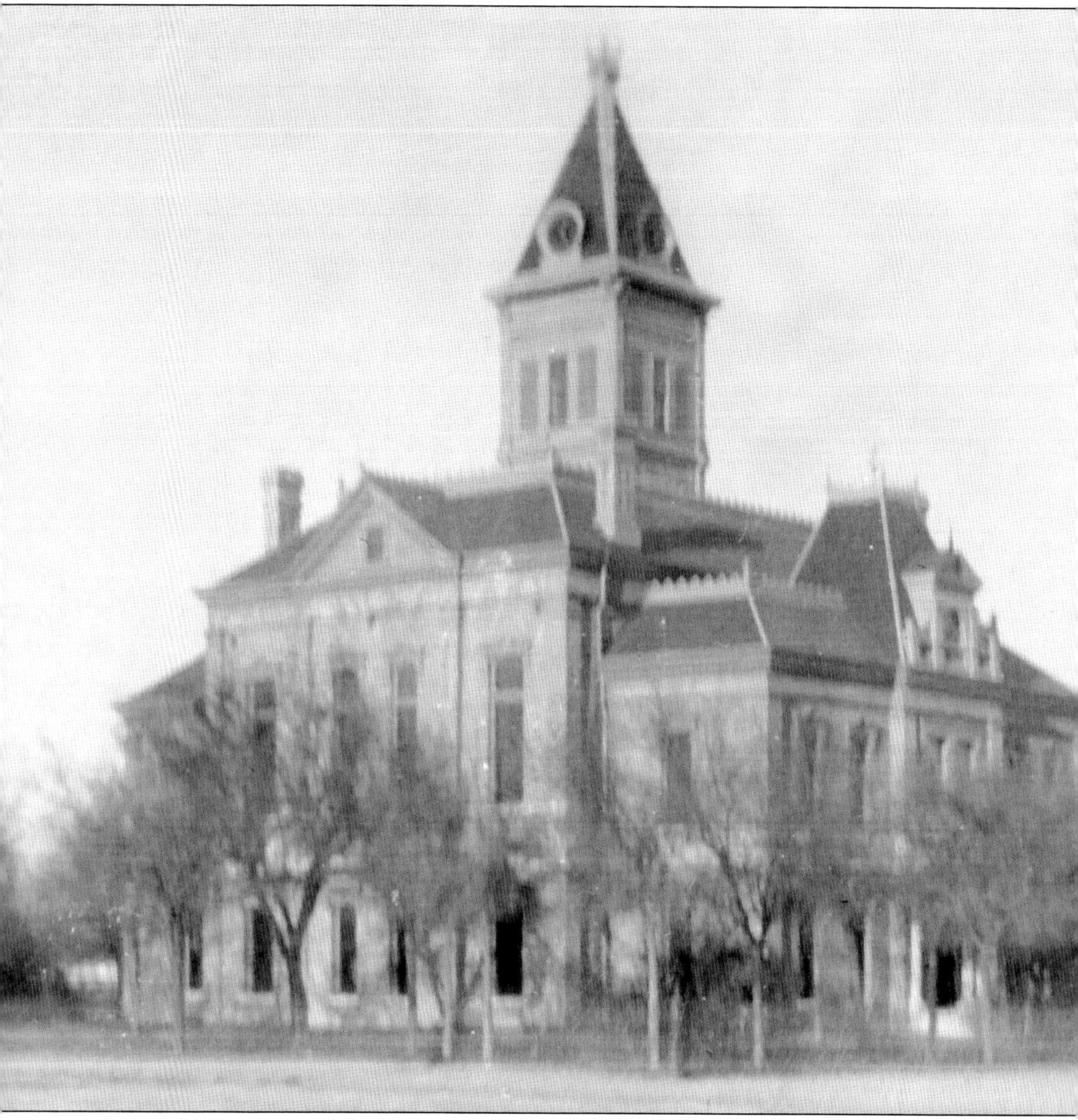

Designed by Benjamin F. Trester, a San Antonio architect, the 1890 Uvalde County Courthouse is considered one of his finest works. Benjamin F. Trester was in vogue during the last half of the 19th century and in much demand for his work. He became one of the most popular architects working in the building boom that spread across Texas in the late 1800s. The courthouse is in the style of Romanesque Revival architecture and combines design elements of 11th-and-12th-century French, Spanish, and Italian architecture. This is very evident in the short squat columns, recessed entrances, and the bands of windows seen in the courthouse design. The 1890 Uvalde County Courthouse and the 1891 Uvalde Grand Opera House were the last works completed by Trester, who died in 1891. The 1890 courthouse was replaced in 1927 with the current courthouse. Only the iron vault of the 1890 courthouse remains today. (Diane Dooley.)

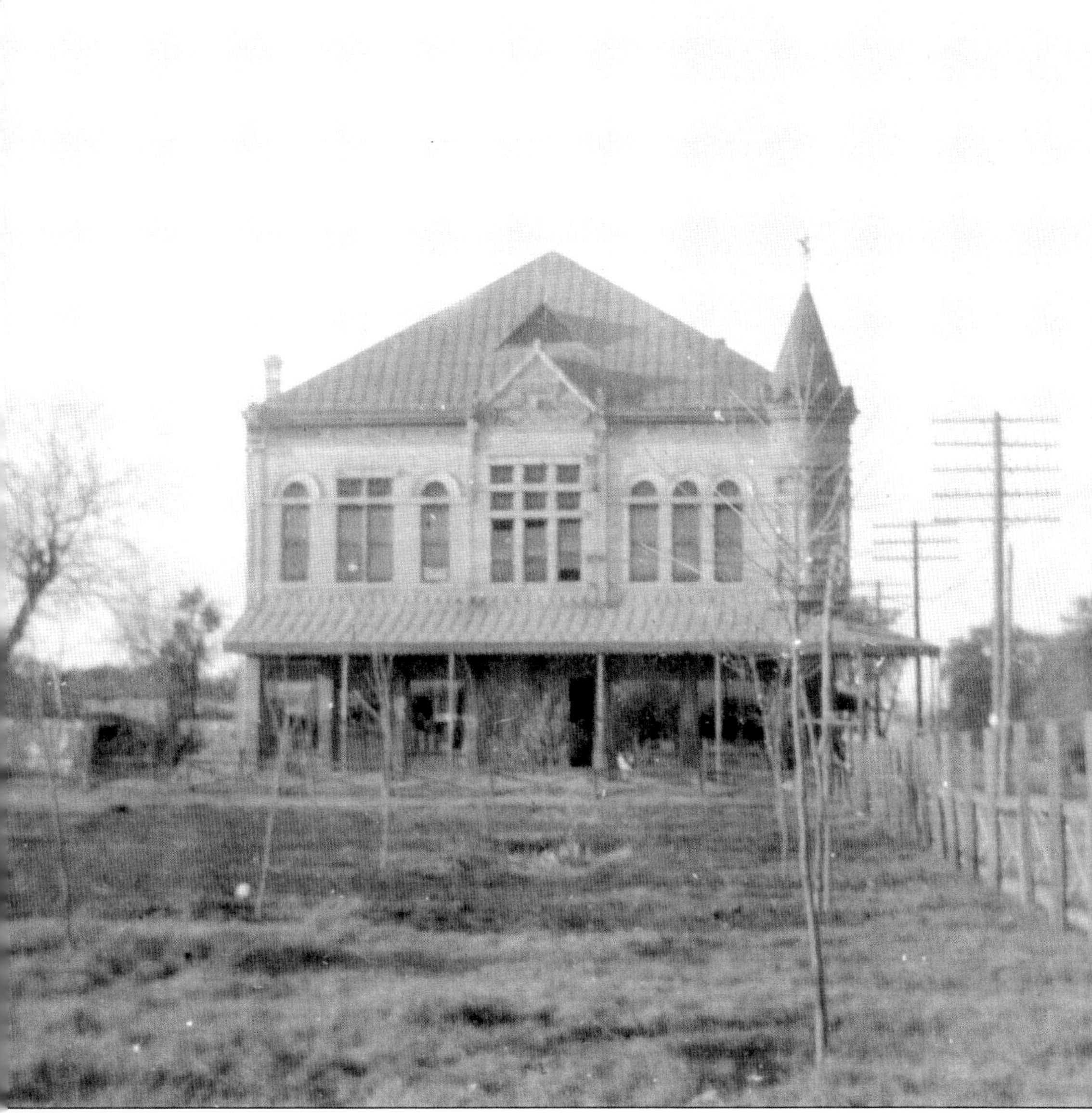

Constructed in 1891, the two-story Uvalde Grand Opera House is located on the town square at the corner of North Street and North Getty Street. Benjamin F. Trester, a San Antonio architect, designed the two-story, 8,500-square-foot building. Grocery, drug, and antique stores, as well as restaurants, have occupied the ground floor. The second floor was dedicated to office space and theater. Reading Wood Black was the original owner of the land. In 1891, the title transferred to the Uvalde Real Estate and Building Company, a partnership between local businessmen, merchants, and ranchers for promoting and building the opera house. In 1916, John Nance Garner bought the opera house and had his office in the large corner office with the oriel bay window so he could overlook the town and all the action. The building stayed in the Garner family until 1978, when it was donated to the City of Uvalde. (Diane Dooley.)

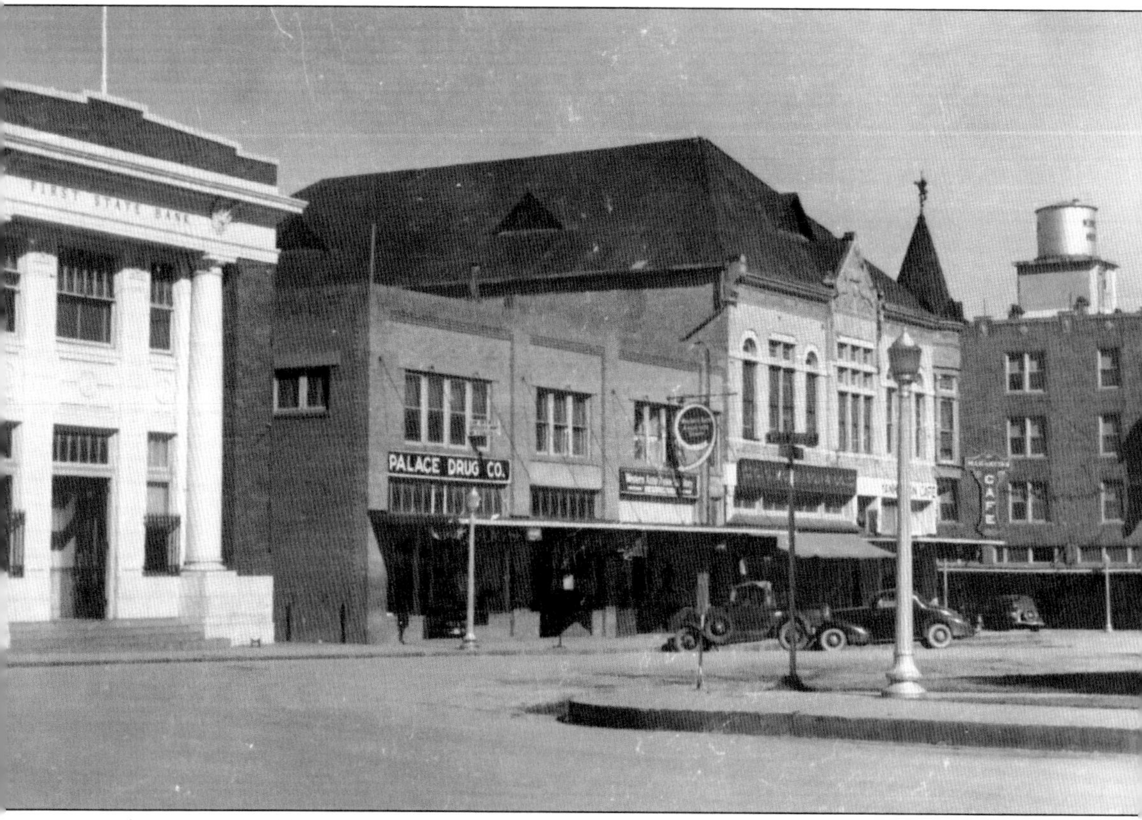

The cost to build and construct the Uvalde Grand Opera House in 1891 was $13,600. From the weathervane dragon greedily eating a snake to the beautiful copper roof, the building was designed to capture the eye. Made with local brick at a long-gone kiln south of Uvalde, it was the pride and joy of early Uvalde. With a unique interior layout that had commercial space on the ground floor, the facility provided a source of income for its owner. The original theater space, with its stage and theater seating, had a main curtain painted with a garden scene and local advertisements. The building hosted not only theater by traveling troupes, but was the social center of the community. The advent of World War I brought the end of traveling theater and the beginning of change for Uvalde's Opera House.

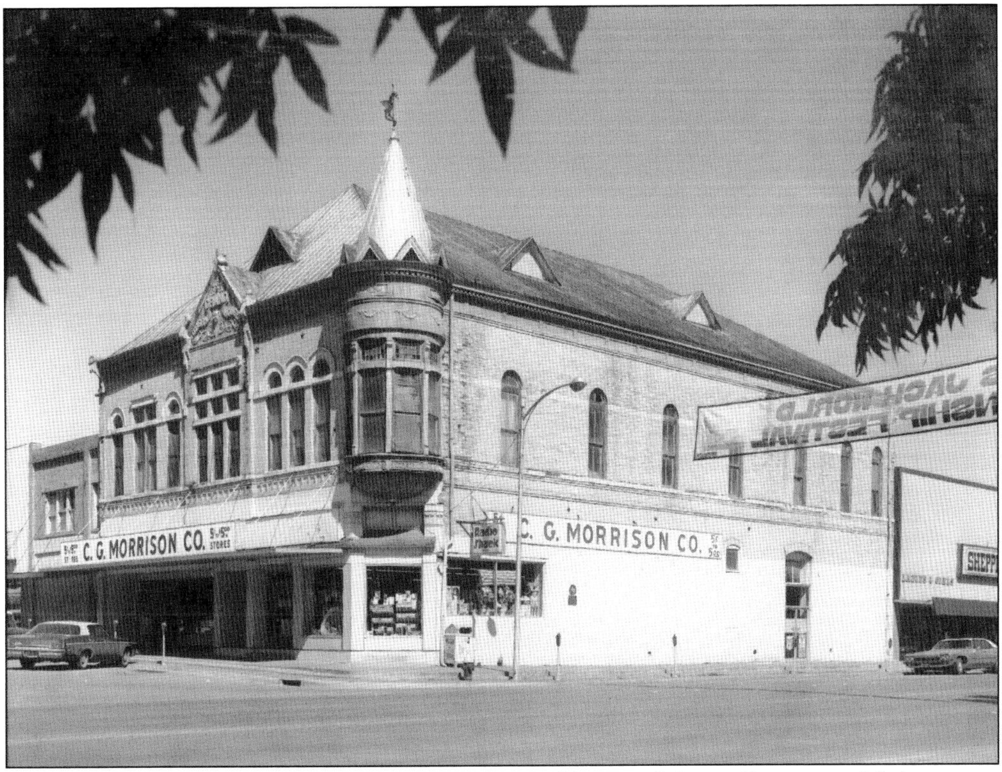

Continually occupied with commercial space, the Uvalde Grand Opera House most likely owes its survival to this unusual arrangement. The ground floor has housed everything from F.A. Piper's general store, the C.G. Morrison Company, and a five-and-dime store that was a forerunner to the dollar store found in today's local strip malls. The second floor was partitioned into offices after World War I and the seats removed. Then the area was leased to local attorneys, dentists, physicians, and later as a storage area for the five-and-dime. Behind the storage room, the old stage is still visible. After time, even these businesses fell by the wayside, and the building fell into disuse.

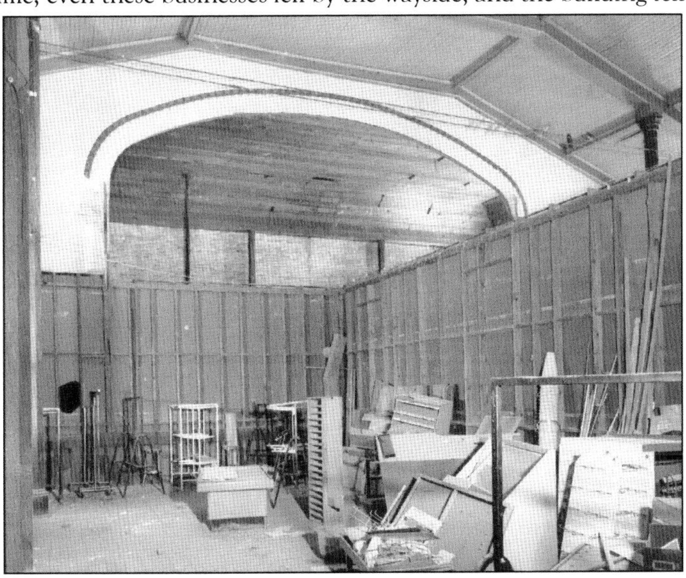

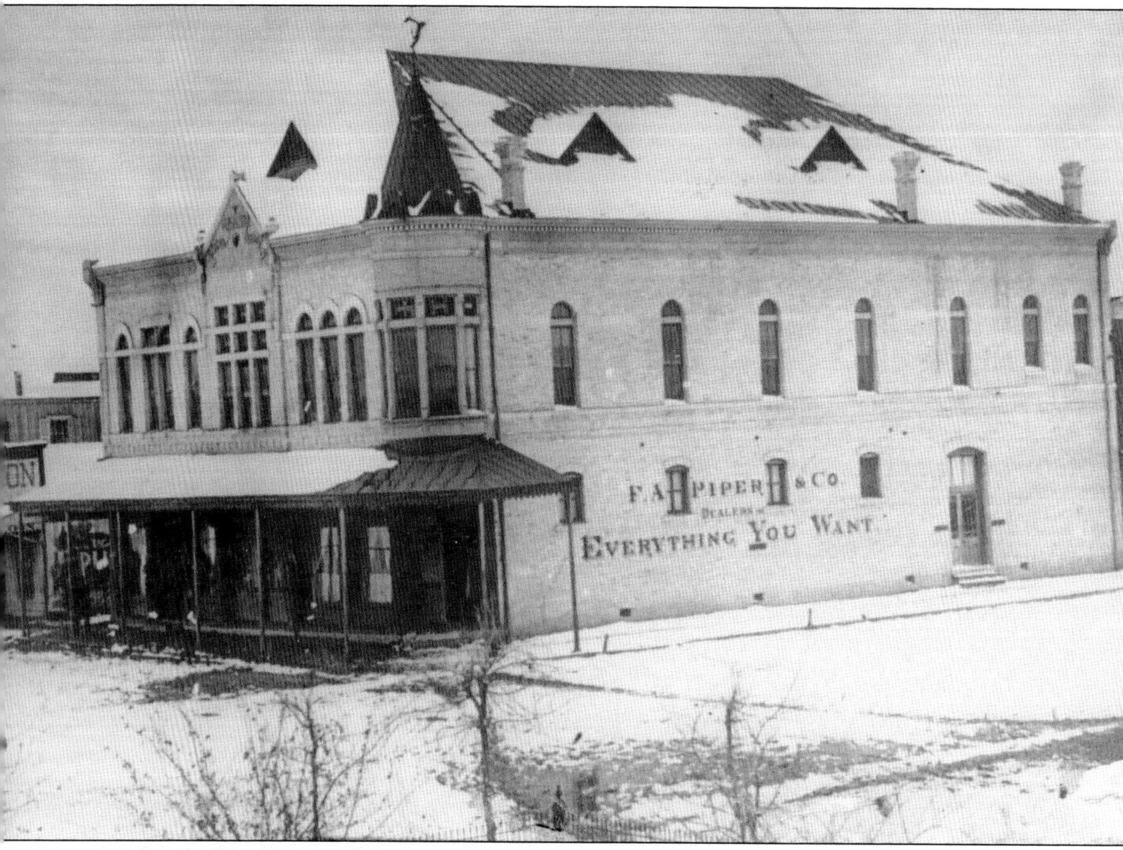

Today, the Uvalde Grand Opera House is the oldest functioning theater in the state. The building was listed in the National Register of Historic Places in May 1978, and in July 1978, the descendents of the John Nance Garner family donated the facility to the City of Uvalde. Restored by the city in 1980, the opera house was brought back to life. Commercial space was still part of the ground floor along with the opera house office. In addition, the ground floor hosts an exhibit area that displays the history of the opera house, her renovations, and Governor Briscoe's gubernatorial campaign. The stage and theater area were restored to their previous beauty and once again host all types of performances. Thanks to the hard work of concerned citizens and the City of Uvalde, today the Uvalde Grand Opera House is once again a "Grand Old Dame."

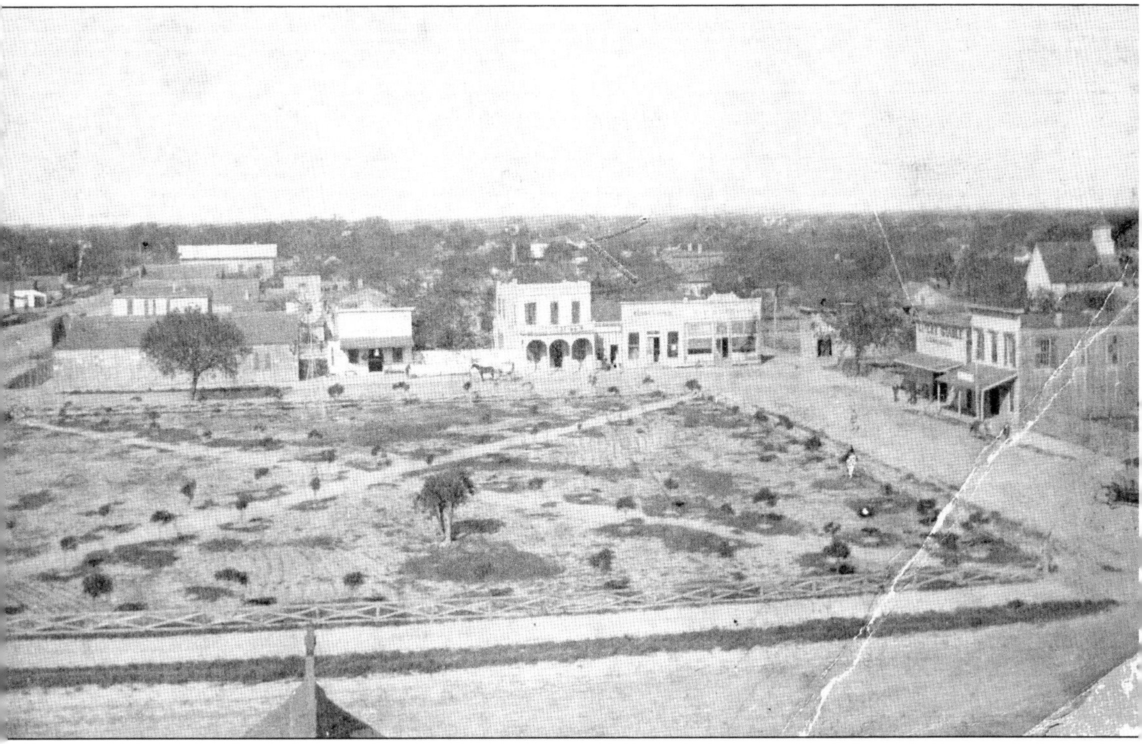

Uvalde's main wagon yard was located on the northwest square, also known as Market Plaza, across from the Uvalde Grand Opera House. Wagon yards were in every town and were a place where drivers and their teams could rest, find a meal, and spend as much time as needed, from several hours to several weeks, while they conducted business. Due to the distance, some Uvalde area farmers and ranchers only made two supply trips a year into town. Those with 15 or 20 miles to travel would need to break the trip up into several days, and the wagon yards provided a safe place to stay. Most wagon yards were located near the business section, had camp houses for cooking and sleeping, and stalls and feed for the horses and oxen. Rental charges at the end of the 19th century ranged from a nickel for a few hours to 15¢ for an overnight stay.

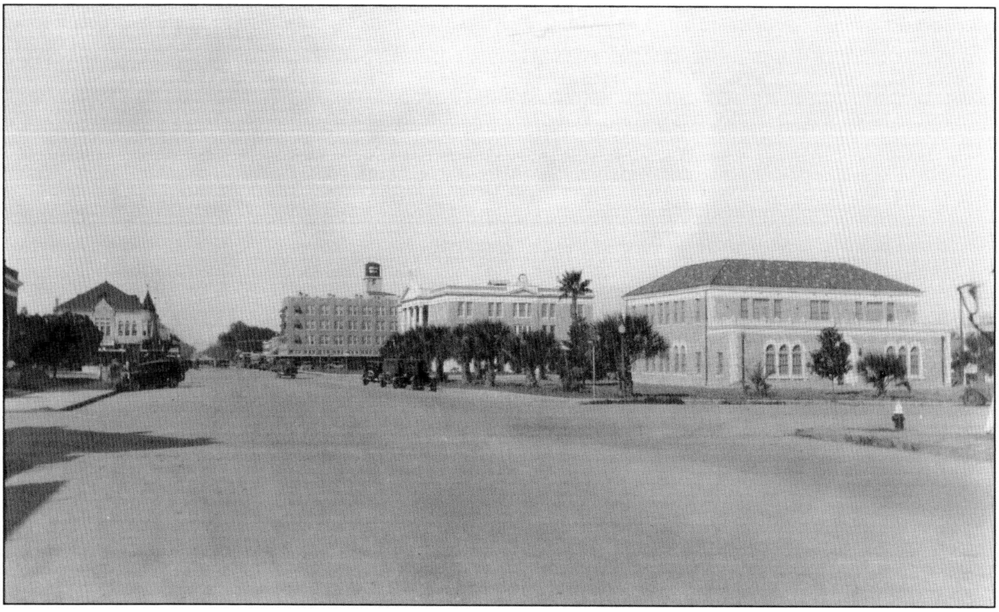

South Getty Street is also US Highway 83, the longest highway running north to south in the United States. On the right are the Uvalde City Hall, Uvalde County Courthouse, and the Kincaid Hotel, and on the left is the Uvalde Grand Opera House.

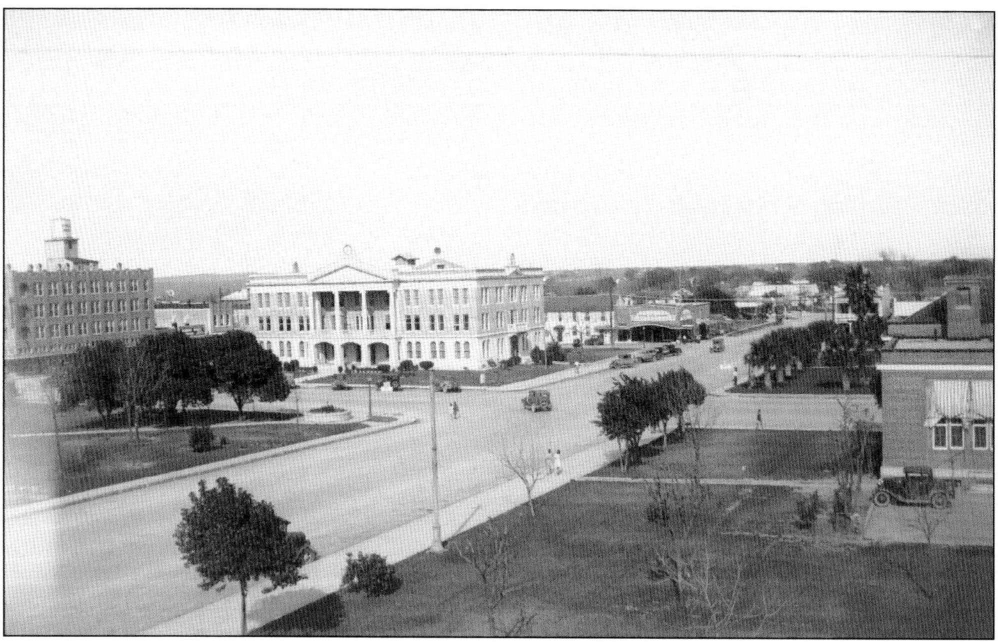

This photograph was taken looking east at Main Street, which is also US Highway 90, the longest east to west highway in the continental United States. With the Kincaid Hotel, Uvalde County Courthouse, and the post office, the view offers a good perspective of the city center. It also shows the crossroads of the two longest highways in the United States.

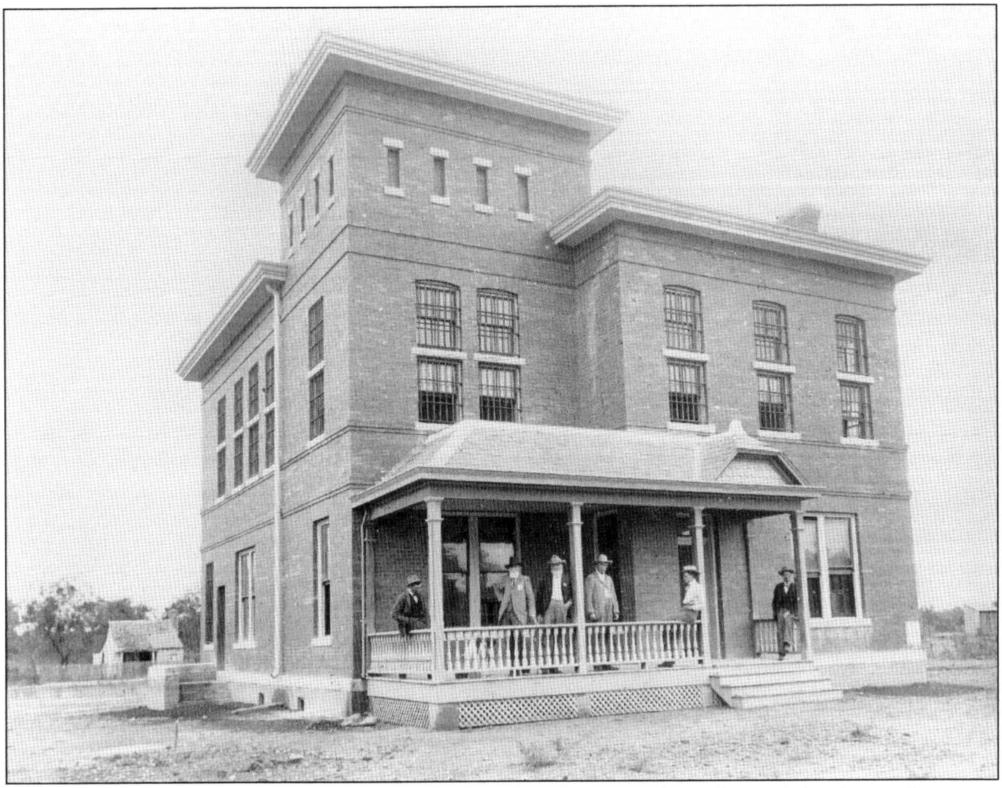

Uvalde had several jails in different locations in her younger days. One of the first jails was in the native stone city hall on Town Hall Plaza. This three-story city jail was built in the latter half of the 1890s. The building had offices on the first floor and the jail on the upper floors. The building of the new jail required some cooperation between the city and the citizens. The cesspool associated with the jail became a little rank, and a number of complaints were received. To remedy the problem, the city constructed a sewer that emptied into the Leona River, a common practice at the time.

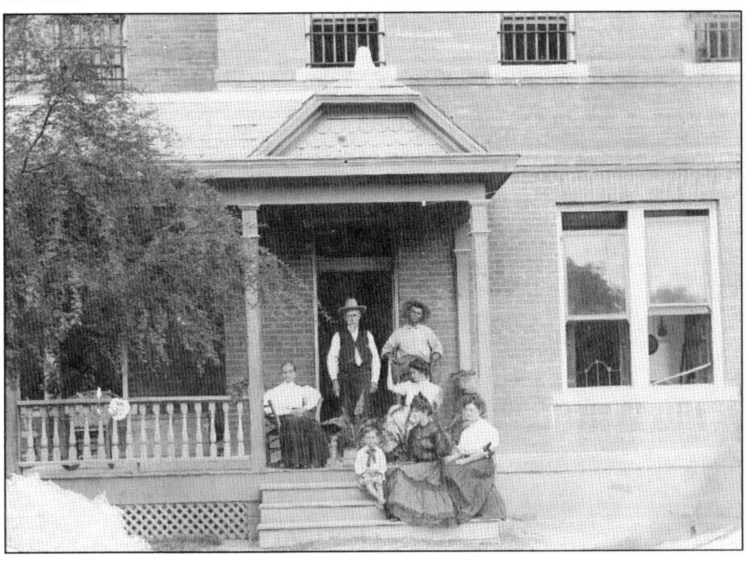

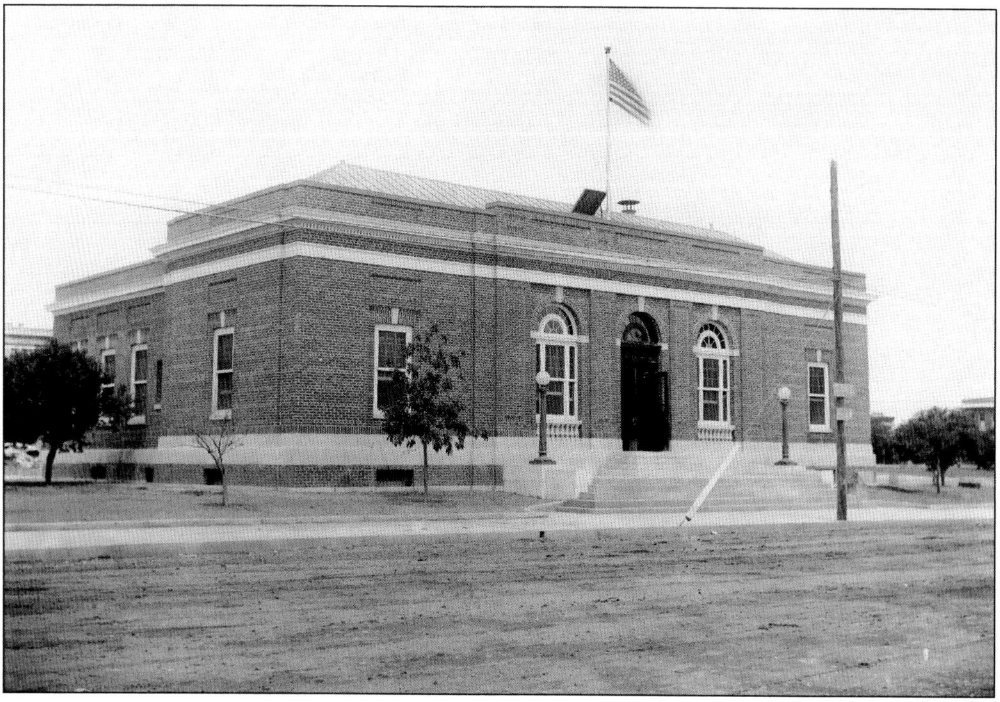

The first post office in Uvalde made several location changes between Fort Inge and Uvalde between 1854 and 1868. However, Uvalde was finally selected as the permanent location for the Uvalde Post Office in 1868. The facility was located in Reading Black's store and on East Main Street. The city donated Fountain Plaza to the US government in 1910 for the future post office and federal building. Construction started in 1915 and when completed, the two-story building had twin iron spiral staircases in the front entry. In 1963, the post office was moved to temporary quarters for five years during renovations and modernization of the building.

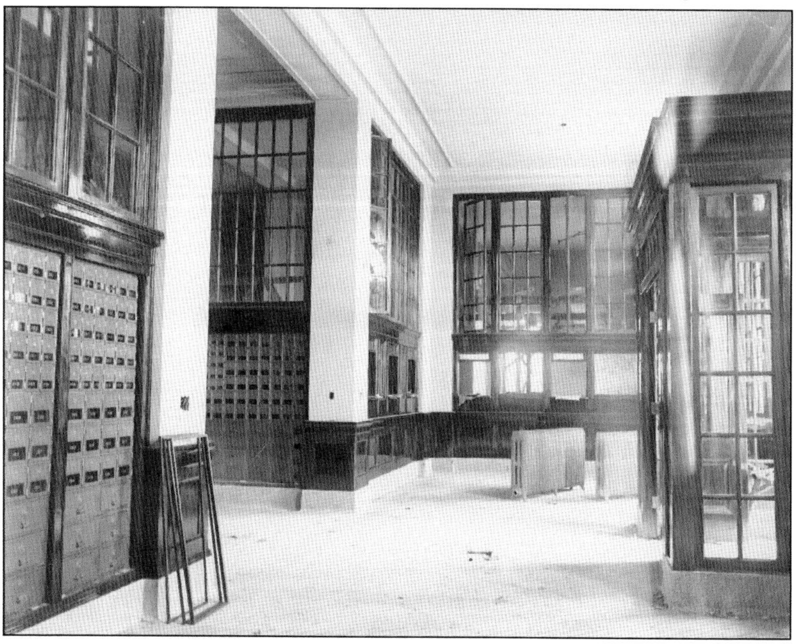

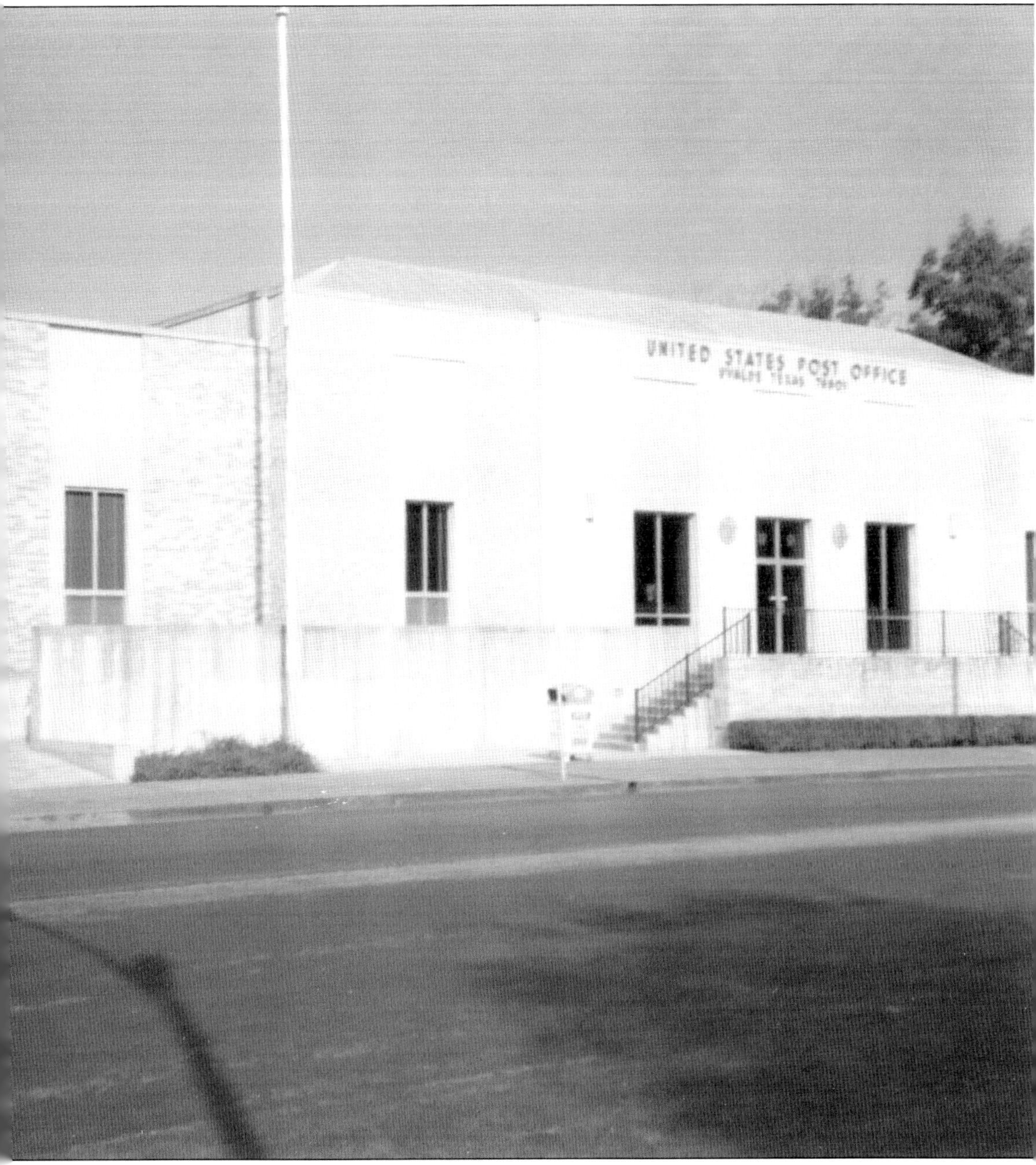

The 1963 expansion of the post office was done to acquire more floor space for the facility. Part of the renovations included a face-lift and the addition of a long ramp along the front of the building. A drive-through mail drop-off lane was also added at this time. During the 110th US Congress, Rep. Ciro D. Rodriguez introduced a bill to designate the facility of the United States Postal Service, located at 103 South Getty Street in Uvalde, Texas, as the "Dolph Briscoe Jr. Post Office Building." Senators Kay Bailey Hutchison and John Cornyn introduced a similar bill into the US Senate. On November 17, 2007, a dedication ceremony renaming the post office occurred and was attended by many in Uvalde. Former governor Dolph Briscoe was on hand to receive the honor from Senator Hutchison and Representative Rodriguez.

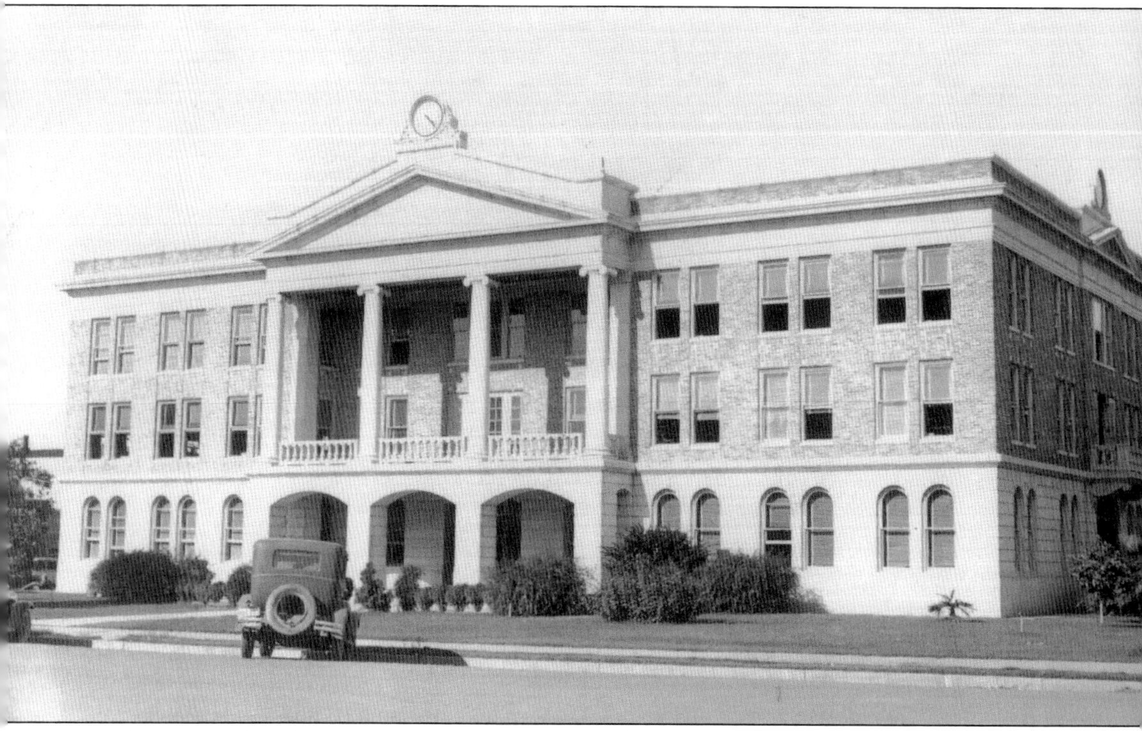

The present-day Uvalde County Courthouse was designed by Henry Truman Phelps (1871–1944), a prominent San Antonio architect. In San Antonio, he designed several commercial buildings including the J.M. Nix Professional Building (1929) and the Maverick Building. His courthouse work included the courthouses in Schleicher, Blanco, and Atascosa Counties. He also redesigned the Dimmit County Courthouse in Carrizo Spring (1925). Built in 1927, the Uvalde building was of neoclassical design with a symmetrical shape, tall columns, and a triangular pediment on each of the four sides of the building. The cost to construct the building was $150,570. The current courthouse was the fifth one built; it replaced the stately Romanesque Revival–style courthouse of 1890. The first courthouse in Uvalde was a combination courthouse and jail contracted to Reading Black in May 1856. Little did he know that he would serve as county judge four years later, in 1860.

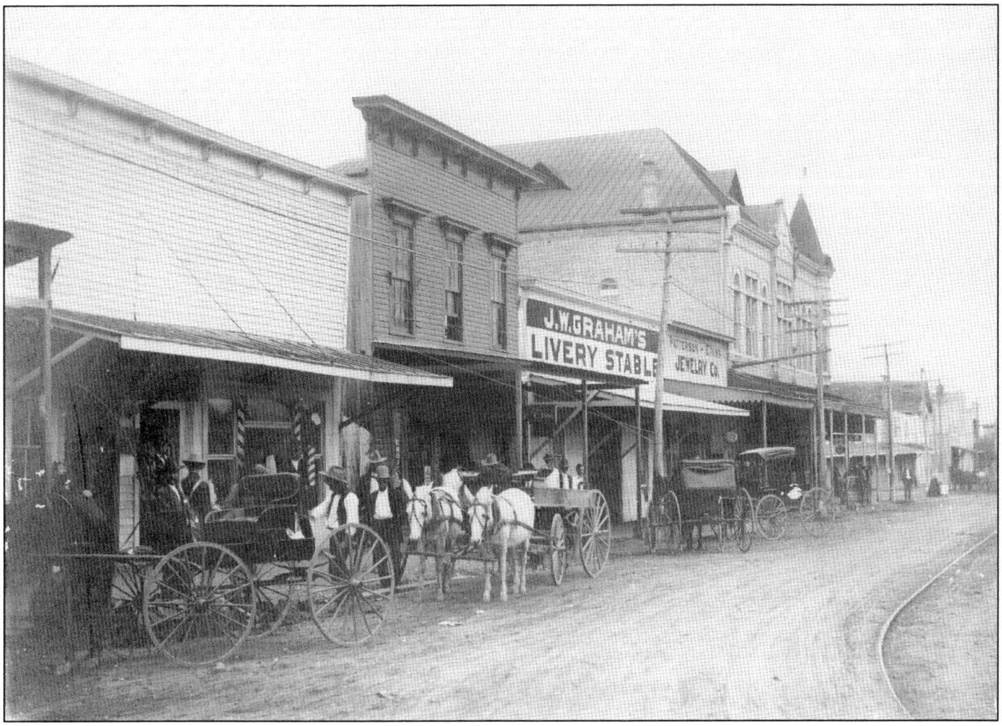

In 1903, there were several businesses on West North Street, just down from the Grand Opera House, including a livery stable, jewelry store, drugstore, and a barbershop. The streetcar tracks on the right were essential to Uvalde's early growth and expansion.

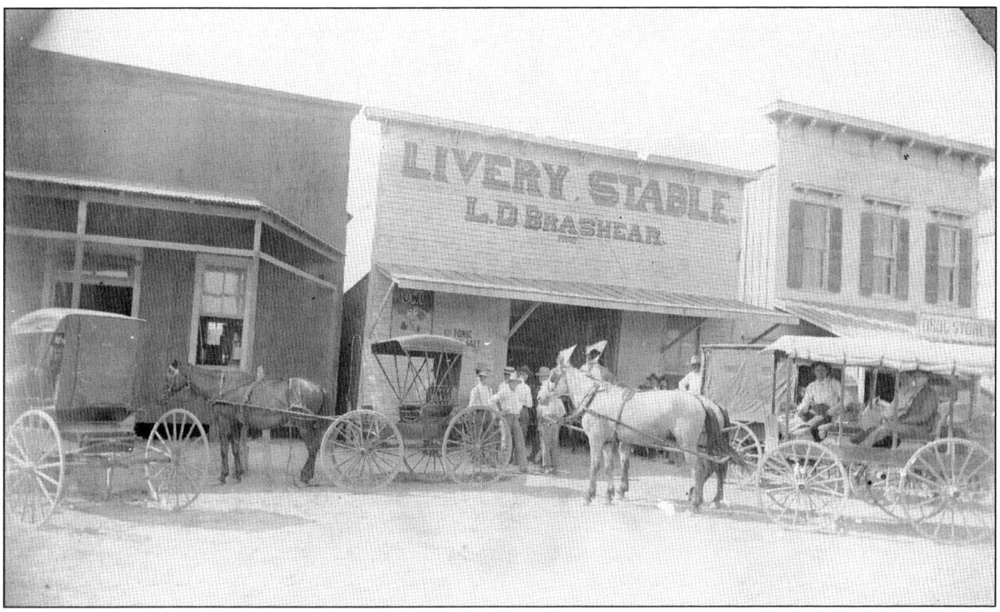

Prior to the automobile, a livery stable could be found in every town. This was a business where horses could be boarded or a horse or wagon team could be hired. Analogous to the rental car companies of today, the livery provided a source of transportation to those who did not have a horse and buggy and only needed one on select occasions.

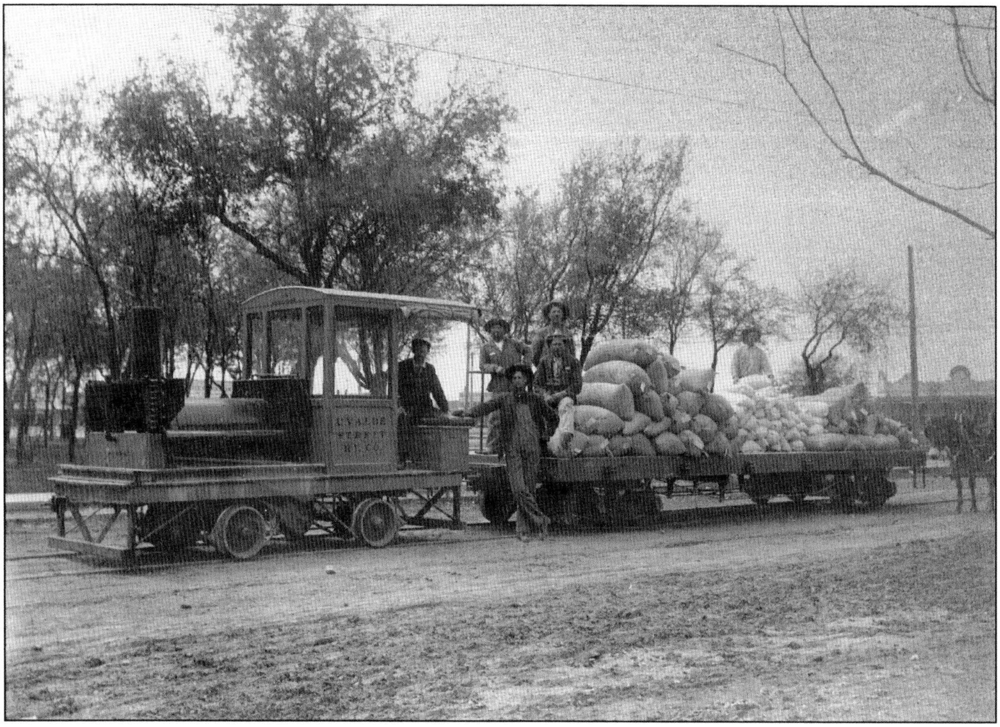

In 1908, M.M. McFarland operated the Uvalde Street Railway Company. The line ran from the downtown plaza area and north on Getty Street. The office for the company was on South West Street. The street railway offered a convenient way to get heavy freight items from town to the rail yard at the north end of town. The freight car above is hauling large sacks of bran and small grains. The passenger car in the c. 1905 photograph below is stopped in front of the city hall. The advertisement on the end of the car says, "To Cross S Land Office.".

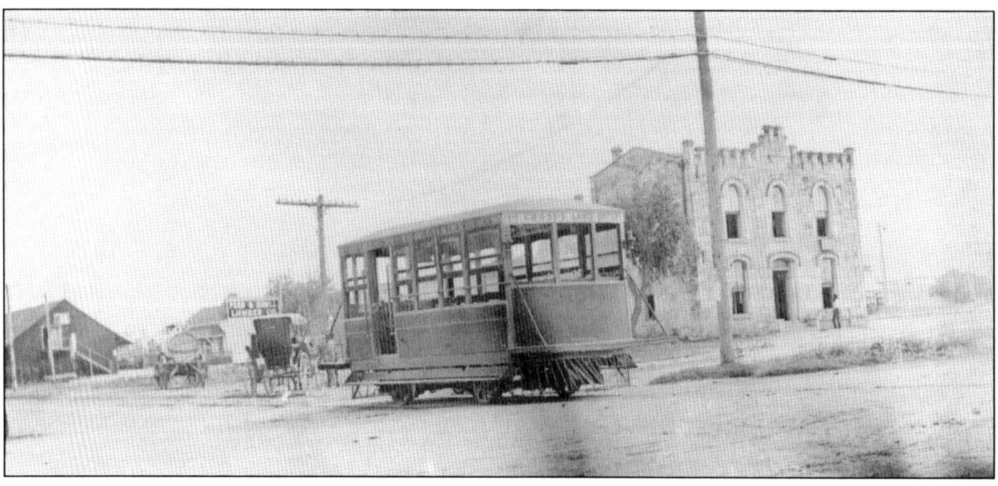

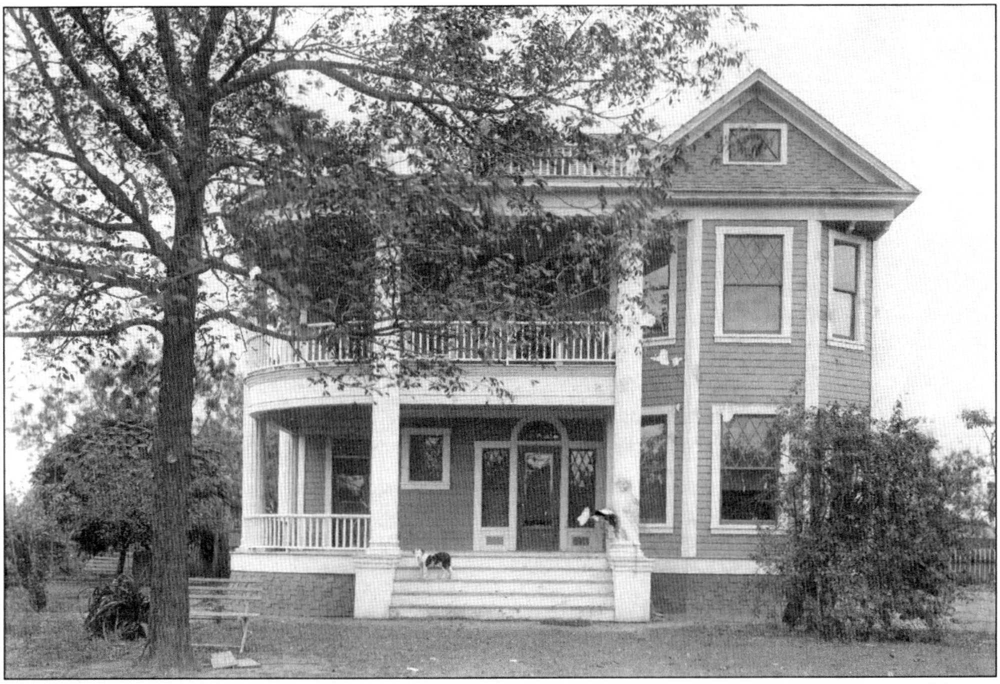

The David Barnhill family moved to Texas in 1887 by way of Leavenworth, Kansas. In addition to his drugstore and newspaper, Barnhill had the first insurance agency in Uvalde. This was the first Barnhill home in Uvalde, which burned in 1919.

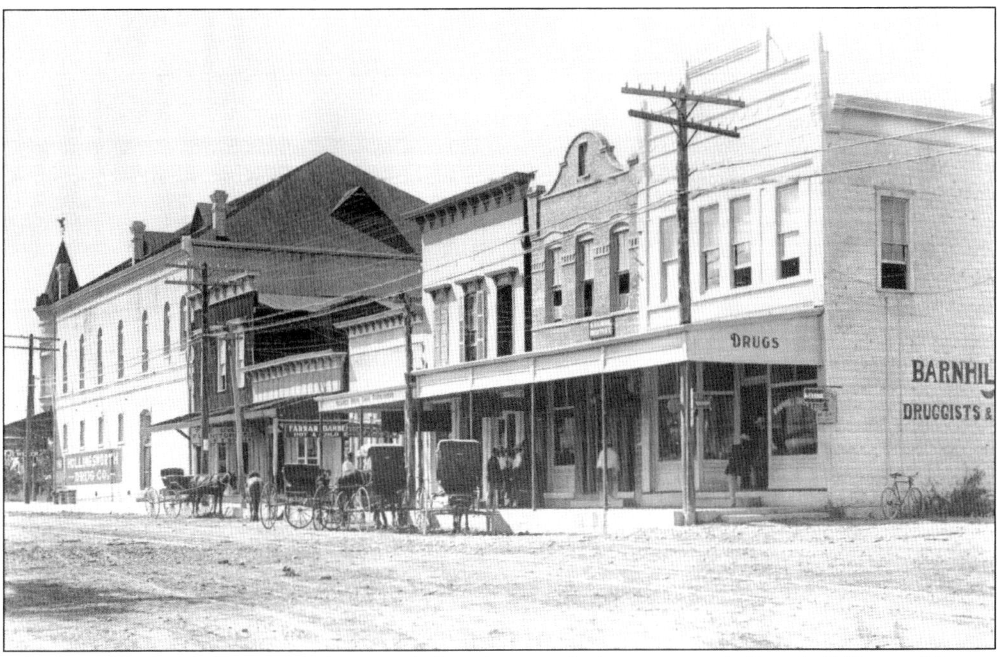

The Getty Street of 1910 was busy and the place to do business with Barnhill Drugs, Meares Brothers Cash Furnishers, Farrar Barber, Uvalde Furniture, and Hollingsworth Drug all in the same block. The keystone of Uvalde, the opera house, is ever-present with her copper roof and arched windows.

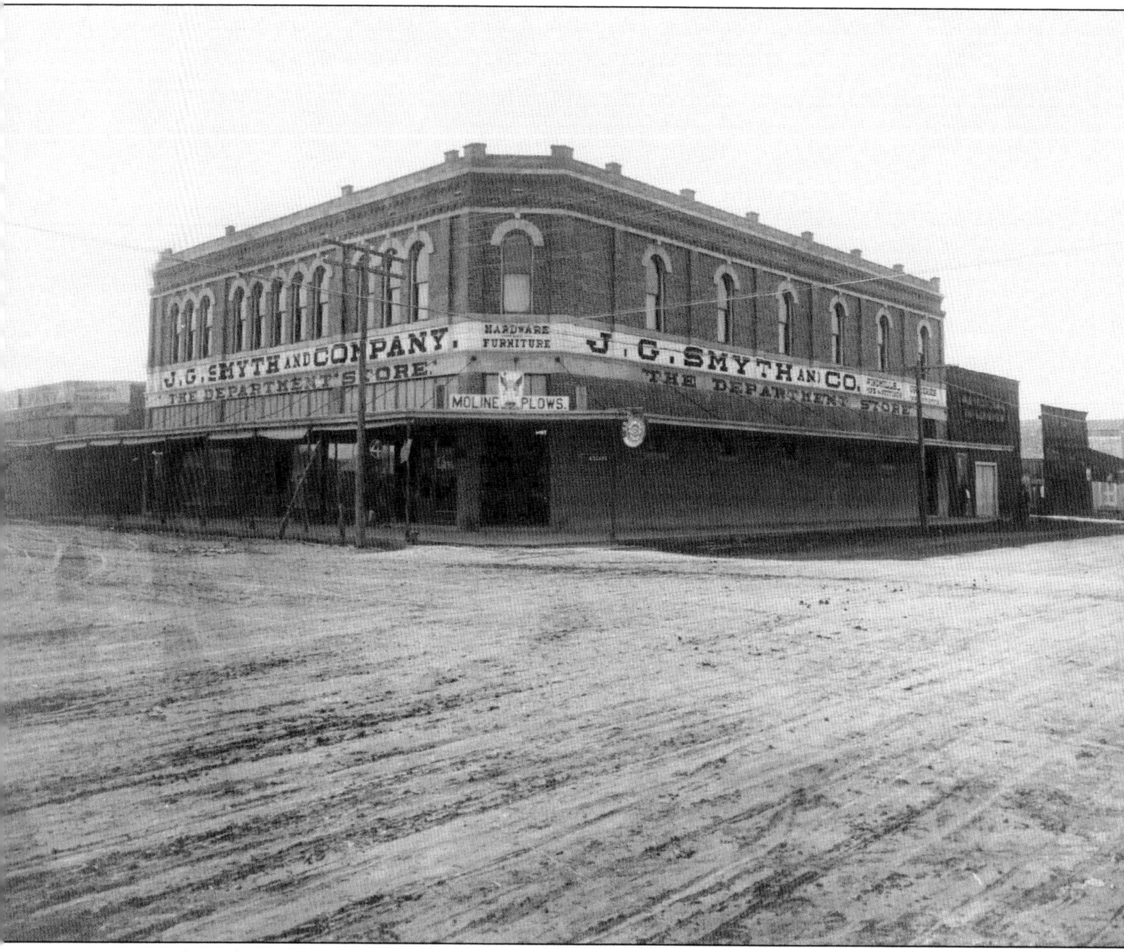

Located at the corner of West Main and South West Street and facing Fountain Plaza, (the location of the present-day post office) J.G. Smyth and Company met the requirement of "location being everything to a business." The business started with the purchase of J.H. Green hardware in 1903. A few years later, it moved to the above address, which allowed for expansion of services in the two-story building with a basement plus neighboring buildings. Much more than just a department store selling "Ladies and Gents Furnishings," the inventory covered just about anything a citizen in Uvalde County would ever need. As the signs on the exterior advertised, the J.G. Smyth Company sold windmills, pipe and fittings, groceries, feedstuffs, Moline plows, diamond edge tools, Kodaks, hardware, and furniture; truly a one-stop store.

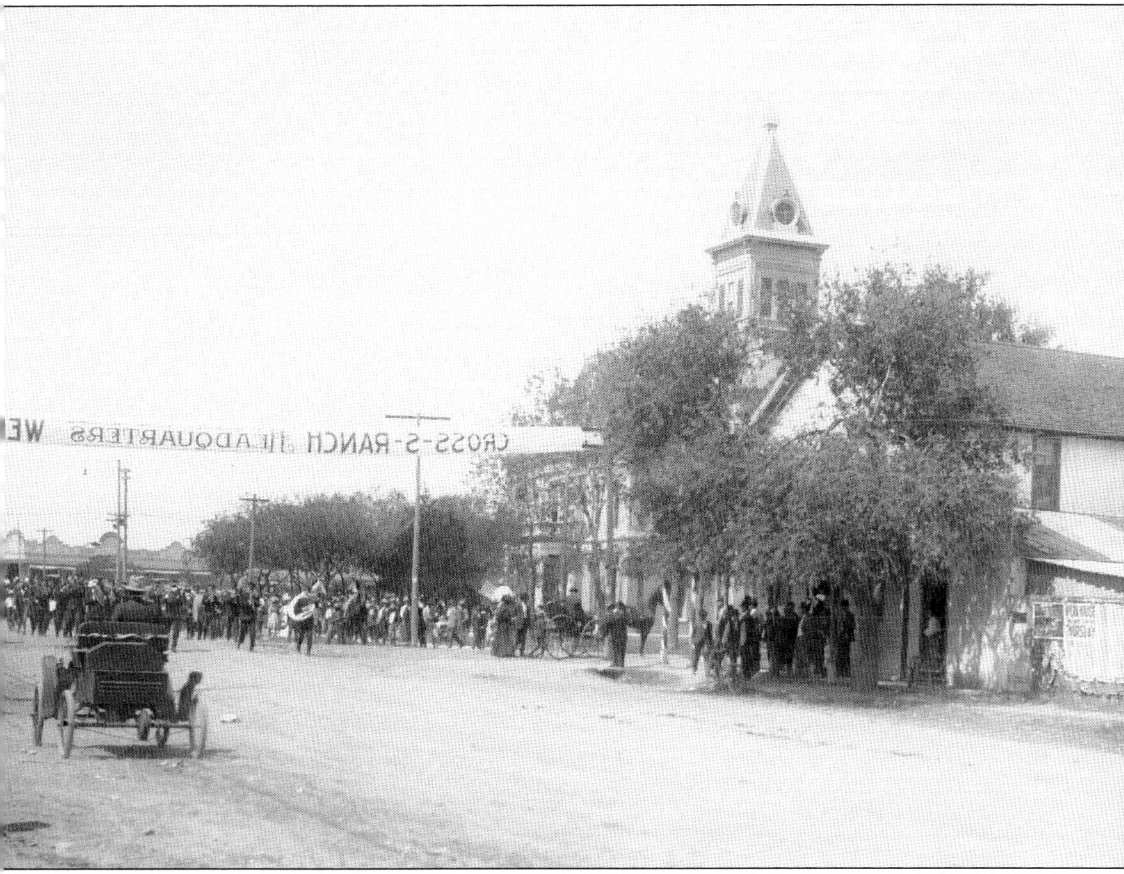

It is another parade in front of the 1890s courthouse! The banner across Main Street is welcoming everyone to the Cross S Ranch Headquarters. The Cross S was a 10,000-acre ranch south of Uvalde near present-day Crystal City. In 1905, two land developers purchased the ranch. Their goal was to partition out the land to sell for farms and to plat out the town. Crystal City was named for the clear artesian water found in the area. Uvalde was the nearest town where the railroad stopped and was the headquarters for prospective buyers looking to purchase land. They would arrive in town and then be ferried the 39 miles by horse and buggy or auto to Crystal City, to view and purchase land. Thus, a new town and community was born in the heart of the Winter Garden area.

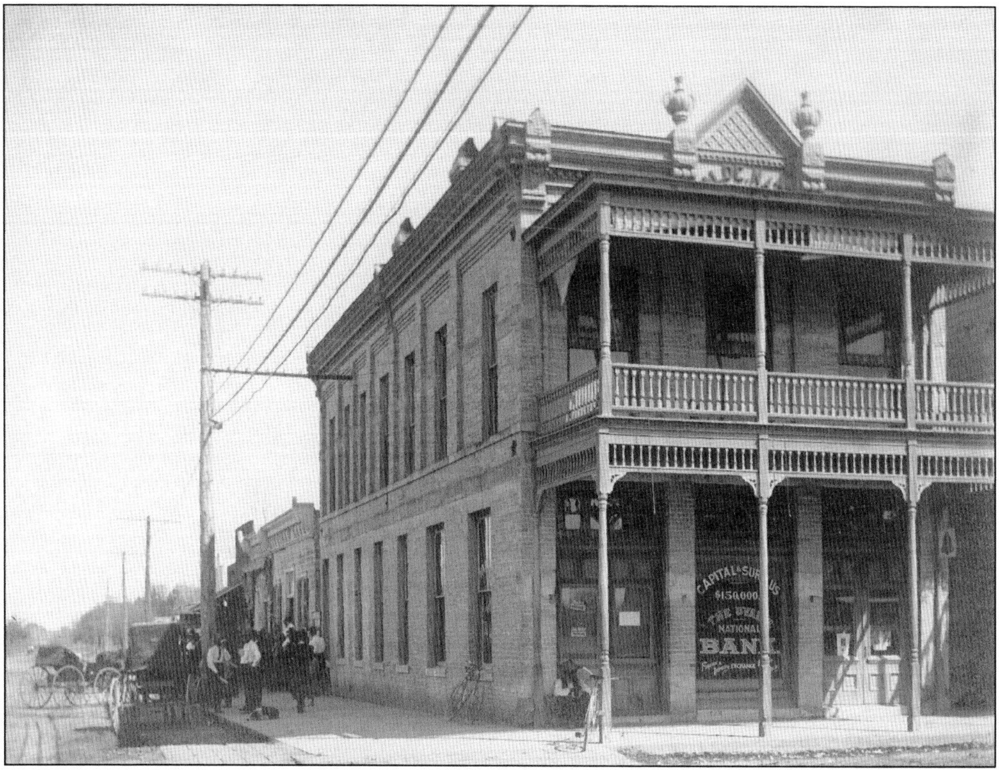

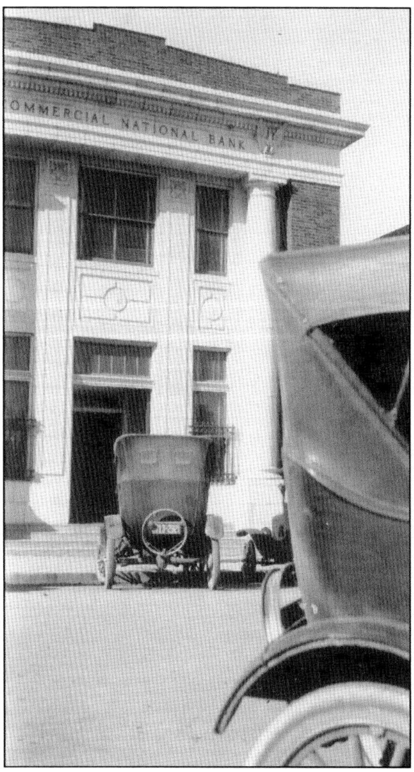

At the start of the 1900s, Uvalde had a number of banks in town to serve the citizenry. The Uvalde National Bank advertised a capital surplus of $150,000 in 1900 plus a foreign and domestic exchange. The second floor of the building housed the Wilson Hotel. Another bank started in the early 1900s was Commercial National Bank, located on the square just down from the Grand Opera House. At the time of the crash of 1933, Fred J. Horner was on the board. After the banking holiday of the Great Depression in March 1933, the bank never reopened. However, Fred J. Horner was asked to serve on the board of First State Bank of Uvalde, which he did until his death.

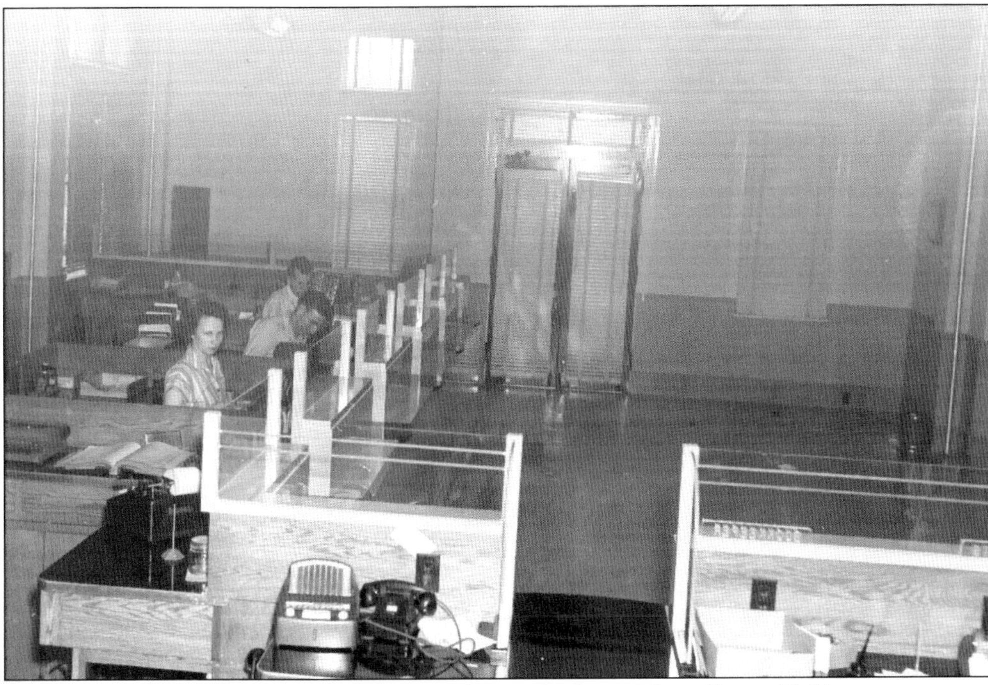

As First State Bank of Uvalde has grown, so has its facilities. The teller and lobby area was quite small when it was located on the plaza in downtown Uvalde. This location was the home of the bank from 1933 to 1970.

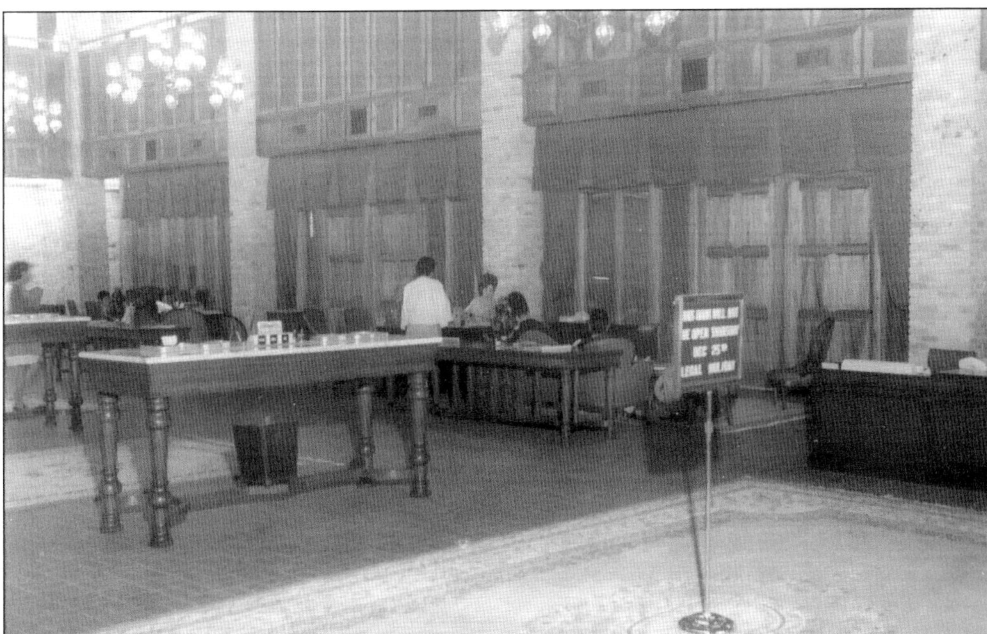

When First State Bank of Uvalde opened its doors at its new location at 200 East Nopal in 1970, the setting was likened to Uvalde's living room. With a soaring lobby that opened to the second floor and the wonderful Briscoe Art Collection, the setting was as Janey Briscoe wanted—"a feeling of warmth and friendship."

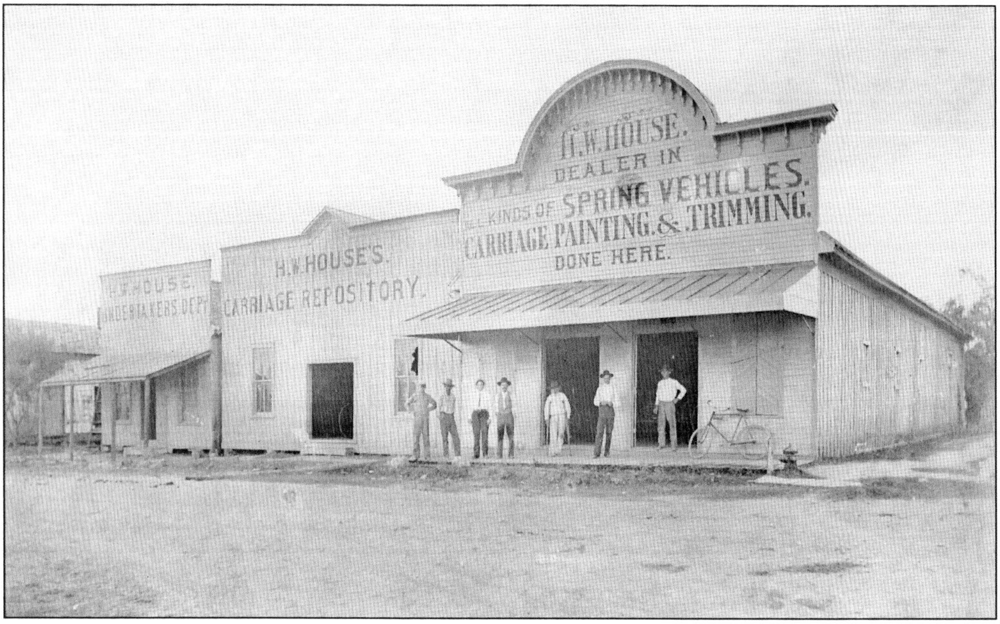

Wagons, carriages, and buggies remained the main mode of transportation into the early 1900s. H.W. House carriage works was located at East South Street and faced Town Hall Plaza. The carriage repository was a combination store, warehouse, and storage area for the carriages. At the time, it was logical for the undertaker's department to be part of the carriage works, since the hearse was a horse drawn carriage. On the right above is a fireplug, which was installed by the city after 1891. The first rules of automobile operation were in place by 1908; this photograph most likely dates to around that time.

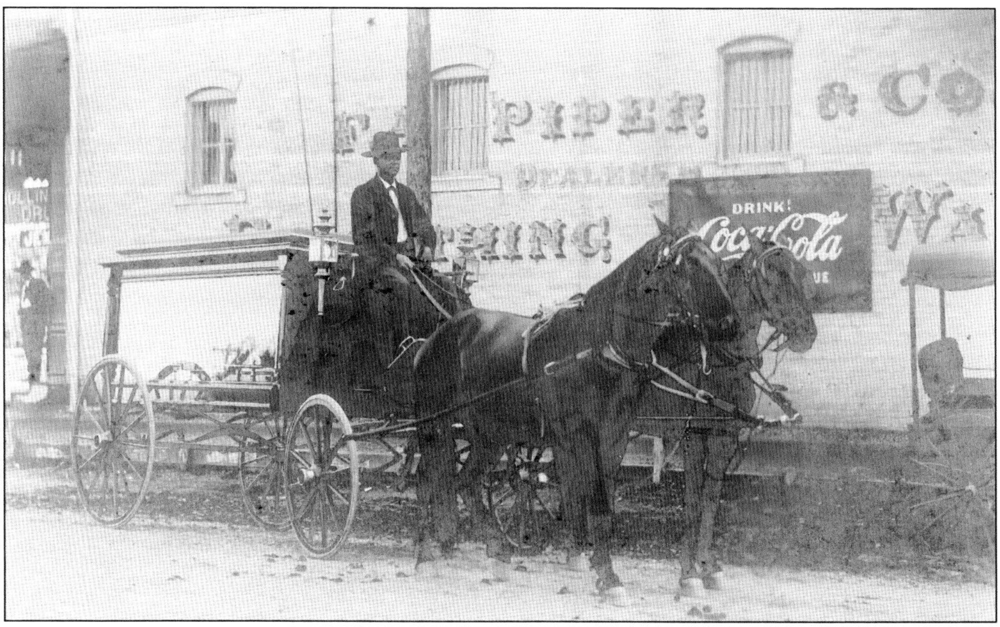

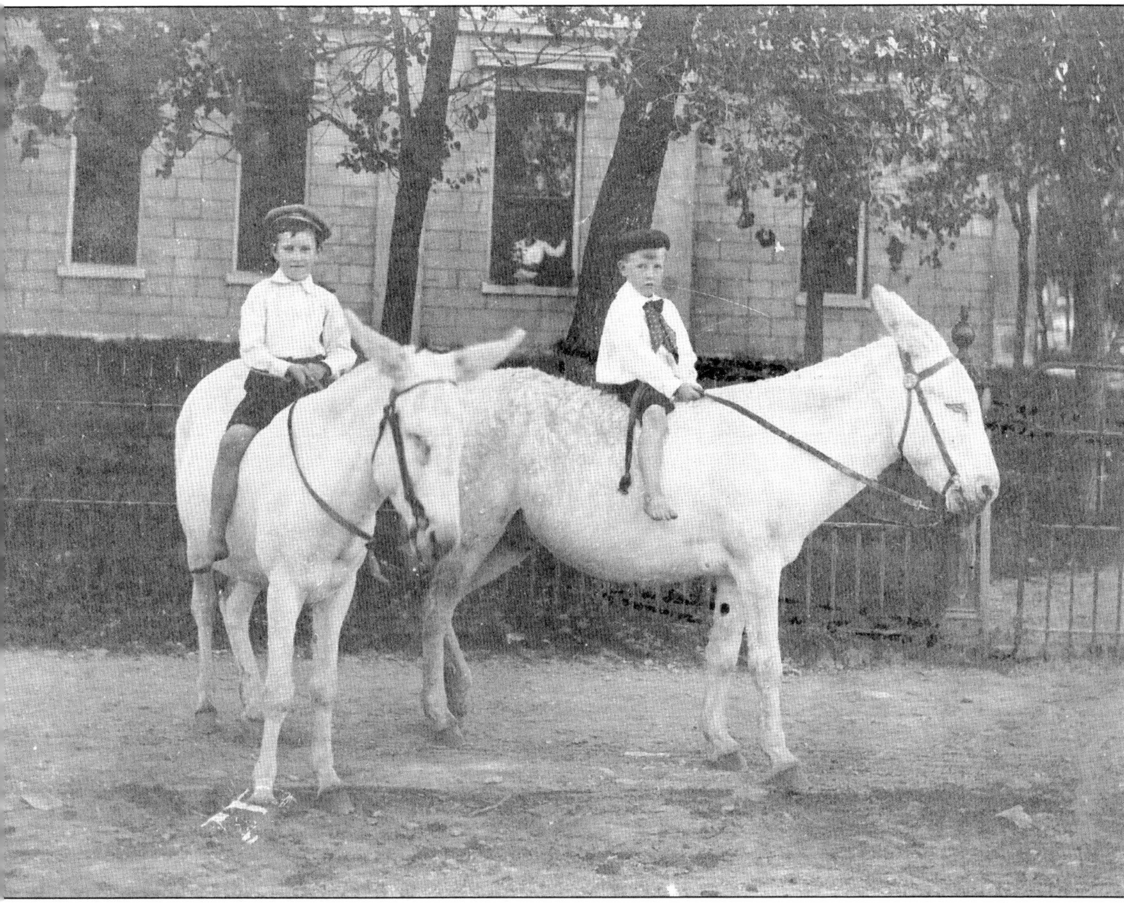

At the beginning of the 20th century, horseback, or in this case mule-back, was still a major mode of transportation for most, if not all, of rural America. This early 1900s photograph of the Ingram children on matching white mules was taken in front of the Uvalde County Courthouse. Mules, the offspring of a male donkey and female horse, were a valuable asset on the farm or ranch. They excelled as draft animals, and their sure-footedness made them excellent pack animals or mounts in the rocky hill country. The US Army used mules extensively as pack animals. Lt. John Bullis—later Brigadier General Bullis—led the Black Seminole scouts on numerous raids around Uvalde and to the west. He used a pack train of over 200 mules because they could cover rough country that no wagon could ever cross.

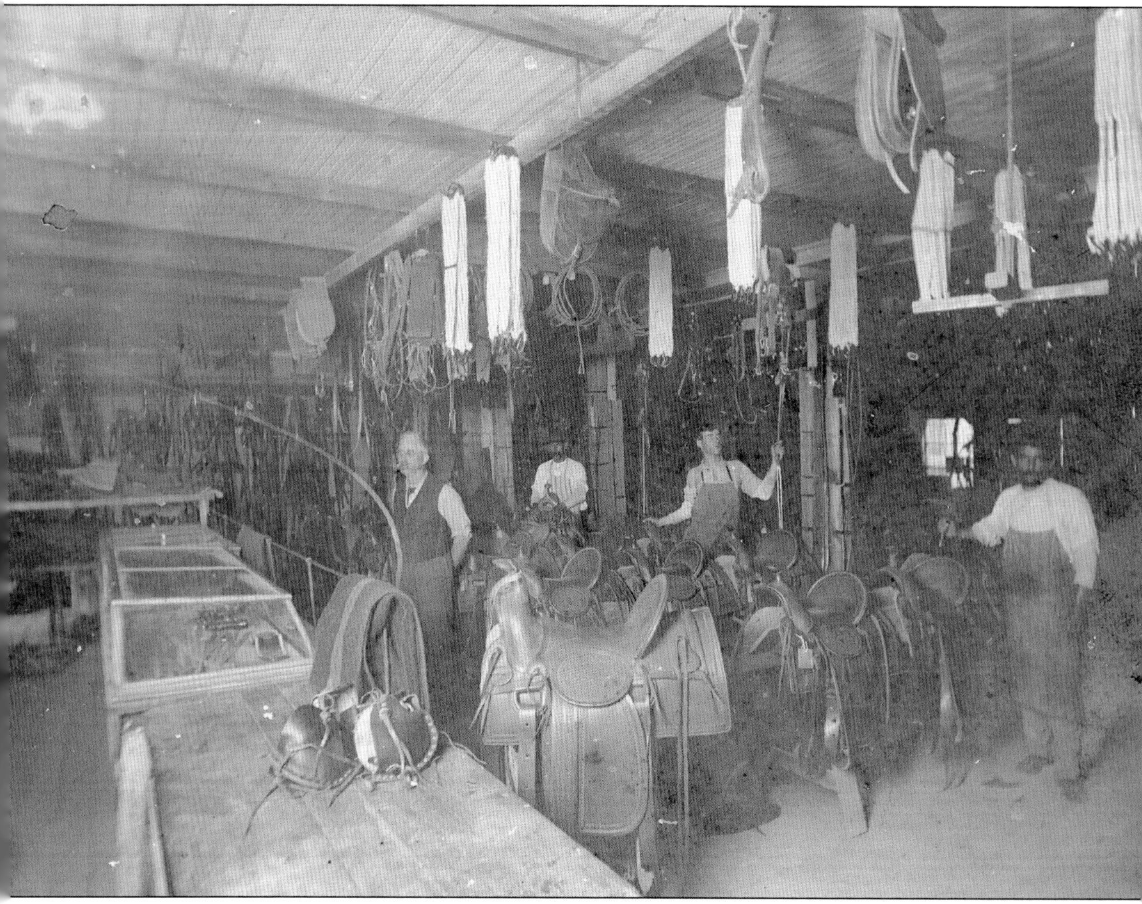

Prentice Rice was an Uvalde saddle and harness maker. In 1913, he purchased a building on the corner of North East Street and East Lane, facing the Uvalde courthouse. He opened his saddle and harness business, Rice Saddlery, on the ground floor. The Rice Hotel occupied the second floor. In 1929, the saddle shop was sold to Will A. Slade, the son of a saddle maker from Waco, Texas. Under Slade's leadership, the saddlery flourished. Slade had customers from far and wide, including Will Rogers, former Texas governor Dolph Briscoe, and even Gen. George Patton. Later, Slade's son-in-law Louis Paradeaux joined him in the saddle business and passed his skills down to his son, Will G. Paradeaux. In 1982, the younger Paradeaux sold the business. After regaining shop ownership, the business was moved to Luling, Texas.

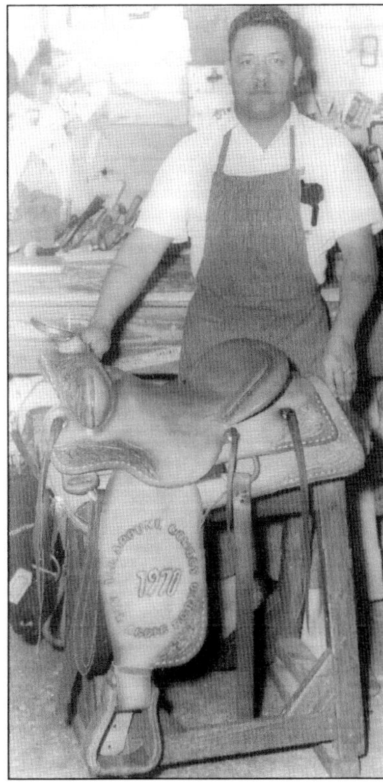

Joe Pena was born in 1923 and by age 12 was working for master saddle maker Will Slade. A very talented young man with the desire to learn, by the age of 16, he had built his first saddle. World War II and the Navy interrupted his saddle-making career, but on his return, he married his childhood sweetheart and returned to saddle making for Slade Saddle Company. Many famous people came to Joe Pena for not only saddles, but also leather belts. Pena's belts held up the trousers of John Nance Garner and John Wayne. Wayne also owned several holsters made by Pena. Today, Joe Pena Saddles are being made by his grandson, Ben Reyes. The saddle shop is now housed amid the farming, ranching, and hunting supplies at Uvalco Supply on East Main in Uvalde.

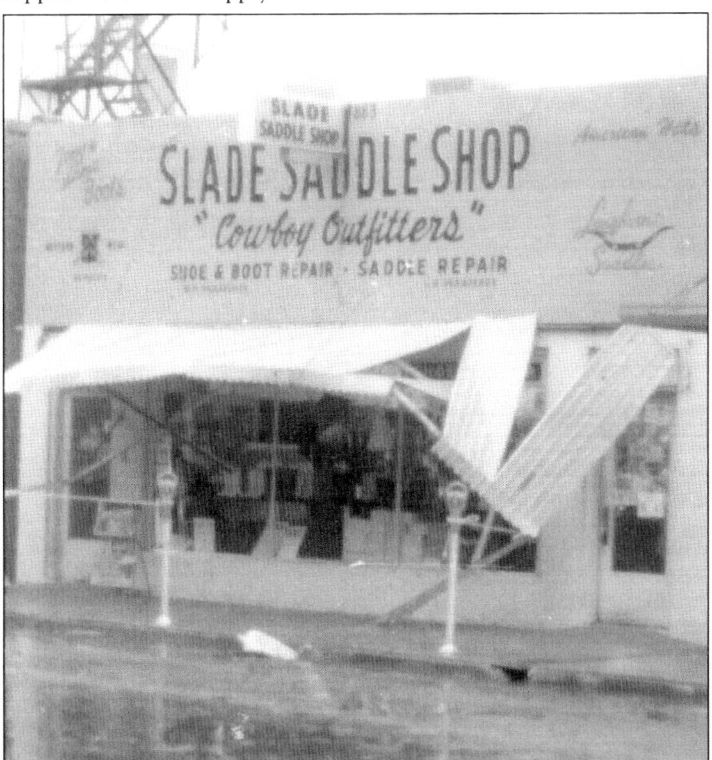

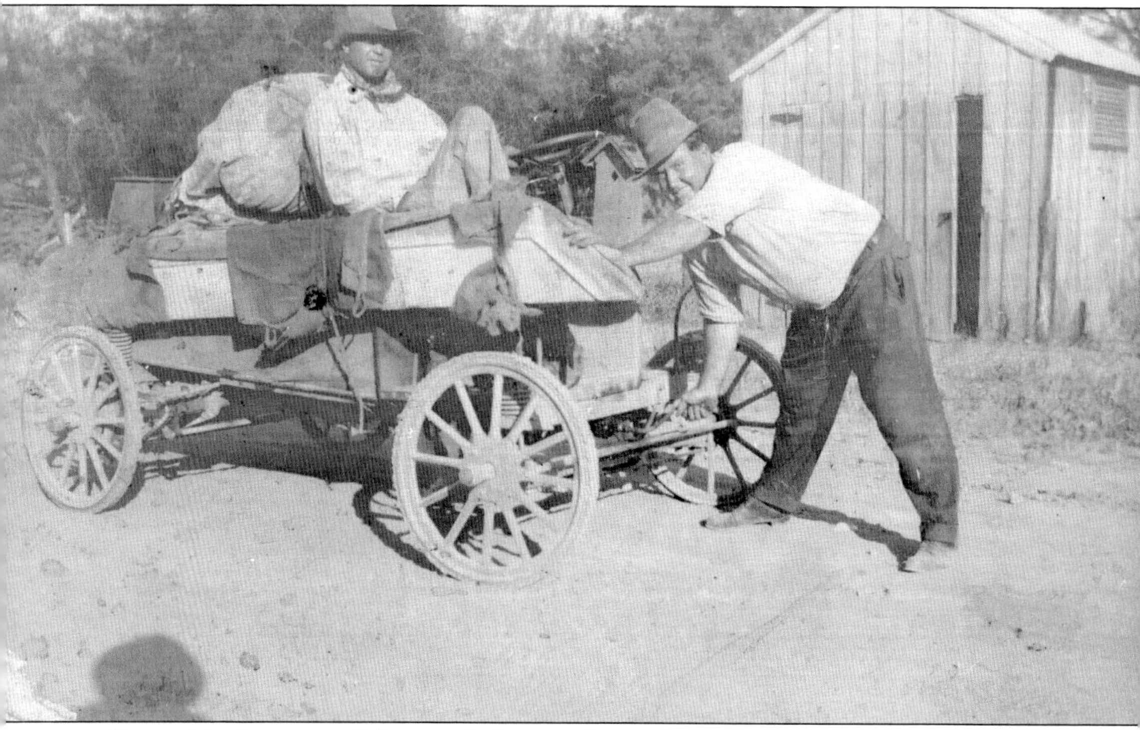

Some of the first automobiles were little more than motorized wagons. A starting battery was not standard equipment and engines were started with a hand crank. The crank turned a magnetic flywheel or electrical generator to produce a spark to start combustion. It was a tricky, finicky way to start an engine and could produce a kickback, which could send the crank handle in the opposite direction and easily break the thumb. The first automobiles were luxury items and not viewed as practical devices. The roads were still unpaved and outside of town little more than wagon tails. The tires were thin and not suitable for the rocks and mesquite thorns that were prevalent around Uvalde. Traveling any distance always resulted in flats. Early automobiles had no spare tire and were equipped with a flat kit and manual air pump for repairs.

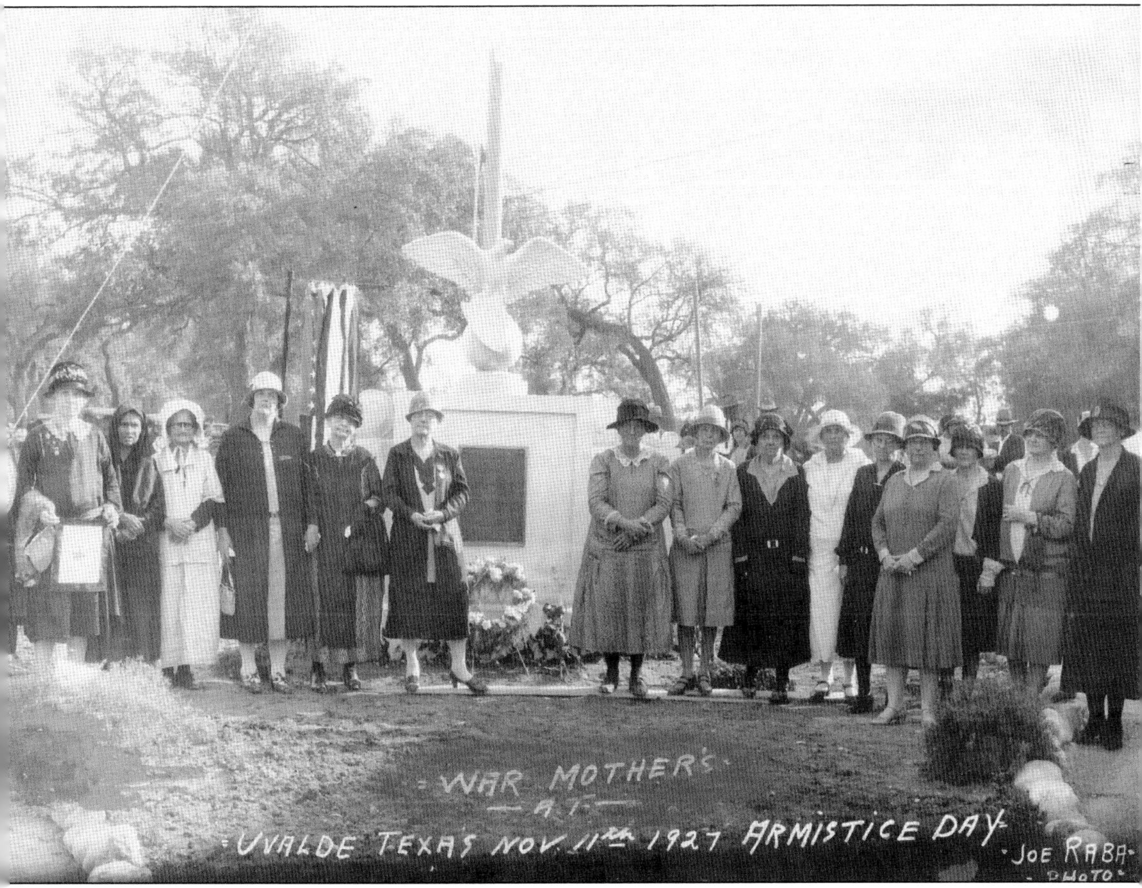

Early Uvaldeans called the land on the banks of the Leona River three blocks east of downtown "the Grove." Basically a barren spot of land with a dry creek bed and a forest of beautiful old live oak trees, it had the potential to be a beautiful location. Concerned that the owner was cutting down the magnificent oaks for firewood, the city purchased the land for $150 in 1898. That began a 29-year transformation of a plot of land into Uvalde's Memorial Park. On Armistice Day, November 11, 1927, a war memorial dedicated to the "Uvalde County Boys who gave their lives during the World War 1914–1918" was unveiled. A number of the Gold Star mothers were on hand to watch the unveiling of the bronze tablet containing their sons' names.

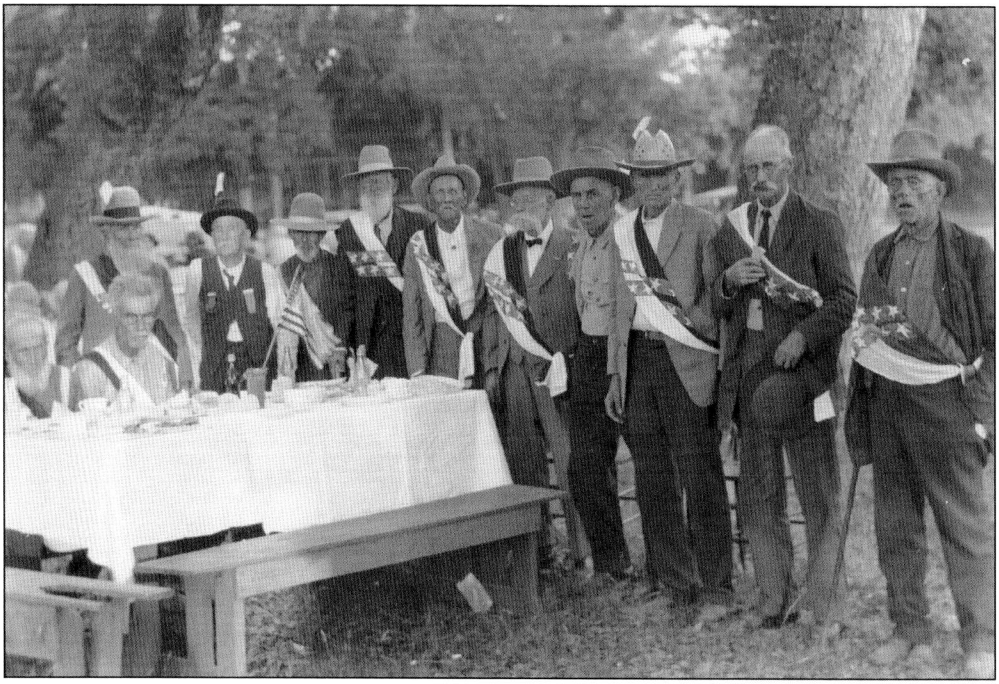

Over the years, the Uvalde Memorial Park has been the sight of many a celebration, picnic, and party. At the May Fete in 1927, the Civil War Veterans of Uvalde County held their reunion in Memorial Park on the banks of the Leona River.

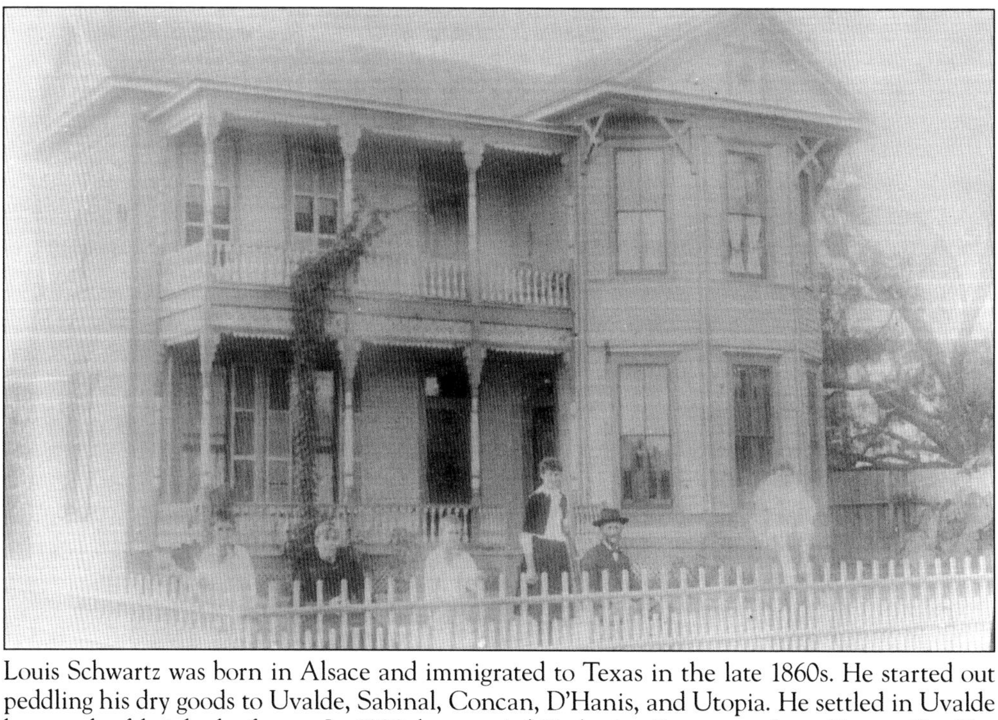

Louis Schwartz was born in Alsace and immigrated to Texas in the late 1860s. He started out peddling his dry goods to Uvalde, Sabinal, Concan, D'Hanis, and Utopia. He settled in Uvalde because he felt it had a future. In 1880, he married Catherine Stevenson from Castroville. She ran the Schwartz Hotel, located near their dry goods store near East Main and Camp Streets.

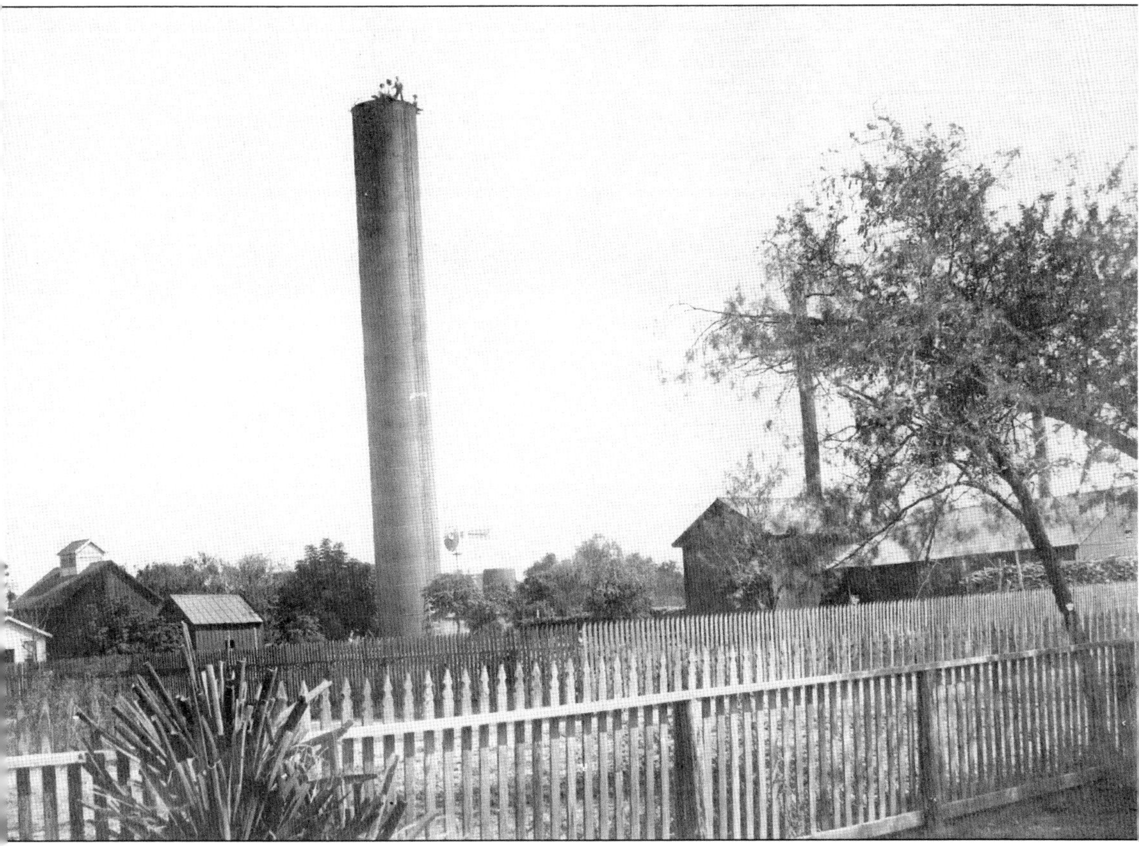

Uvalde Water and Power Company received a contract from the City of Uvalde in 1891 to construct the waterworks for the city. The contract called for the installation of 22 water hydrants with water mains. The initial plan was to pump water out of the Leona River. However, since the area was in the midst of a hard drought, there was no water in the river to be pumped. The decision was made to dig a well at the site of the waterworks. These was lean times for the fledgling city; the combined forces of the drought, national economic depression, and a smallpox epidemic stretched the budget of city hall. The unlucky victims of the smallpox epidemic were sent to the county's "smallpox camp," but the care and feeding of the ill fell on the City of Uvalde.

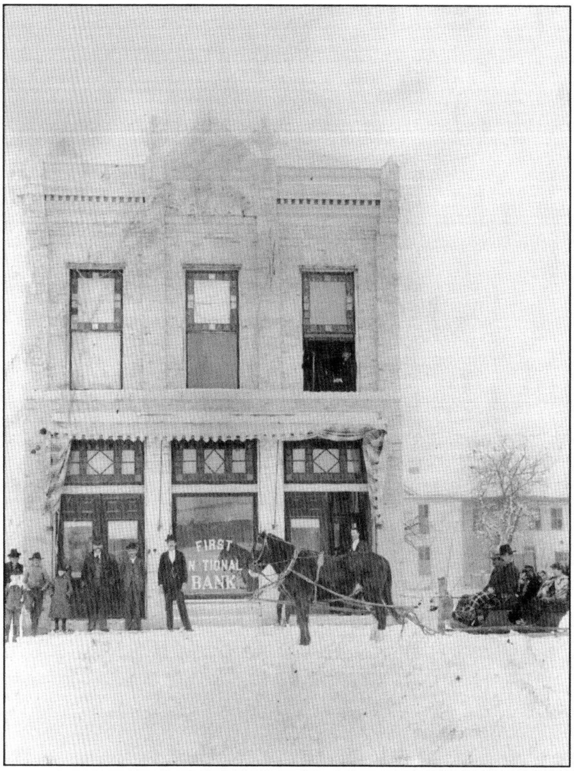

Snow is a rare sight in Uvalde. Winters are usually mild, with the January temperature range falling between the mid-60s and mid-40s. The lowest recorded temperature was six degrees in February 1951. Evidently this rare snow did not keep anyone indoors.

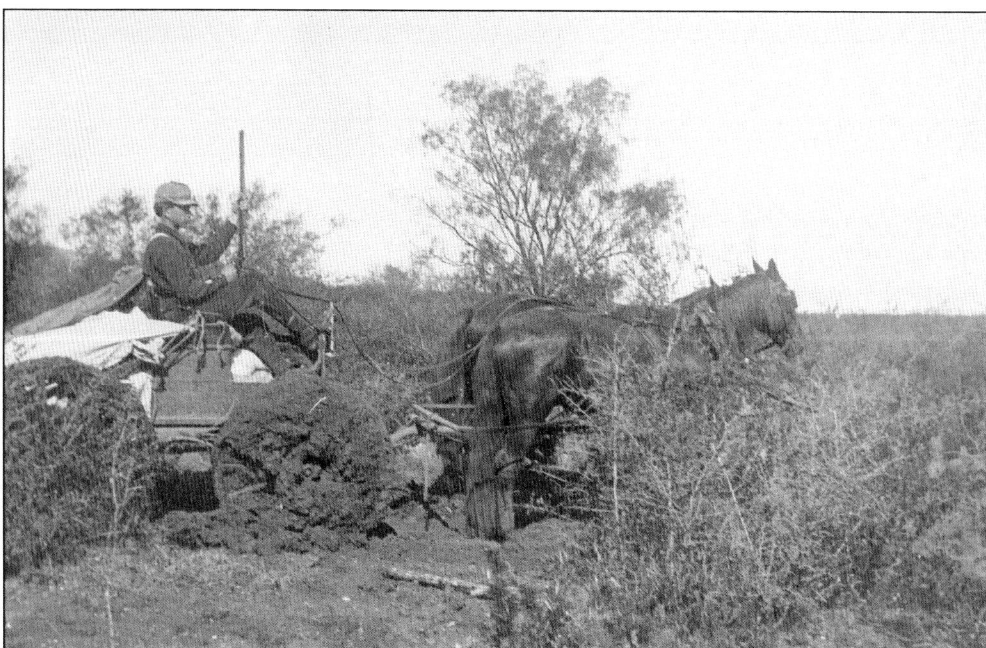

Rain—like most of nature's resources—is always welcomed in Uvalde. When droughts can and do last years, moisture in any form is a delight to see. Getting stuck in the mud was just one of the side affects of a nice rain.

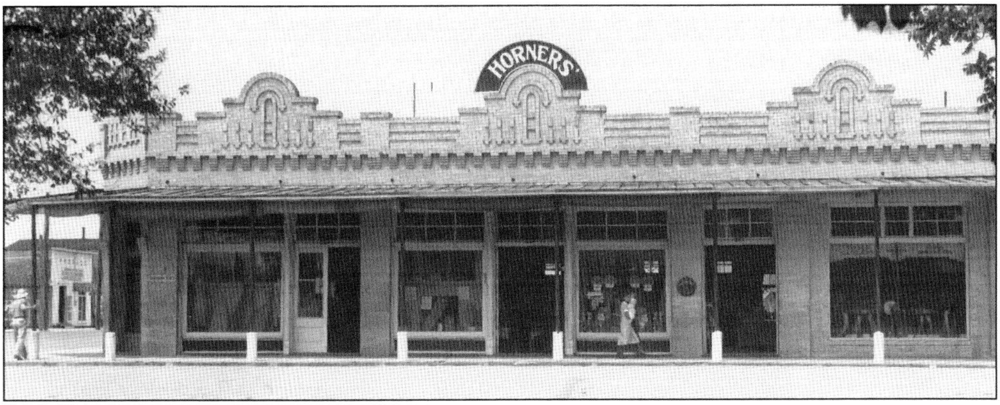

George Horner Jr. was one of 14 children born to George and Josephine Horner of San Antonio. In 1878, the younger Horner moved to Uvalde to work in his brother-in-law's hardware store, F.A. Piper Company. In 1900, the store became George Horner Hardware. More than just a hardware store, Horners' became the Buick agent in 1913 and the Ford agent in 1914. A store with a little bit of everything, as with most stores of this era, Horners' was a combination grocery, dry goods, ranching supply, and hardware store, as well as car dealership. George Horner Jr. and Nellie Robb married in 1855, and their children and grandchildren continued the family business. The photograph above with the Horners' sign over the center of the building is from the 1940s, and the view below with the sign on the corner was taken in the 1970s.

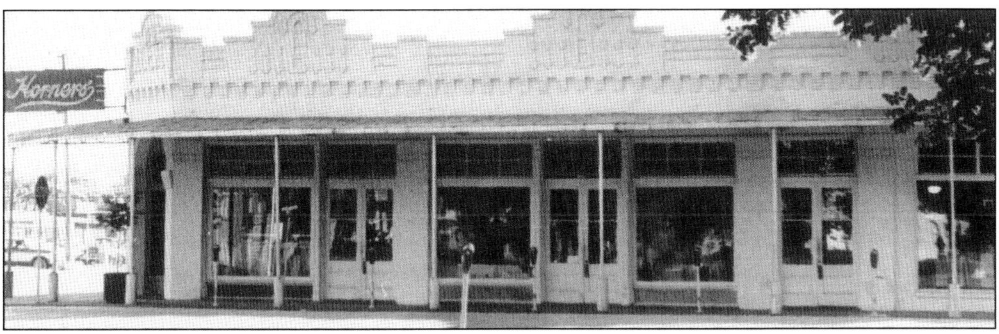

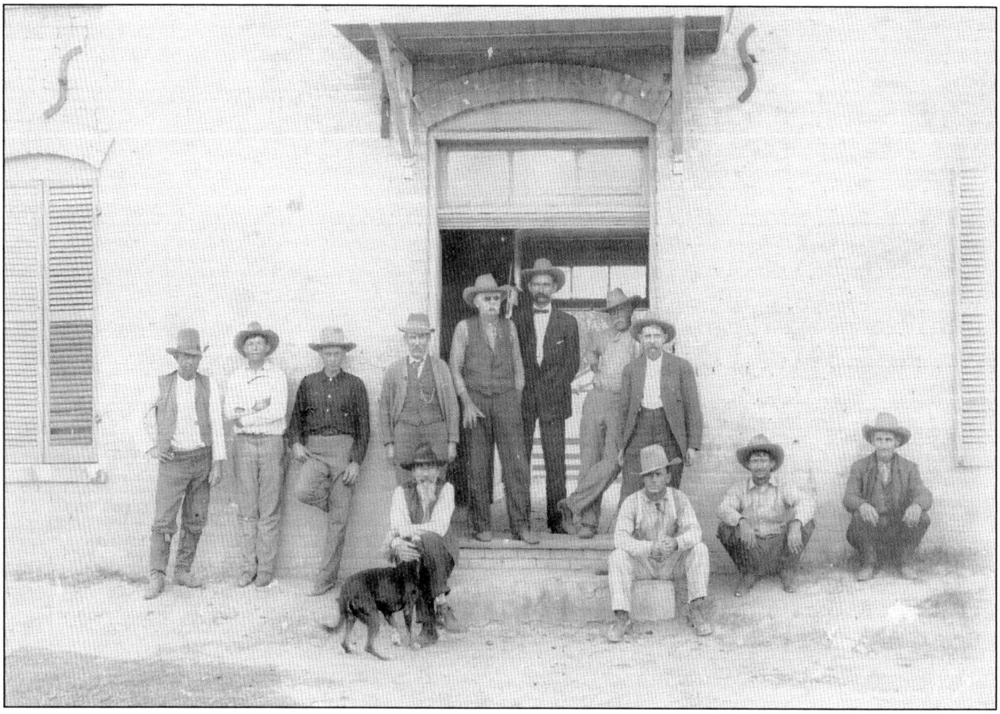

This bank on the square at North West Street, next to George Horner's Hardware Store, was not identified by name. It was not rare for general stores to extend credit to their customers and perform services similar to a bank.

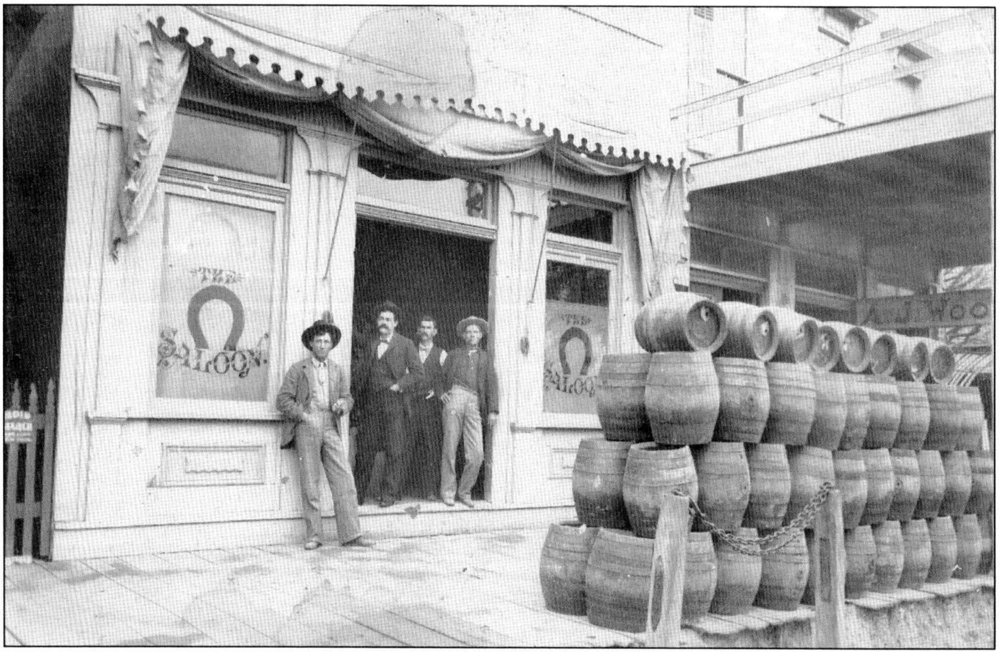

From the number of kegs on the sidewalk, it appears the Horseshoe Saloon did a brisk business in 1900. In 1908, the city voted out saloons, but it took a number of years for all the buildings to remove their signs.

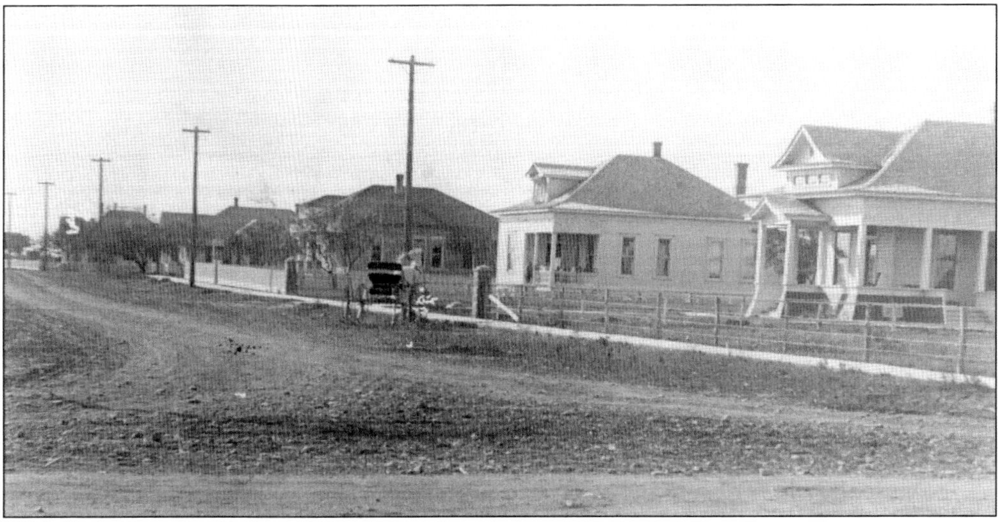

This unidentified scene (the note on the back of the photograph indicated it may be Myrtle Street) shows the wide streets preferred by Uvalde's city planners. There is plenty of room to leave a rig hitched to the hitching post while visiting a neighbor.

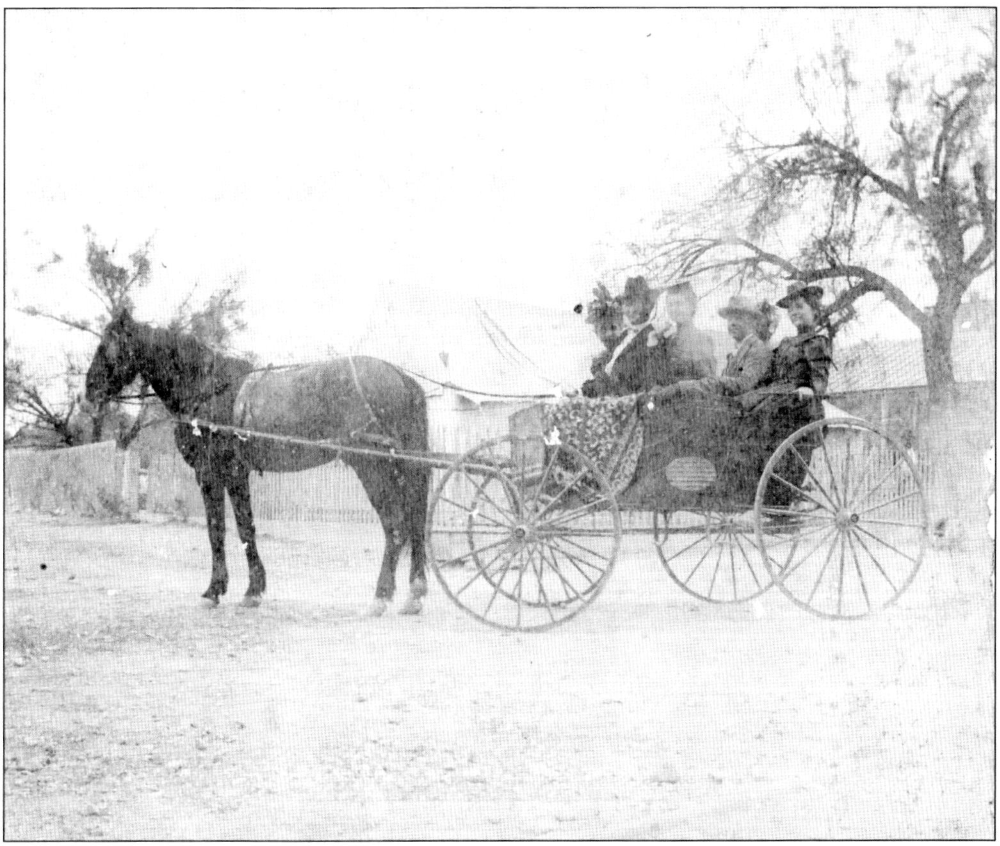

Out for a pleasant carriage ride are, from left to right, (first row) Maud Stucky, Fred Rhiner, and Meta Muller; (second row—partially hidden) Lola Derr, Hewett Kelso, and Alma Renolds. It must have been a cool day, as the lap blankets are out.

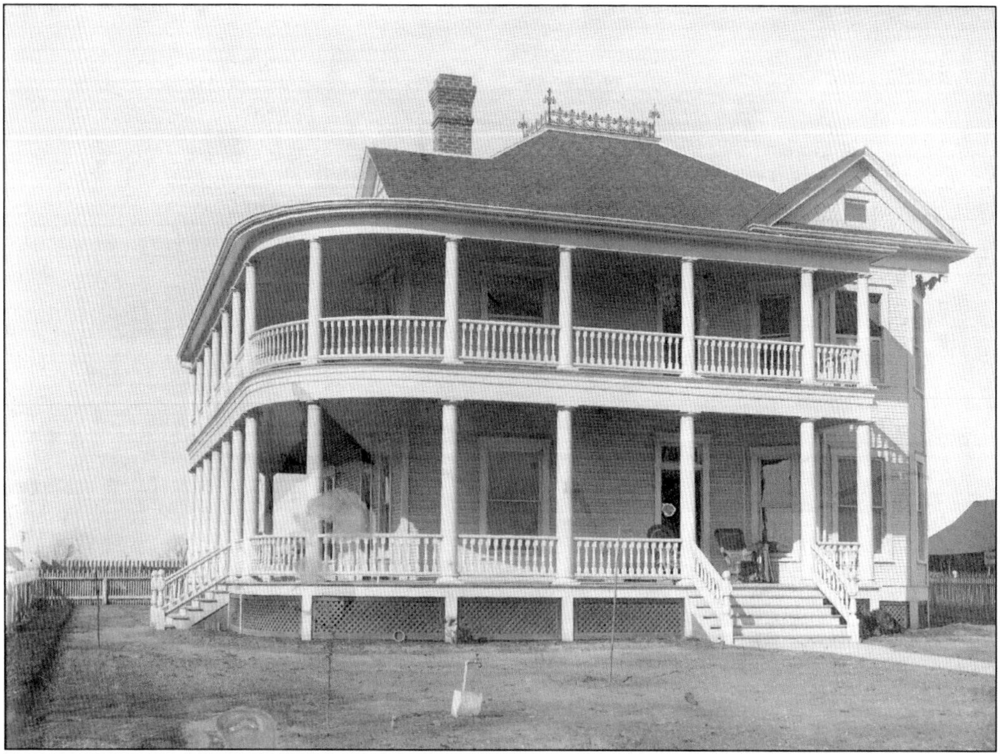

The Moore home is a large two-story structure with wide porches, or verandas, for the hot summer days Uvalde is known for. The home is still standing today at 757 North Getty Street. It was built in 1910.

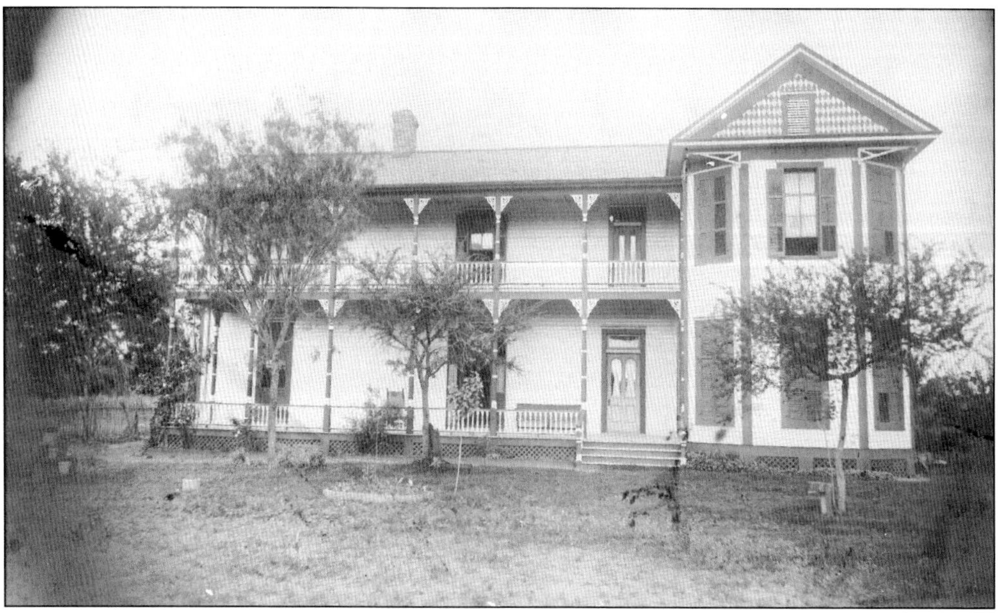

This large two-story home was built on the Leona River by Stephen Hoag and was part of the 3,600-acre Hoag Ranch that included Mount Inge and all of the Fort Inge property. The floor-to-ceiling windows were typical for the era and were designed to catch the summer breezes.

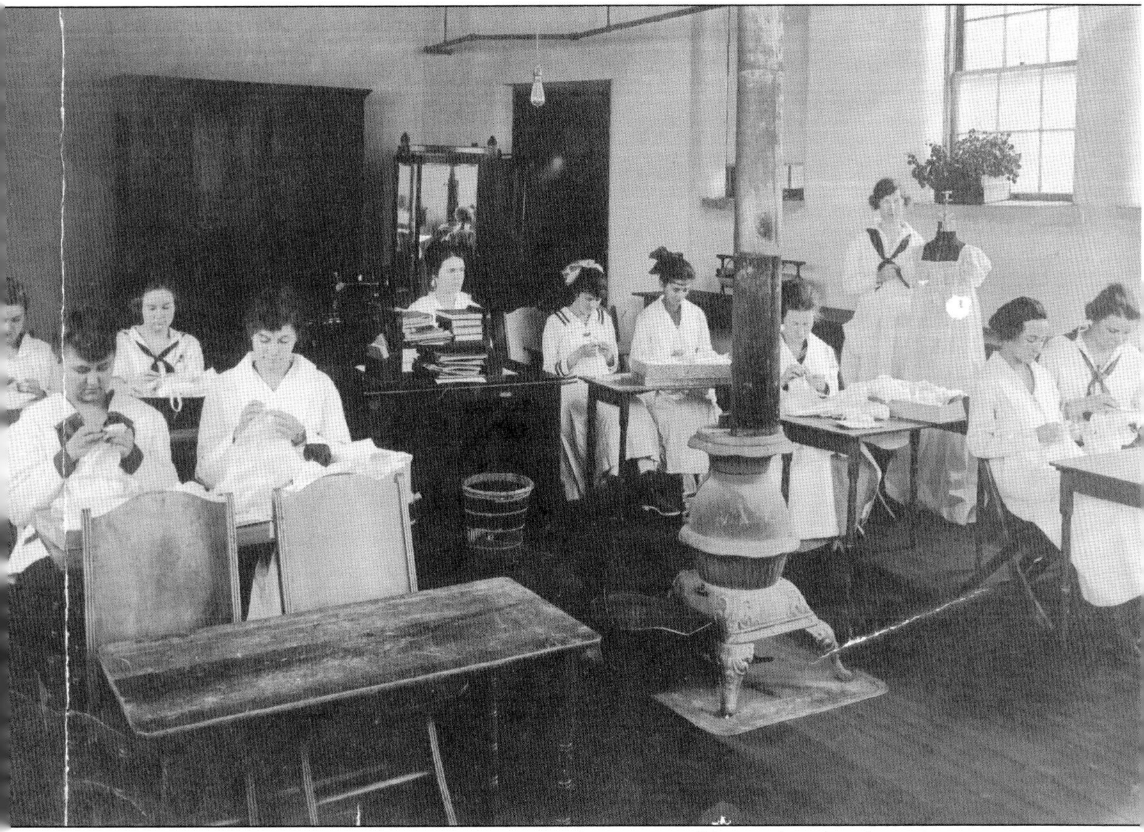

In the 1920s, homemaking was part of the curriculum at Uvalde High School on West Main Street. Early 20th-century home economics classes were designed to prepare young women for a life of raising a family and caring for the home. Classes in sewing, weaving, cooking, canning, soap making, and other domestic skills were all designed to help prepare her for life as a married woman. With the advent of coeducational land grant institutions, women could break into higher education. As women's liberation took hold in the 1960s to 1980s, combined with more women obtaining college degrees, joining the workforce, and education budget cuts, home economic classes fell out of vogue. The feminist movement claimed that home economics classes were designed to keep women in the kitchen.

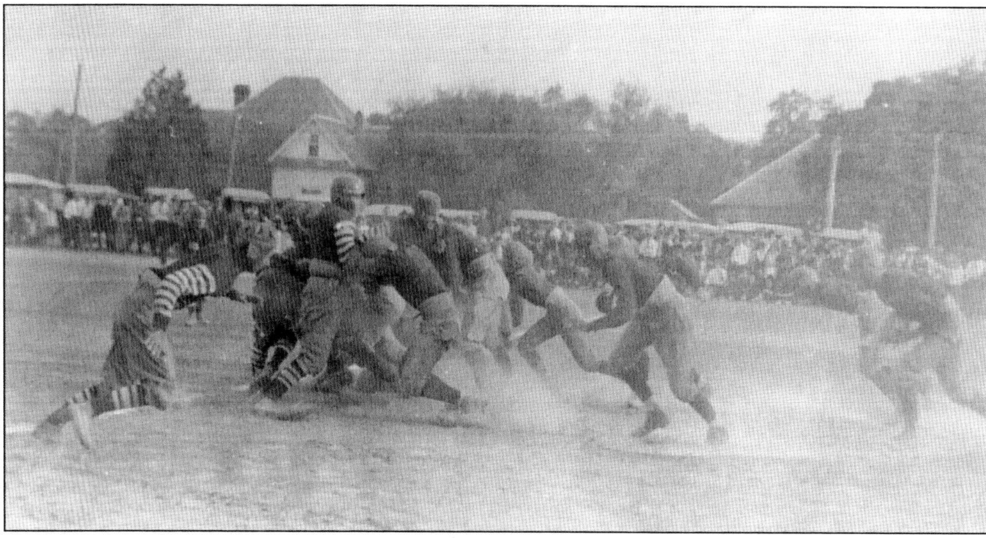

This Uvalde football team from the 1920s is playing at the old West Main School on West Main and South Park Streets. The Uvalde schools joined the University Interscholastic League in 1925. The Uvalde teams drew a large crowd to these early games.

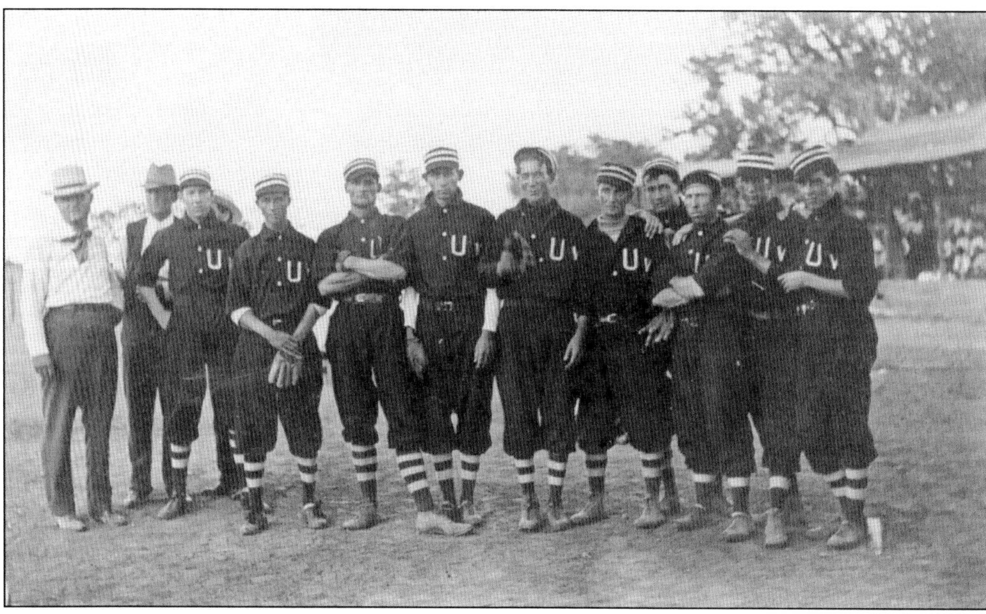

In the 1920s, baseball games were played on the west bank of the Leona River, although the specific location was not given. This Uvalde team looks like they were ready to play ball; they have a great swagger about them.

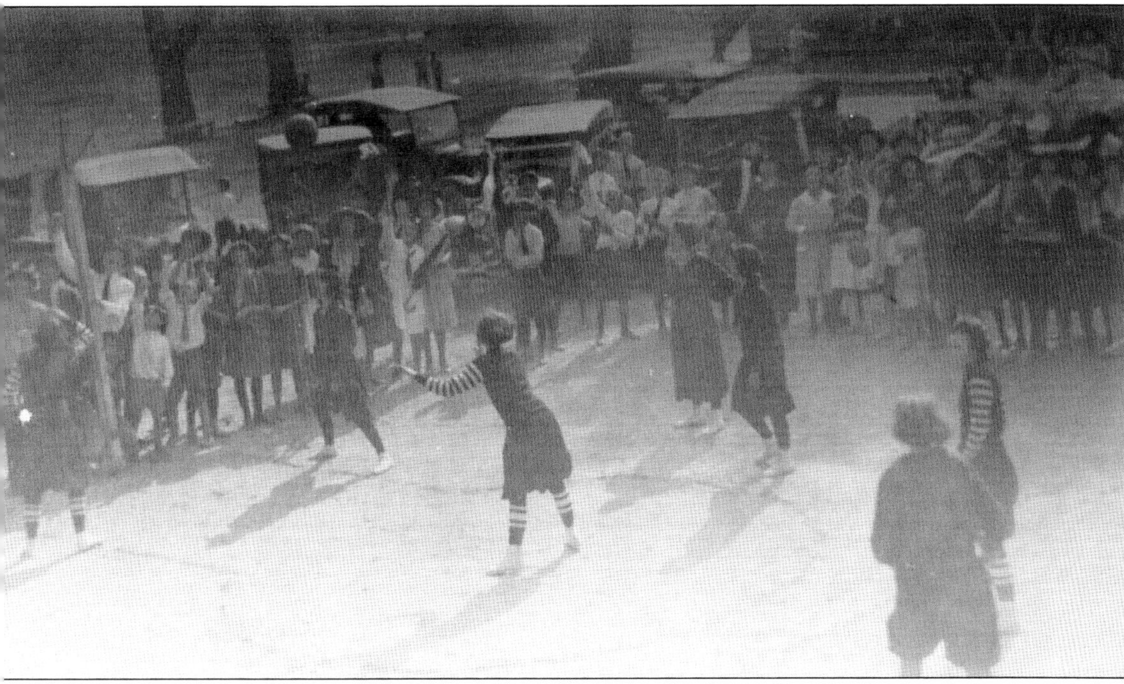

Girls' basketball in 1910 was a great deal different from the game that is played today. Aside from the conservative uniform, the basketball key area was actually shaped like a keyhole. The style of shooting was different, and there was no jump shot. To shoot the basket, the ball was tossed underhanded. The young girl in the middle of the circle is shooting a free throw. The release for shooting the ball was always below the shoulders, and these girls would never try to dunk the ball. Women also played a nine-person game where they could only hold a ball three seconds, take three dribbles, and could not snatch or bat the ball away from an opponent. This game is being played on a dirt court in 1910. Evidently hats were an option when playing the game.

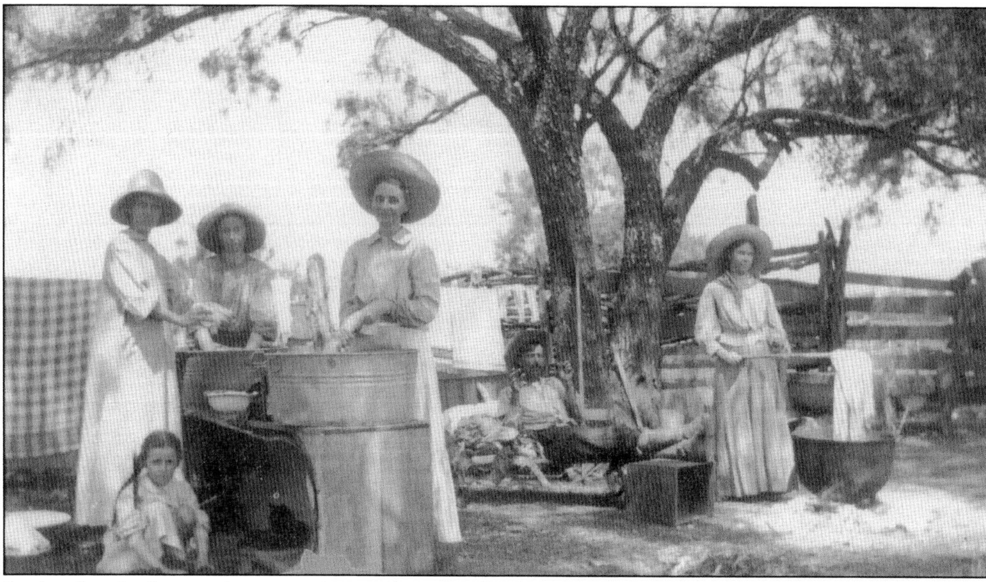

In the days before washing machines, laundry day literally took all day for a large family. Laundry was a chore done by the women of the family. Water was heated in large kettles over an open fire, which added an element of danger with long skirts close to open flames.

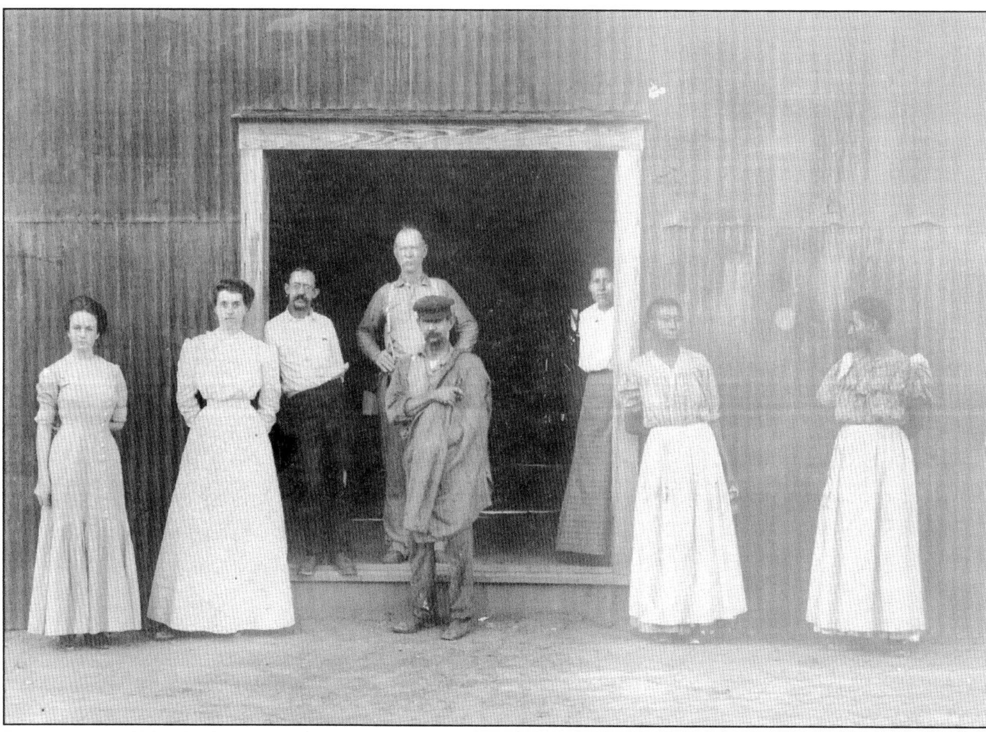

Laundry in 1910 had come a long way since the days of cleaning clothes by pounding them on rocks. The first electrical washing machine had been introduced in 1908. Still, it was difficult work dealing with the hot water, hot clothes presses, and irons. Here, the employees of Kelly's Laundry are posing in front of the establishment.

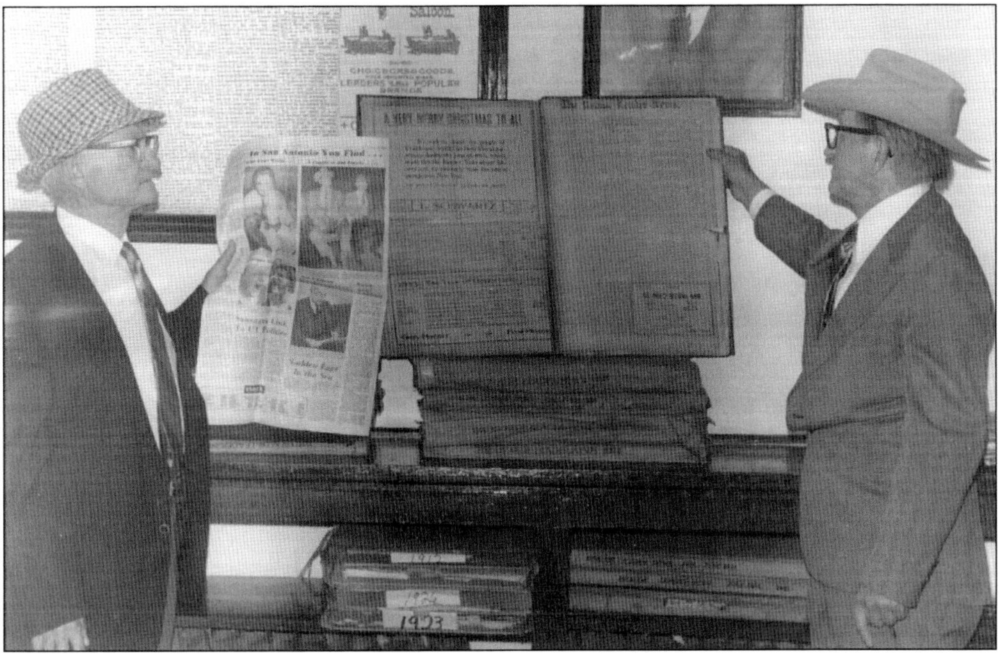

The Newton Boys have long held the interest of those enthralled with the stories of the 1920s. This wild bunch of young men robbed over 80 banks from Texas to Canada and managed to rob six trains. The "robbery take" was quite profitable as the amount stolen by this one gang exceeded all other robberies in the era combined. Willis Newton (above, left) was arrested for vagrancy and stealing cotton in 1909. By 1914, he had robbed his first train in Uvalde and fell into a life of crime. After release from prison, Willis and Joe Newton (above, right) returned to the Uvalde area. They are seen reviewing a *Uvalde Leader News* headline story about their crimes.

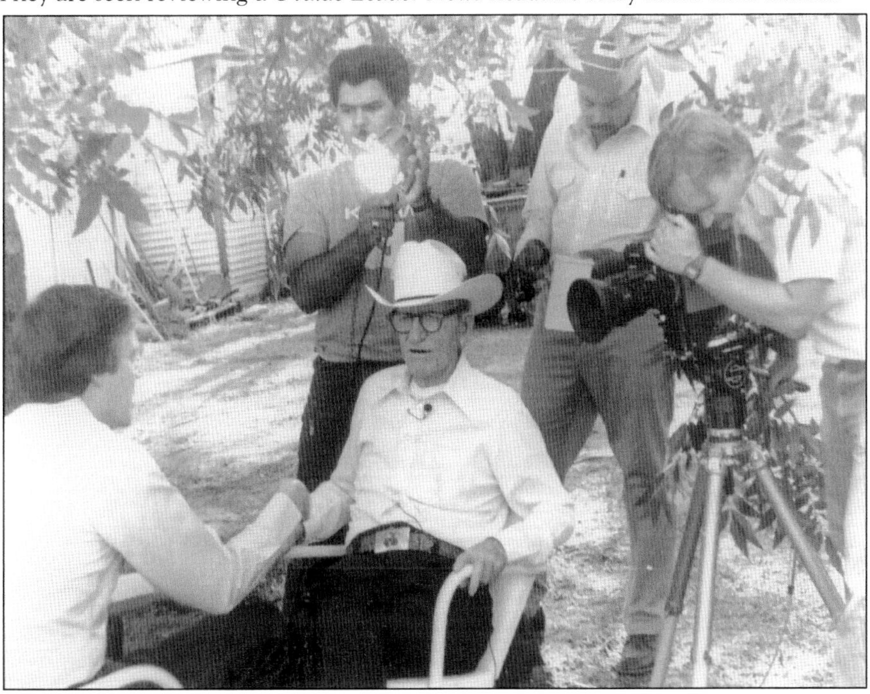

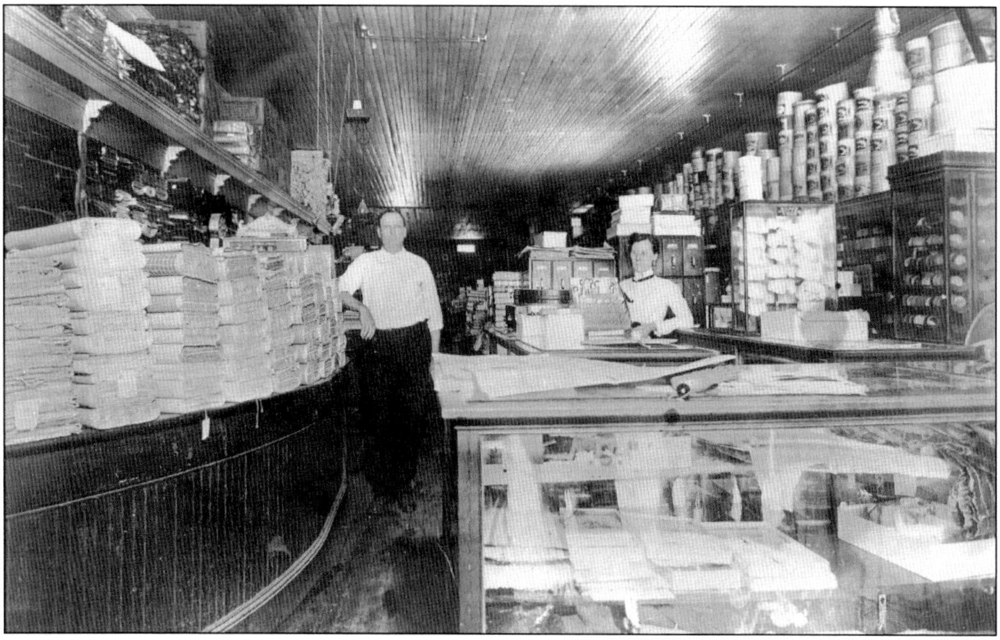

At the start of the 20th century in rural southwest Texas, the general store had to meet the needs of everyone in the community. Such was the case with Robert's General Store, pictured here around 1913; it sold dry goods such as fabric, ribbon, lace, and men's collars (in the glass display case on the counter at right), in addition to groceries and hardware.

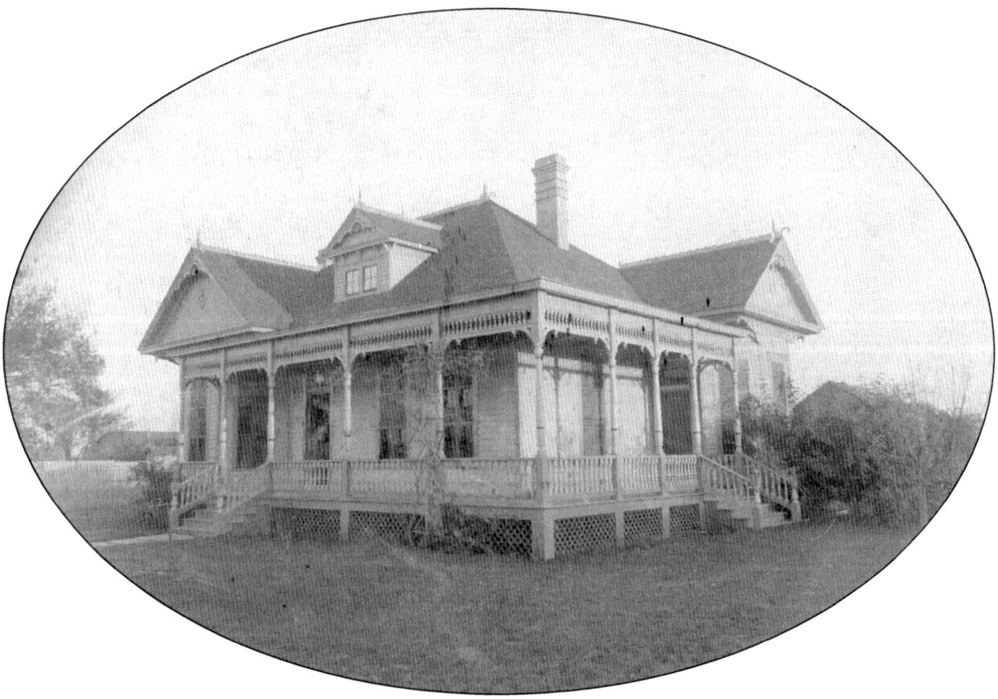

This home was the residence of Dr. A.R. Bowman. A successful physician and surgeon, he came to Uvalde after medical school in Missouri and New Orleans. He also had business interests in Barnhill Drug Company and Uvalde Wholesale Company, and in Uvalde area land and ranches.

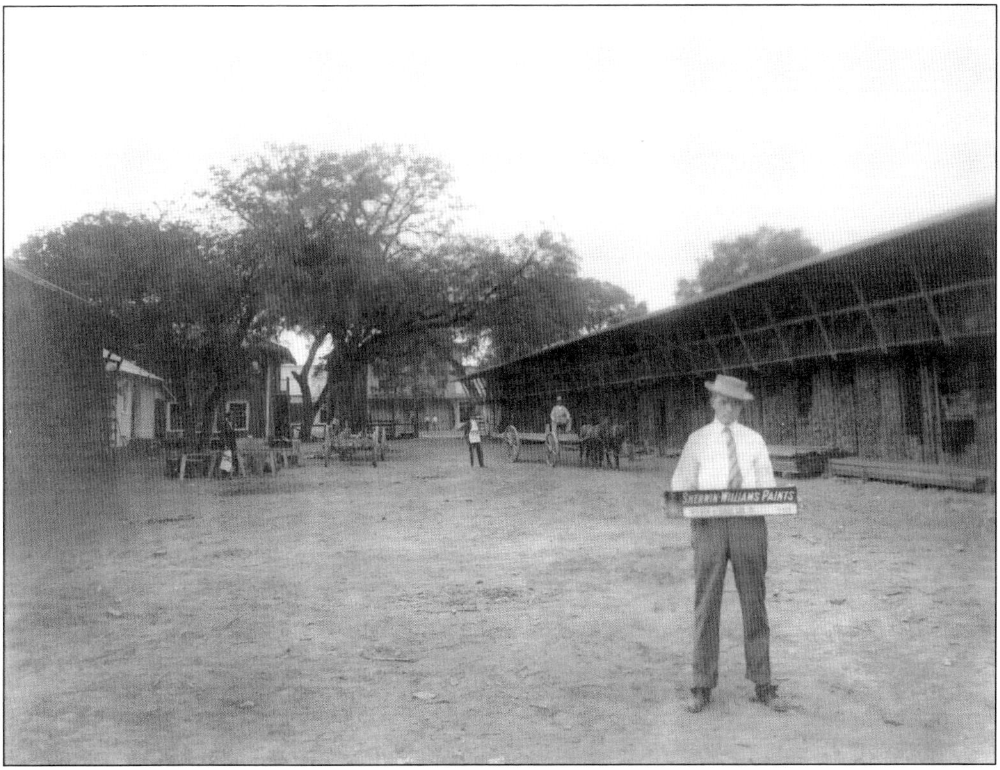

Mayhew & Isbell Lumber Company was an early-20th-century Uvalde business. By 1900, the population of Uvalde had grown to 1,889, and by 1910, it was 3,998. A large lumberyard was needed to meet the demands of a growing community as the majority of homes, barns, and outbuildings at this time were still made of wood.

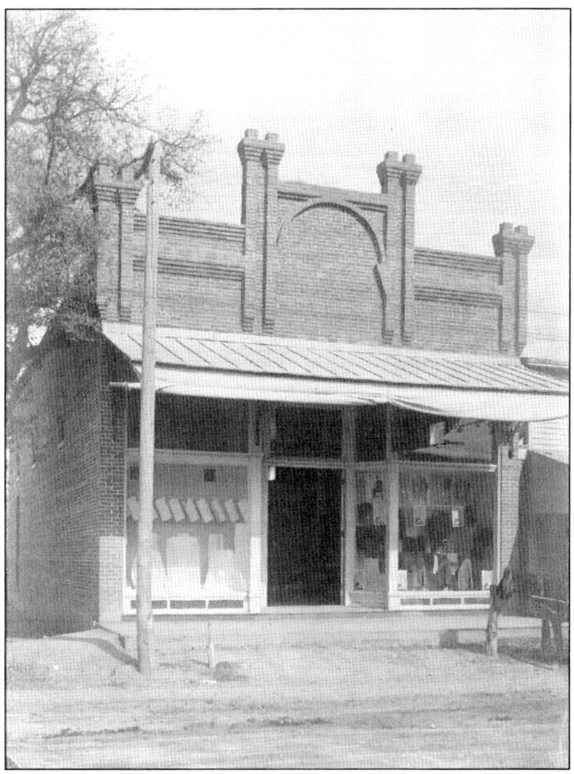

This tailor's shop has fabric, trim, and lace on display in the left window. The right display window has men's suits and slacks. There are also a number of different suit styles on display on posters. The exact location of this store is unknown but the photograph was taken in the early 1900s.

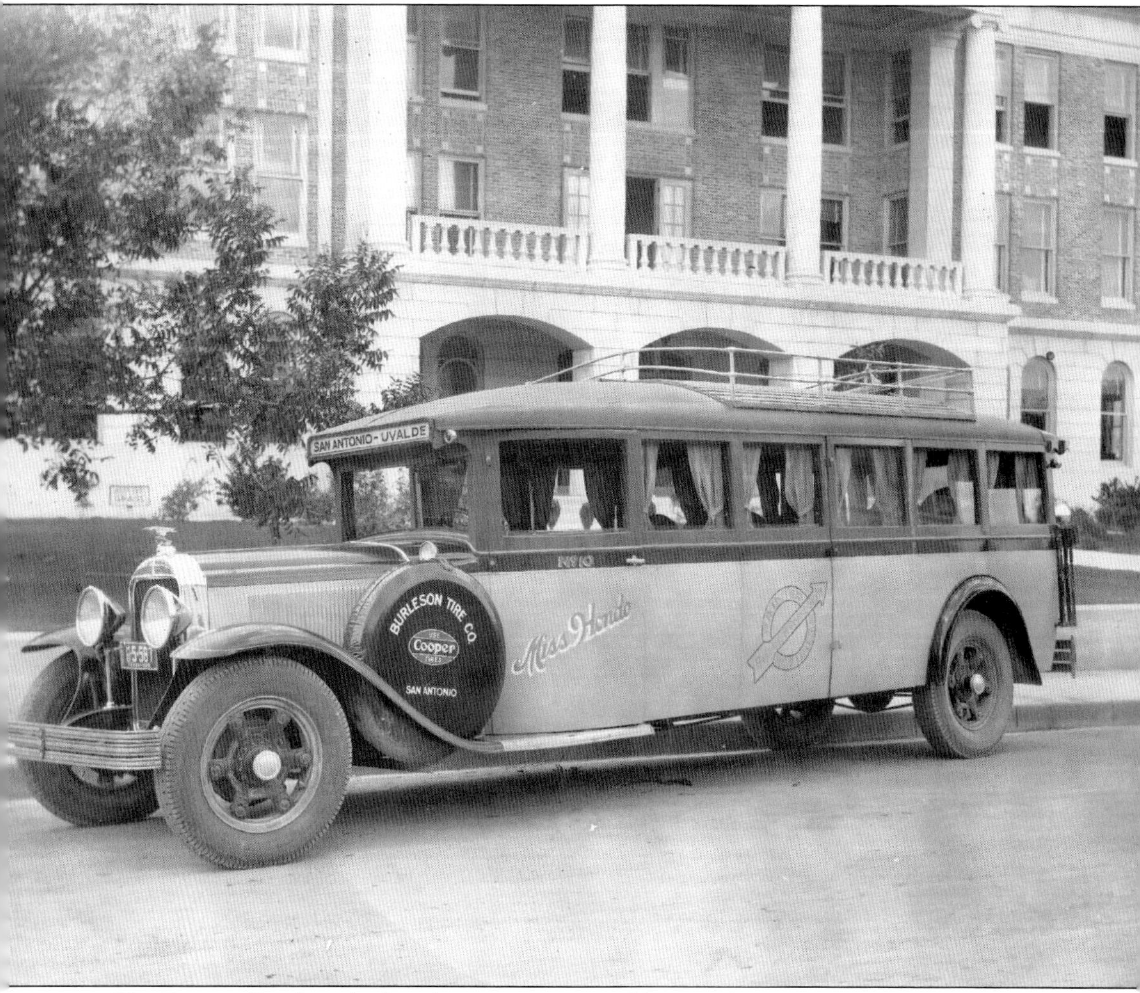

The Painter Bus Line had its beginning in Uvalde on July 4, 1924. With a seven passenger Studebaker Red Ball Bus, Walter Painter drove the daily 90 mile round trip from Uvalde to San Antonio. The business grew with routes to Carrizo Springs, Del Rio, and the Winter Garden area added to the itinerary. By 1927 services were expanded to Eagle Pass; with each destination, busses were added to accommodate the business. This 1929 photograph shows the "Miss Hondo" bus, and the Painter Bus logo, which states "Painter Bus Lines Inc. Serving 8 County Seats." Congressman John Nance Garner was often a passenger in the early 1920s when Painter was the only driver. During their conversations over the 90-mile trip Garner learned of Painter's expansion plans and loaned him $600. Painter, ever grateful for the 1925 loan, felt that Garner really helped jump-start his bus company. By 1933 the bus line had 12 buses and 23 employees. In 1966 the company was sold to the Kerrville Bus Company.

This building is still in use today on East North Street. The lower stairway has been enclosed, but the upper outdoor balcony still exists. However, over the years the lower facade has been changed to offer more storefront windows.

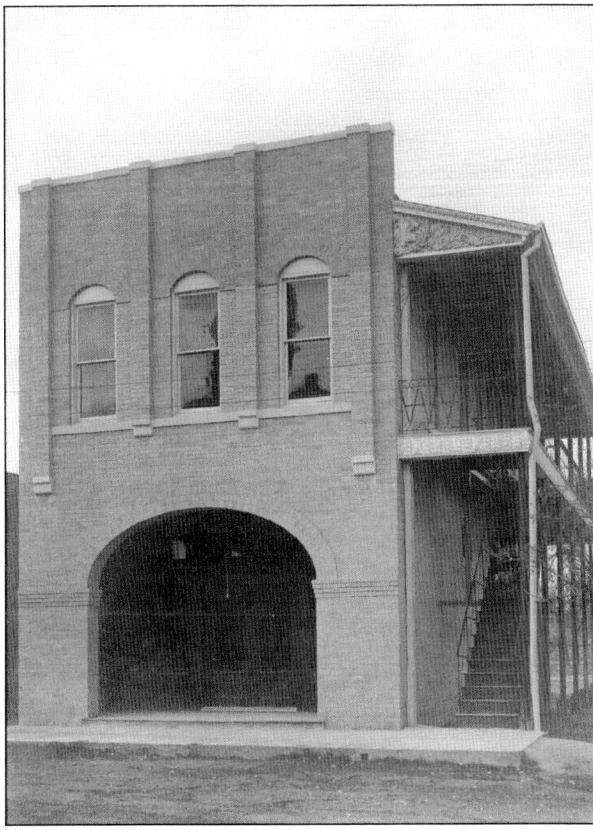

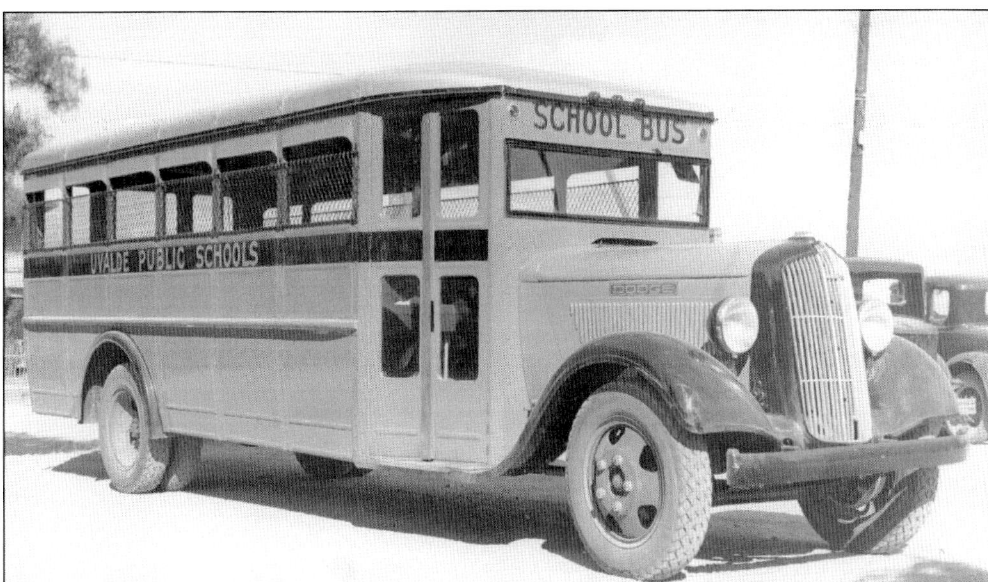

Prior to the automobile, the earliest school bus was known by several names, such as kid hack, school car, or school truck. Kid hacks were horse drawn wagons with a rear entry, so as to not spook the horses when loading or unloading children. The Uvalde Schools acquired their first enclosed school bus, a Dodge, around 1936.

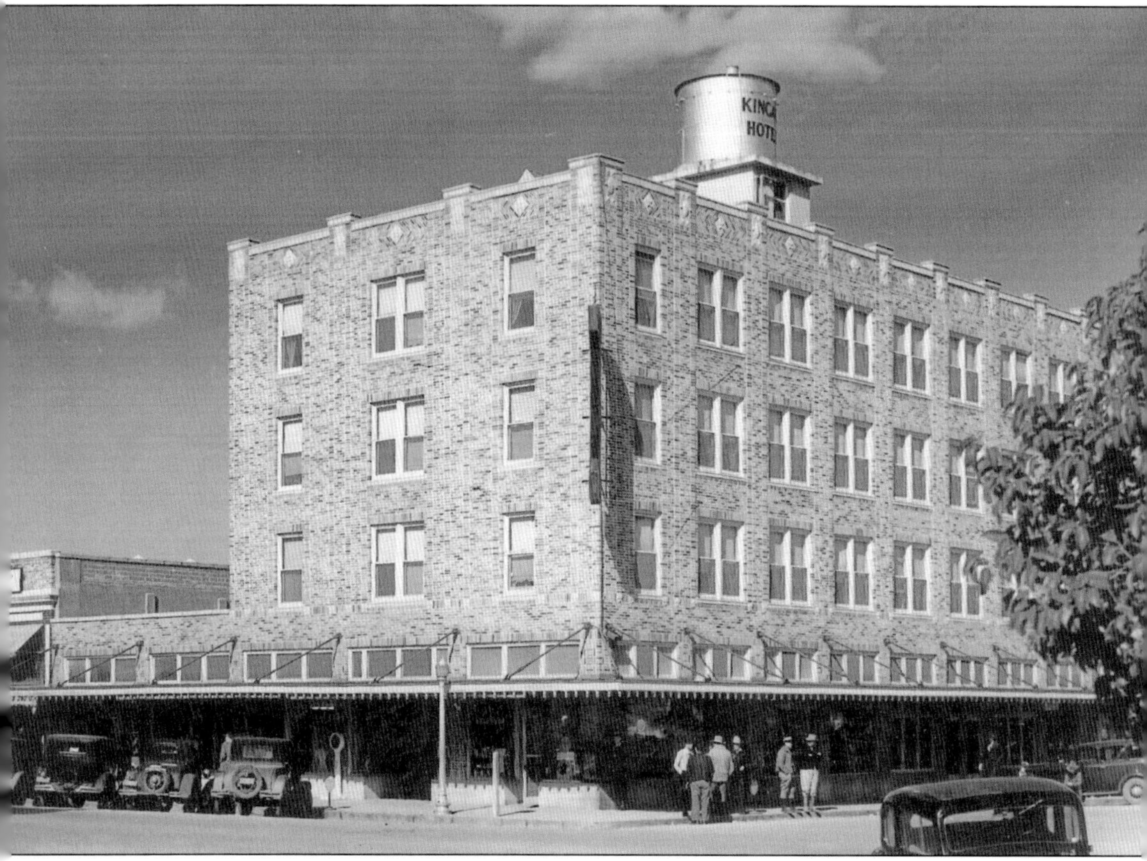

Today the Kincaid Hotel still stands at the corner of North Getty Street and East North Street. It was built in memory of William David Kincaid by his widow, Cordelia Taylor Kincaid, and their children, Eugene, Frank, Tincie, and Mae. From opening day on August 18, 1927, the Kincaid Hotel hosted just as many dignitaries as the lawn of the John Nance Garner home. Quickly becoming the social and business center of Uvalde, the ground floor shops included a barbershop, beauty salon, candy and dress shops, a large lobby, coffee shop, and restaurant. There were 54 guest rooms on the second, third, and fourth floors. When cattlemen came to Uvalde to buy cattle, the Kincaid was where they hung their hats. From receptions for Pres. Harry S. Truman and his wife to a cup of coffee for Lyndon B. Johnson, the Kincaid was the place to be seen and was the social hub of the community.

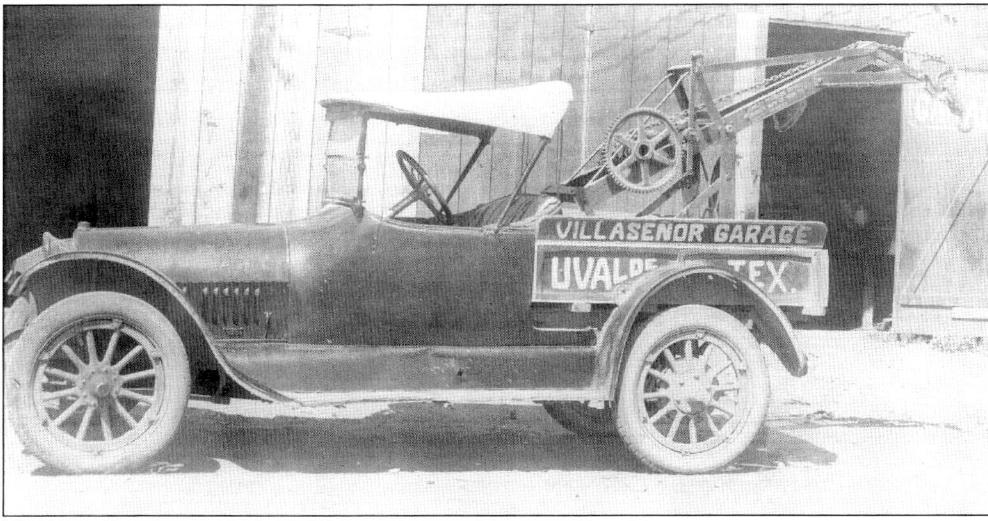

Every garage needs a good wrecker and such was the case for Villasenor Garage. This Uvalde business was a needed addition with the advent of the automobile and was much better than dragging the car to the garage with a team of mules.

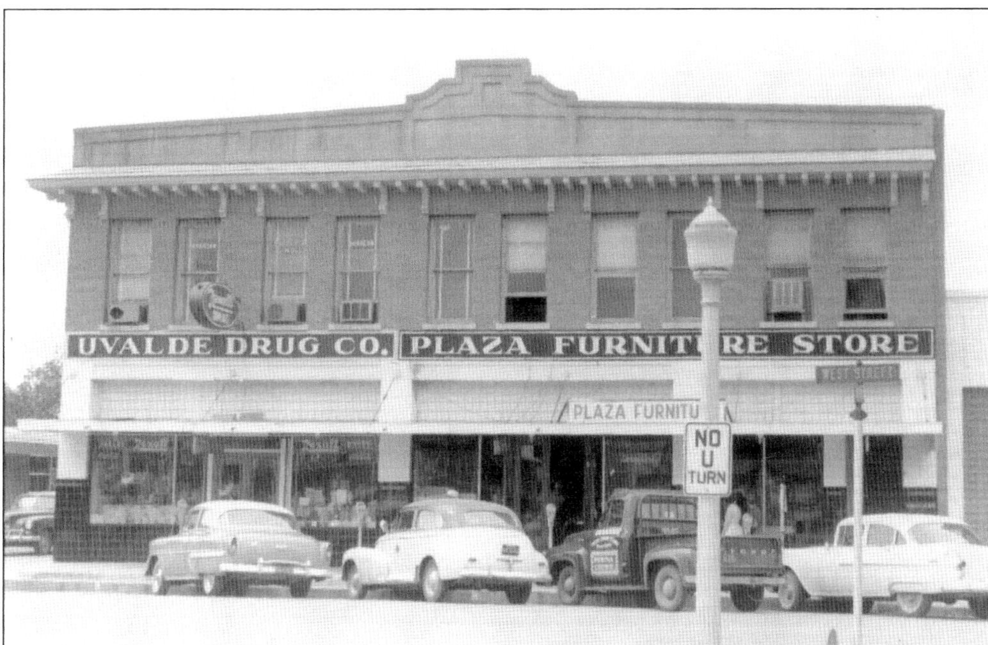

This building still stands on the corner of West North Street and North Piper Lane in the same block as the Grand Opera House. Once home to the Uvalde Drug Company and the Plaza Furniture Store, it now houses a beauty school.

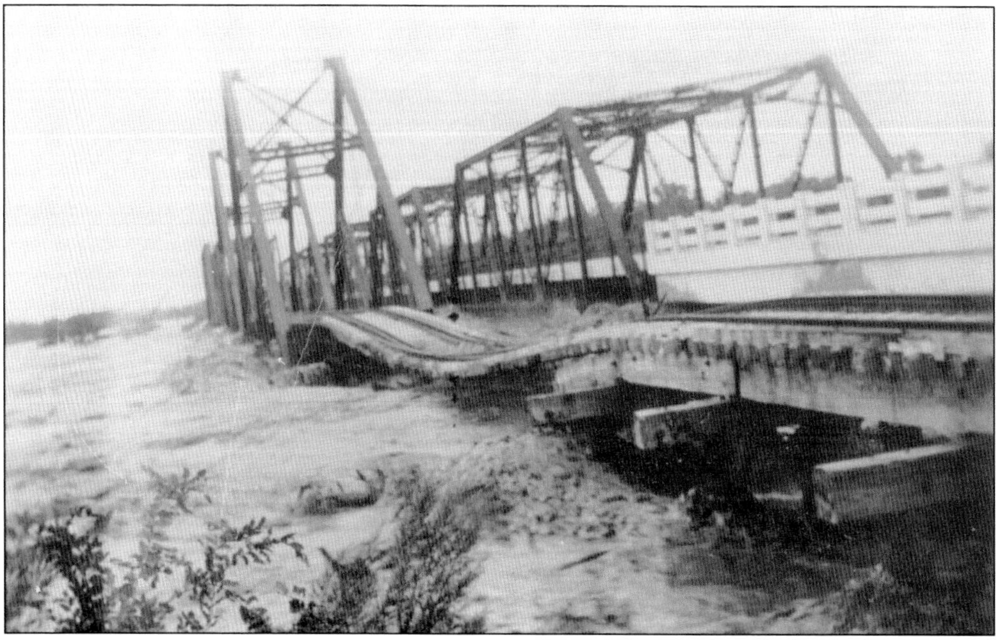

In June 1935, another set of storms and rain settled over the Uvalde area and produced major flash floods. The Nueces River travels north to south in the western portion of the county as it winds its way toward Corpus Christi Bay. US Highway 83 crosses the Nueces River just south of Uvalde. It is the major transportation artery taking goods and people to Crystal City, Laredo, and points south. This flash flood was severe enough to take both the railroad trestle and the bridge out and send them downstream. In the "after" photograph below, notice how the railroad rails are wrapped around the concrete bridge support.

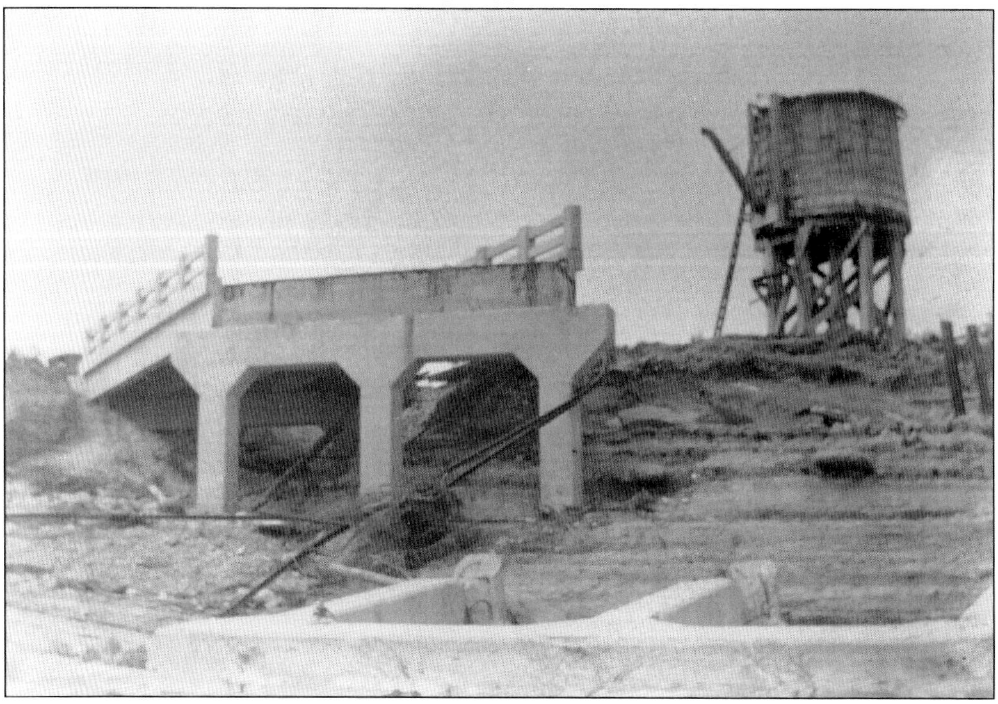

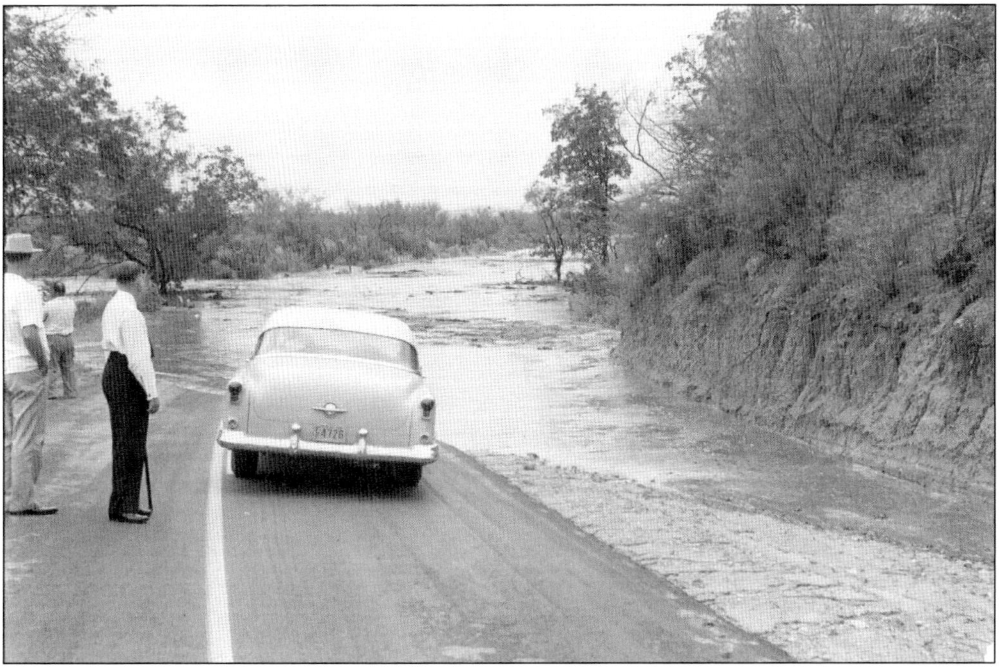

Nothing can rise faster than a creek or river in Uvalde County during or after a hard rainfall. The dry creek beds with numerous hillside draws feeding into the creeks and rivers make for a funneling influence that can turn a dry ditch into a raging wall of water. Everything in its path is destroyed, from fence gaps to livestock that happens to be trapped by the rising water. This 1950s scene is still typical during times of heavy rainfall. All one can do is wait for the water to subside and hope the roadway is still there and not covered with debris so the next trip to town can be made.

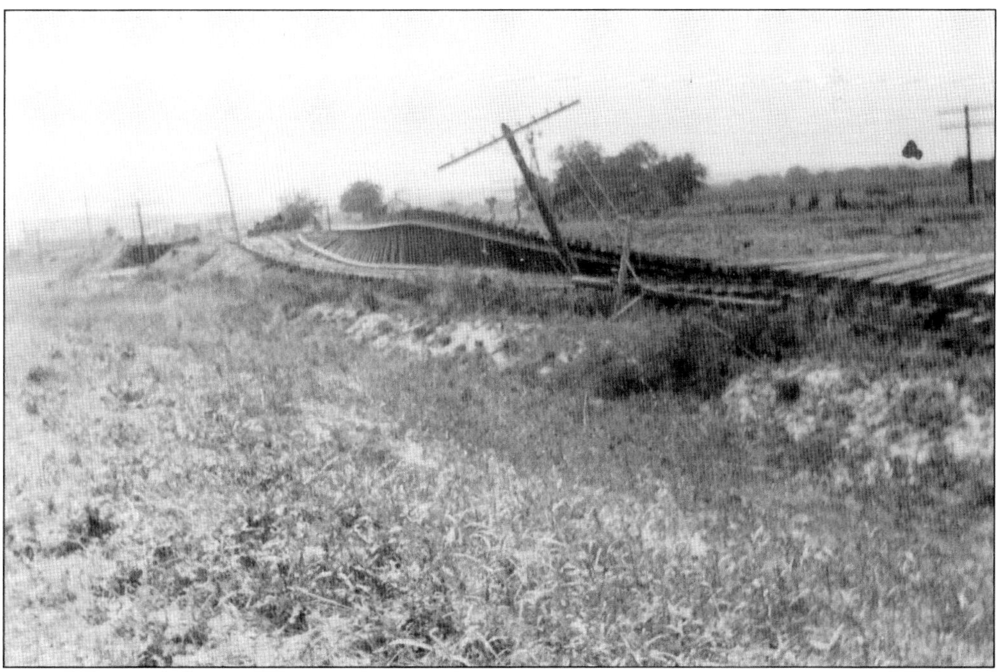

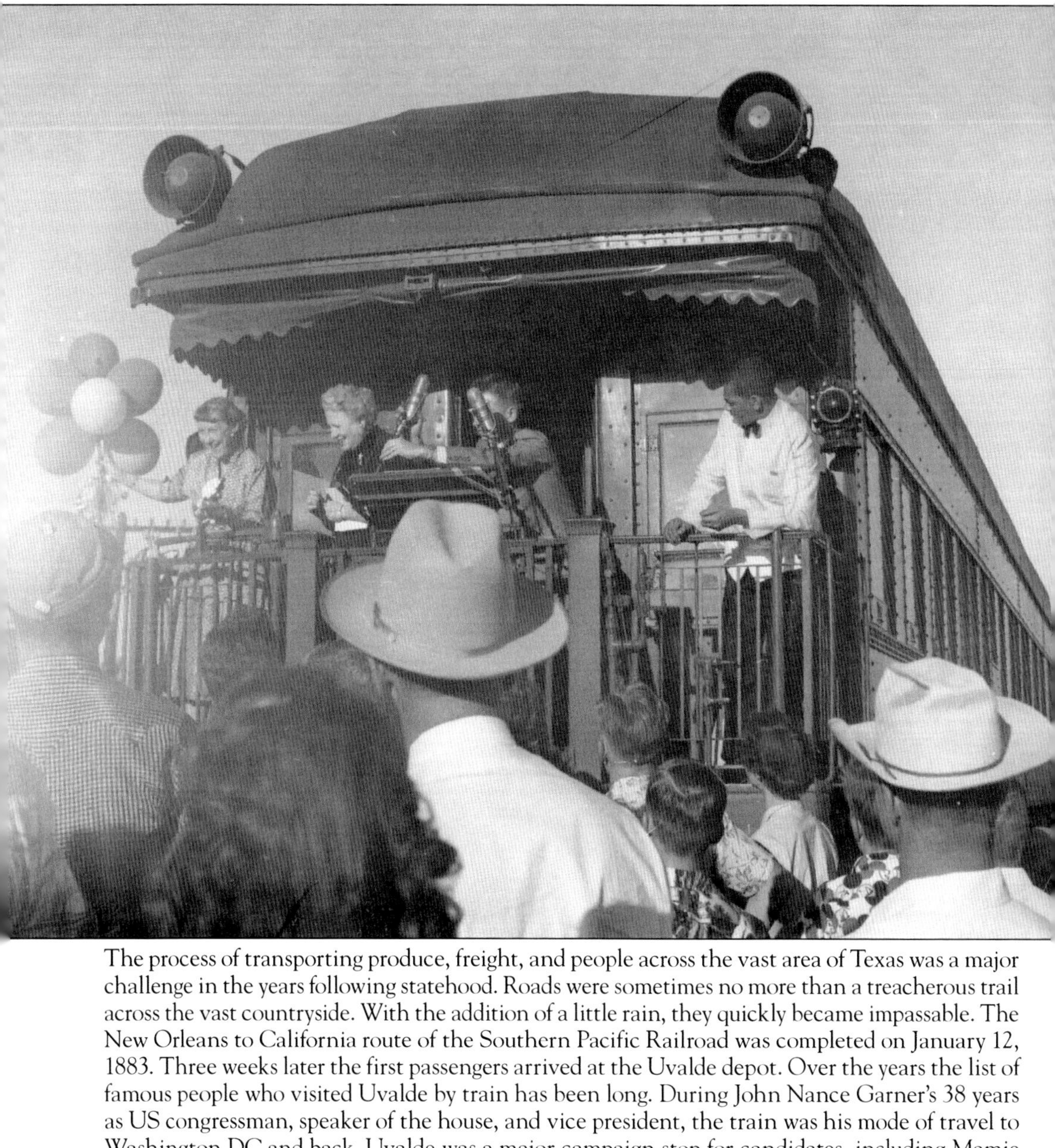

The process of transporting produce, freight, and people across the vast area of Texas was a major challenge in the years following statehood. Roads were sometimes no more than a treacherous trail across the vast countryside. With the addition of a little rain, they quickly became impassable. The New Orleans to California route of the Southern Pacific Railroad was completed on January 12, 1883. Three weeks later the first passengers arrived at the Uvalde depot. Over the years the list of famous people who visited Uvalde by train has been long. During John Nance Garner's 38 years as US congressman, speaker of the house, and vice president, the train was his mode of travel to Washington DC and back. Uvalde was a major campaign stop for candidates, including Mamie Eisenhower (at left with balloons) who visited during her husband's 1952 bid for the presidency.

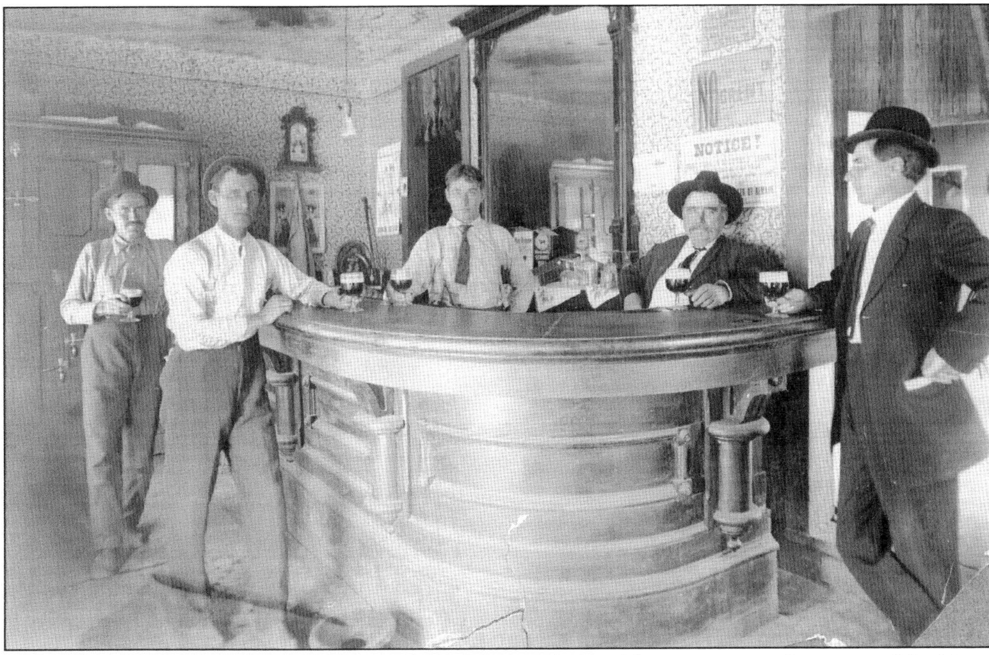

This saloon with its classic mirror and wrap-around wood bar was one of many in Uvalde at the turn of the century. Signs on the wall read "PLEASE Donot [sic] Use Profane LANGUAGE HERE," "No Checks Cashed, No Credit," and a warning to minors that these gentlemen are relaxing and enjoying a cold brew. Note that the spittoon is close at hand.

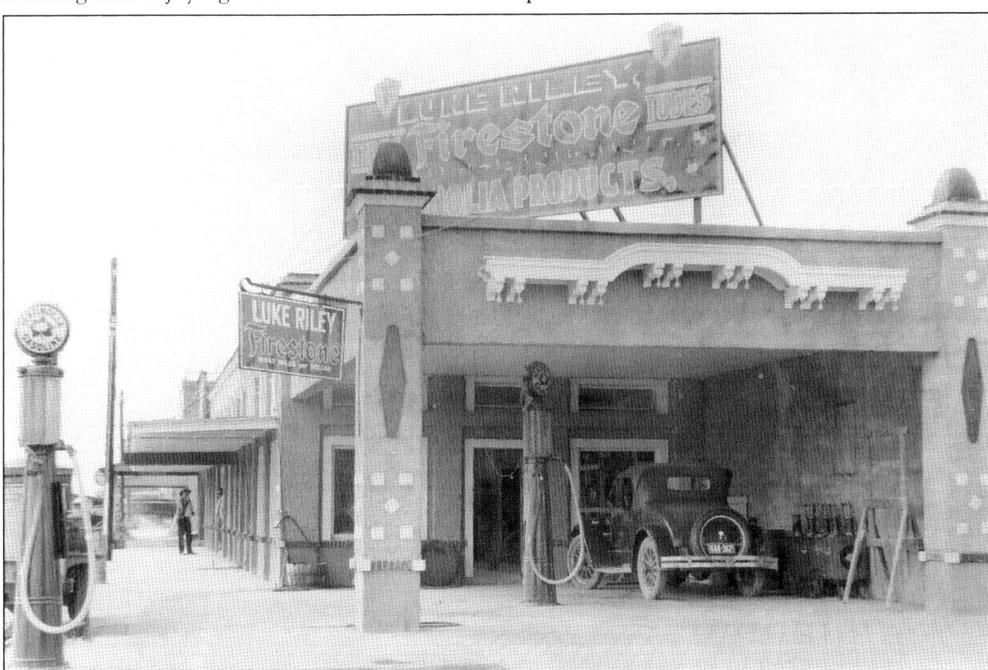

Luke Riley's Firestone and Filling Station selling Magnolia gasoline was located at 111 South Getty in the 1930s. In the same building row just beyond the filling station was the Walker Grocery Company. The 111 South Getty address is on the town square.

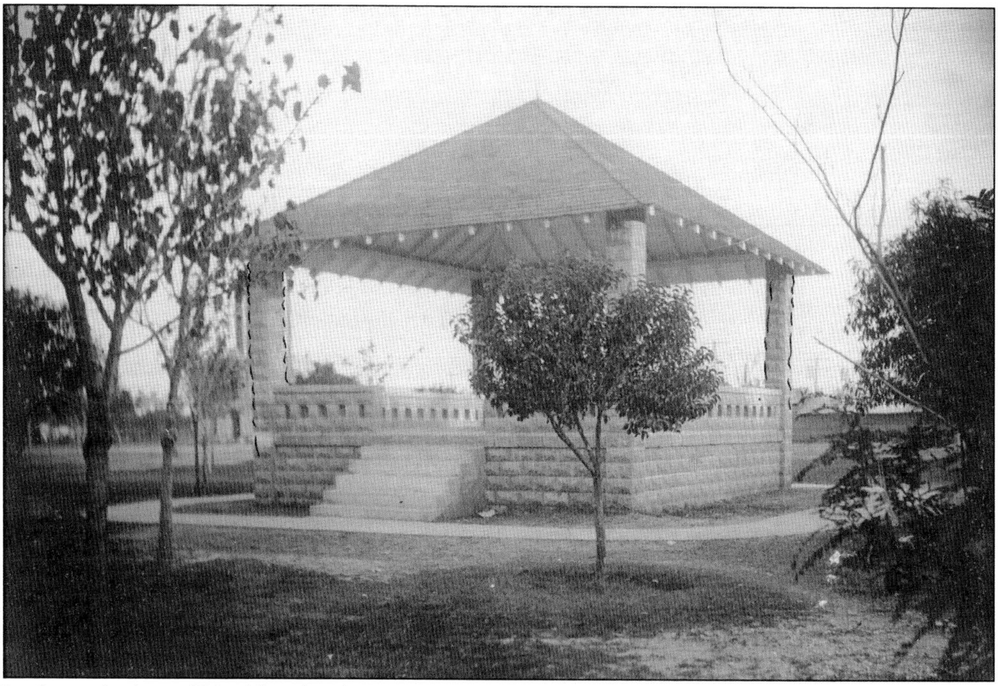

In the early days of Uvalde's development, Market Plaza was one of the main wagon yards for the town. However, by the turn of the century, the town put the plaza back to its intended use as a pleasant place for the townsfolk to enjoy, complete with a bandstand.

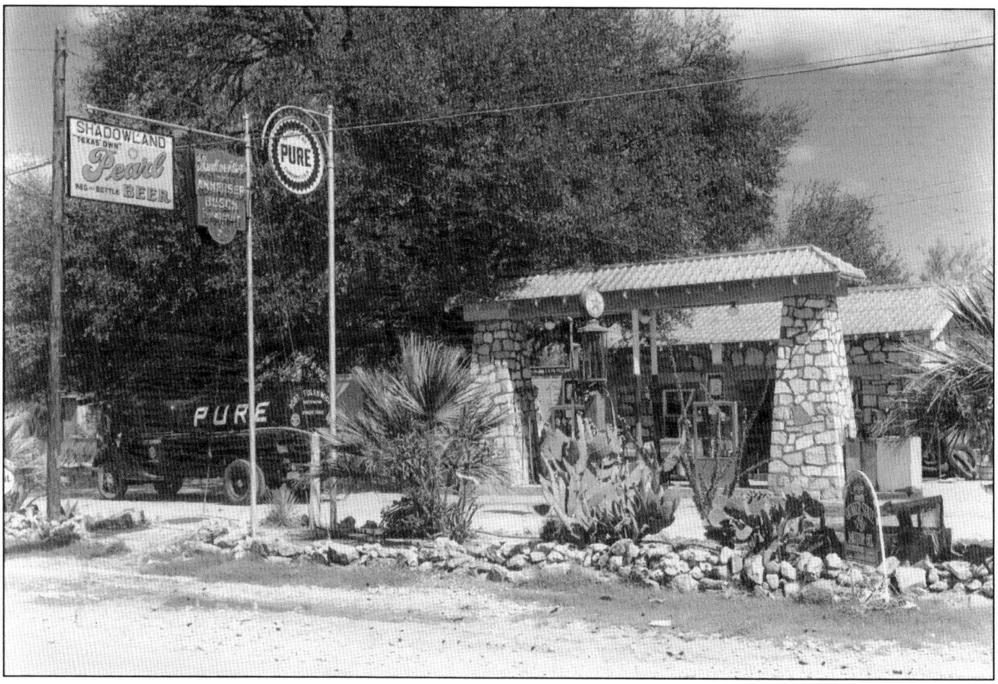

There are several generations of Americans that have no idea what "fill her up" means. The full service station would have someone to pump the gas, clean off the windshield, and check the oil, all at no extra charge to the customer.

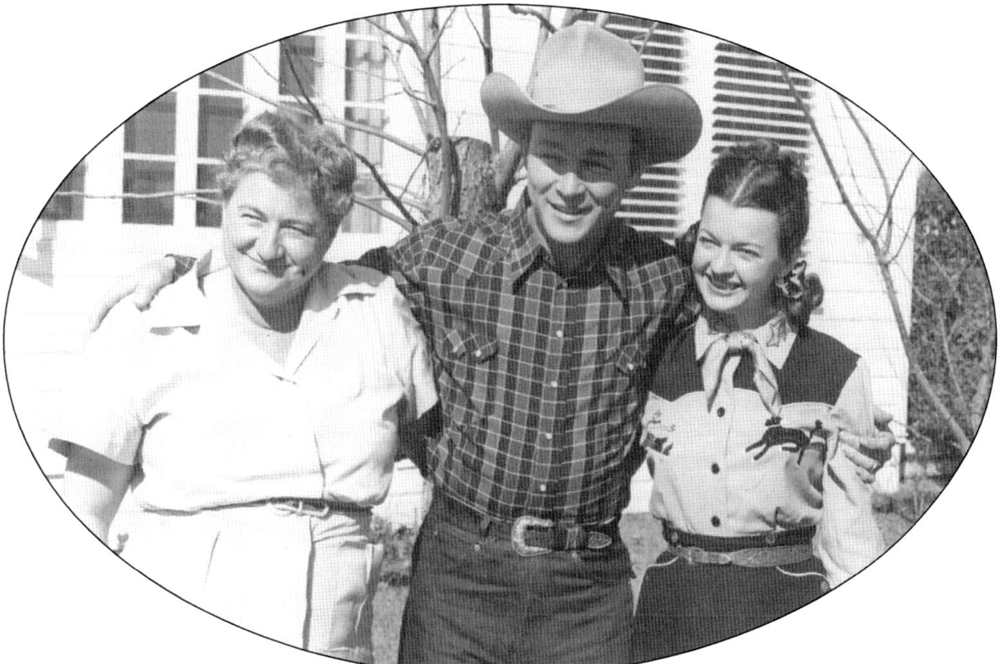

Happy Trails To You! Dale Evans was born Frances Octavia Smith in Uvalde on October 30, 1912. As a child, she spent many a summer and Christmas with her maternal grandparents in Uvalde. She married Roy Rogers on January 1, 1947. They honeymooned in Uvalde to visit friends and family. Here they are photographed with Dale Evan's aunt, Mrs. Bryon Pulliam, at her Uvalde home.

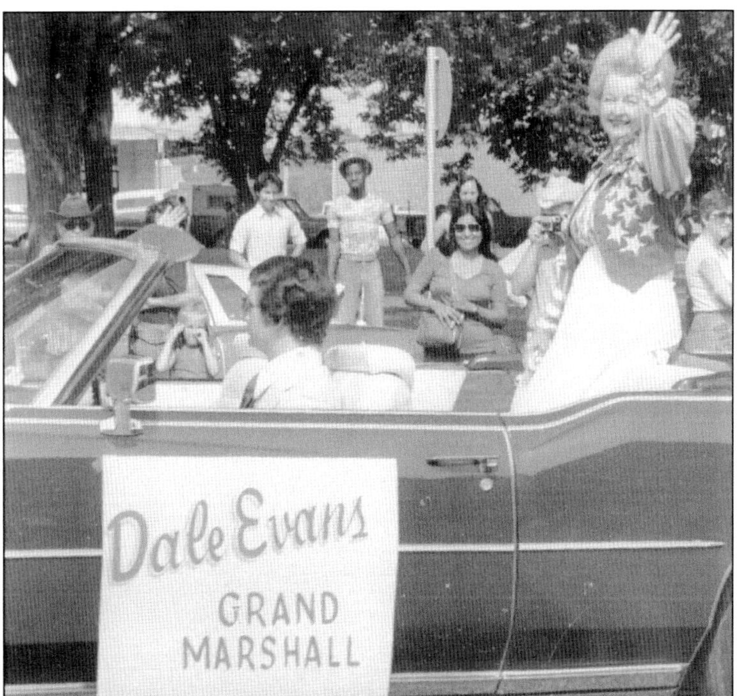

Movie and television star Dale Evans was proud to call Uvalde home. In 1956, she was queen of the Uvalde Centennial. On June 5, 1976, she returned and served as grand marshal and helped Uvalde celebrate the US Bicentennial.

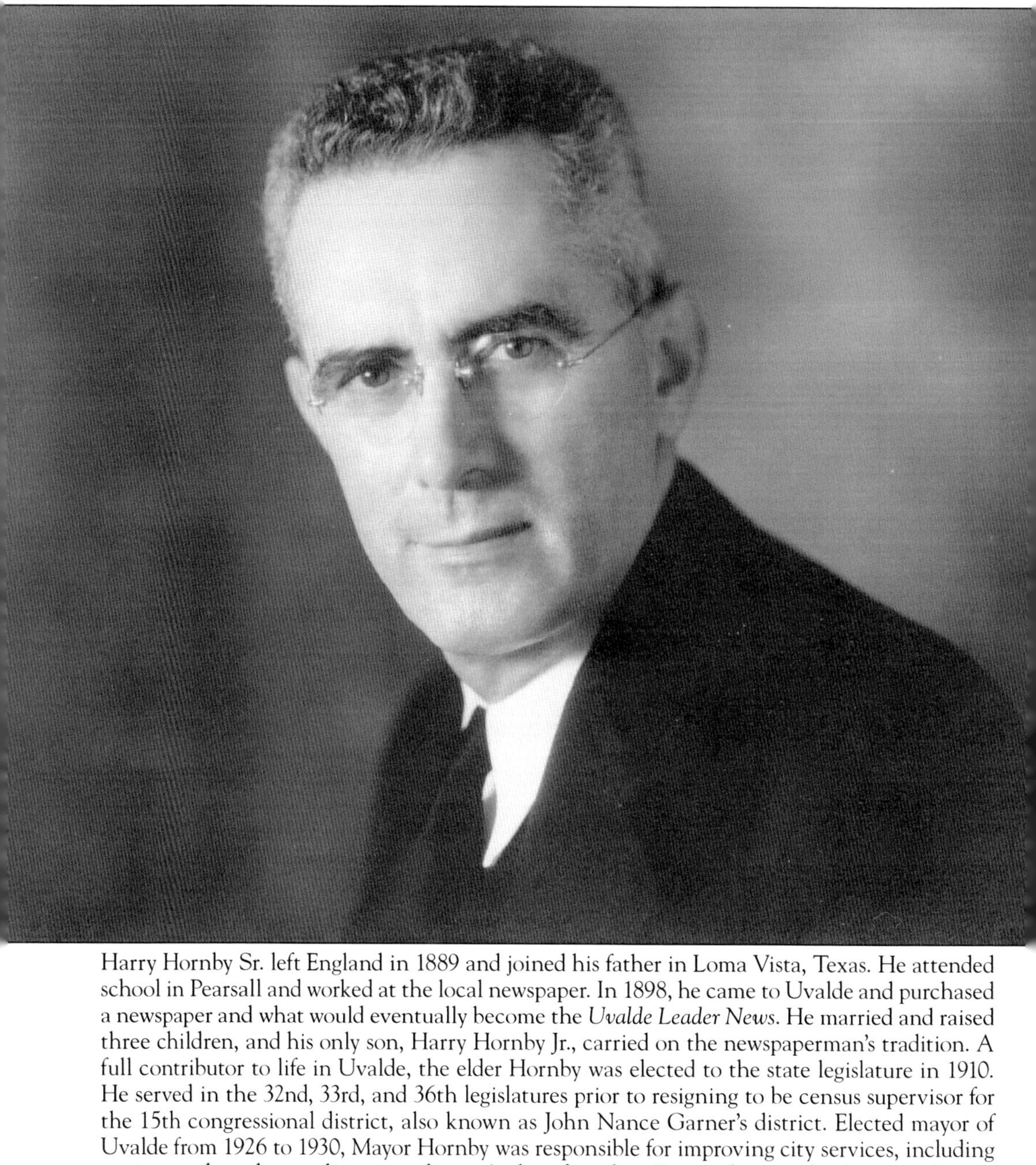

Harry Hornby Sr. left England in 1889 and joined his father in Loma Vista, Texas. He attended school in Pearsall and worked at the local newspaper. In 1898, he came to Uvalde and purchased a newspaper and what would eventually become the *Uvalde Leader News*. He married and raised three children, and his only son, Harry Hornby Jr., carried on the newspaperman's tradition. A full contributor to life in Uvalde, the elder Hornby was elected to the state legislature in 1910. He served in the 32nd, 33rd, and 36th legislatures prior to resigning to be census supervisor for the 15th congressional district, also known as John Nance Garner's district. Elected mayor of Uvalde from 1926 to 1930, Mayor Hornby was responsible for improving city services, including paving roads and extending sewer lines. A close friend to Garner, he was the first president of the "Garner For President" club.

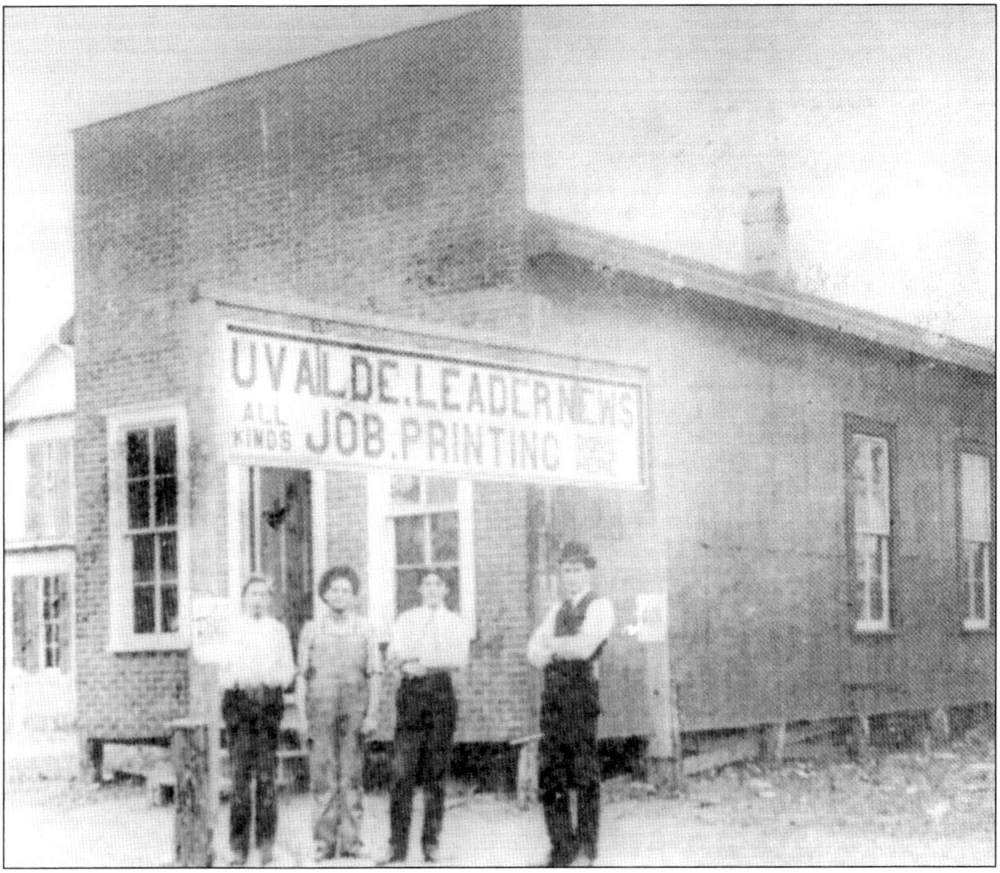

In 1902, the *Uvalde Leader News* was located on East Main Street. Pictured above from left to right are "Bum" Spurgeon, Finney Martin, Roy Mortin, and unidentified. Since the newspaper business involved printing presses and typesetting, most newspapers diversified and offered printing services to the public. Harry Hornby moved to Uvalde in 1898 and purchased the *Uvalde Leader News*. The 1910 photograph at right of the same building demonstrates how the business had expanded to rental houses and insurance in addition to printing. The building facade had been improved with a front awning, improved front steps, and new brick.

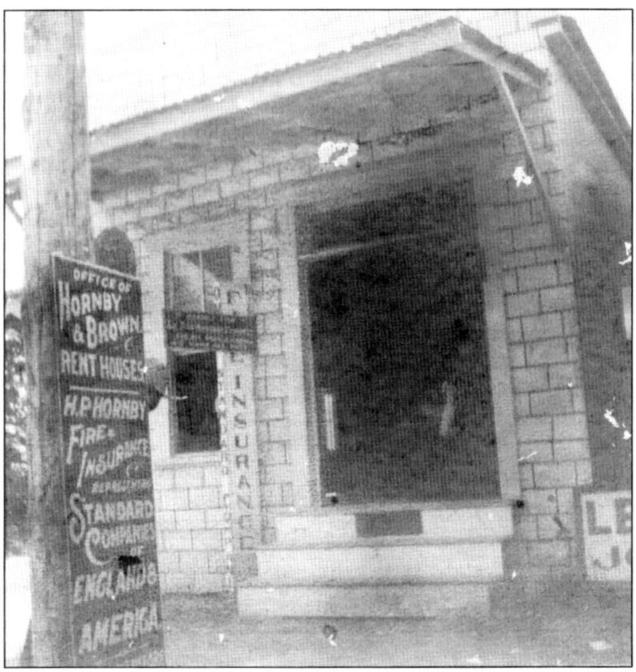

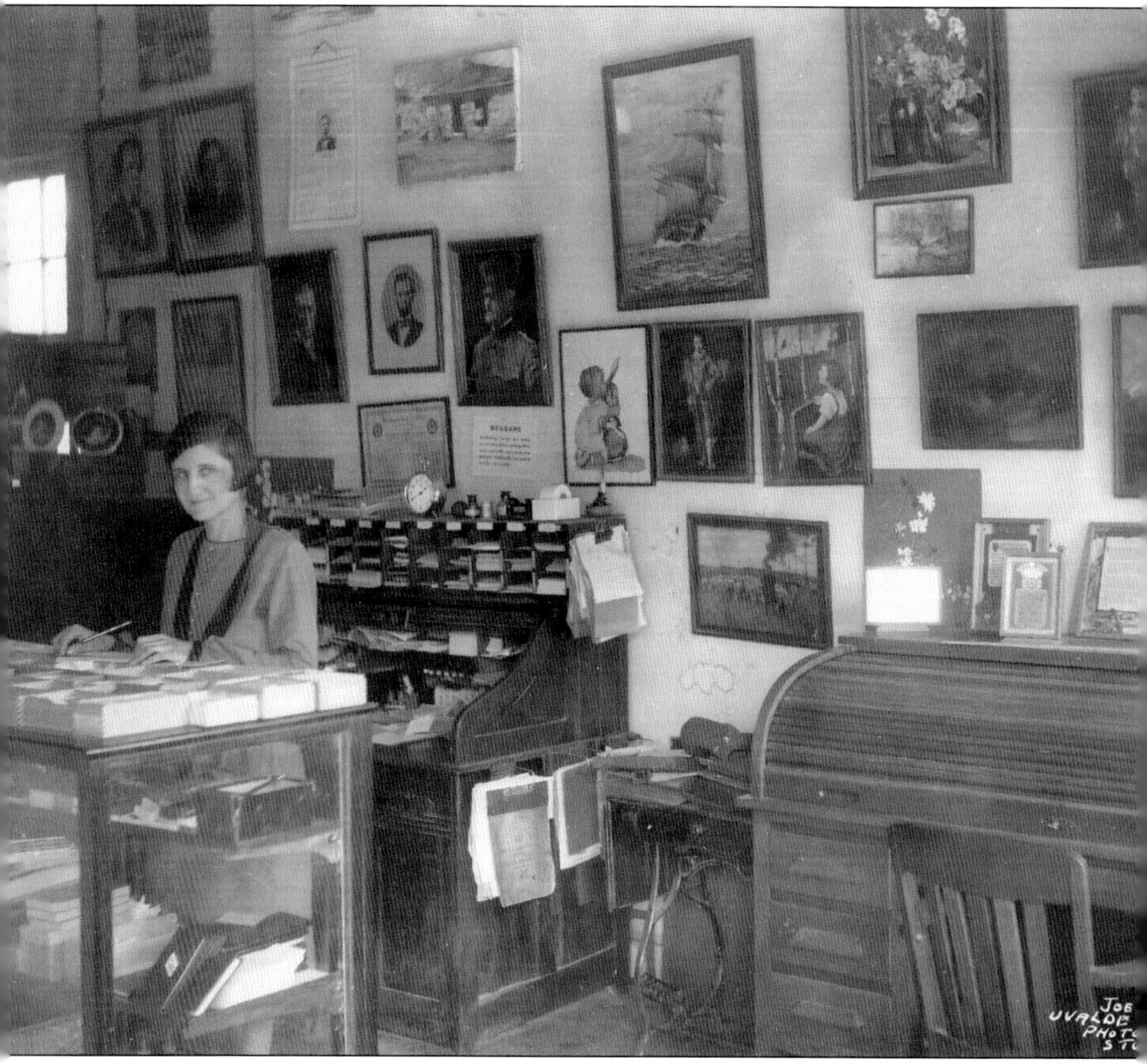

Mattie Thompson was the bookkeeper for the *Uvalde Leader News* in 1927. By this time the newspaper office was located on North East Street next to the Kincaid Hotel. Above Thompson's left shoulder and flanking the picture of Abraham Lincoln are Pres. Woodrow Wilson (president from 1913 to 1921) and Gen. John Joseph "Black Jack" Pershing, heroes of World War I. On the rolltop desk below the pictures are a number of items from bottles of ink to a white ceramic envelope roller with water basin that were common office supplies through the 1950s but today are considered antiques. Office supplies including pencils, ledger books, and invoice clipboards are for sale in the glass cabinet. The rolltop desks were also very popular at the turn of the century. They offered the convenience of hiding a messy desk very quickly.

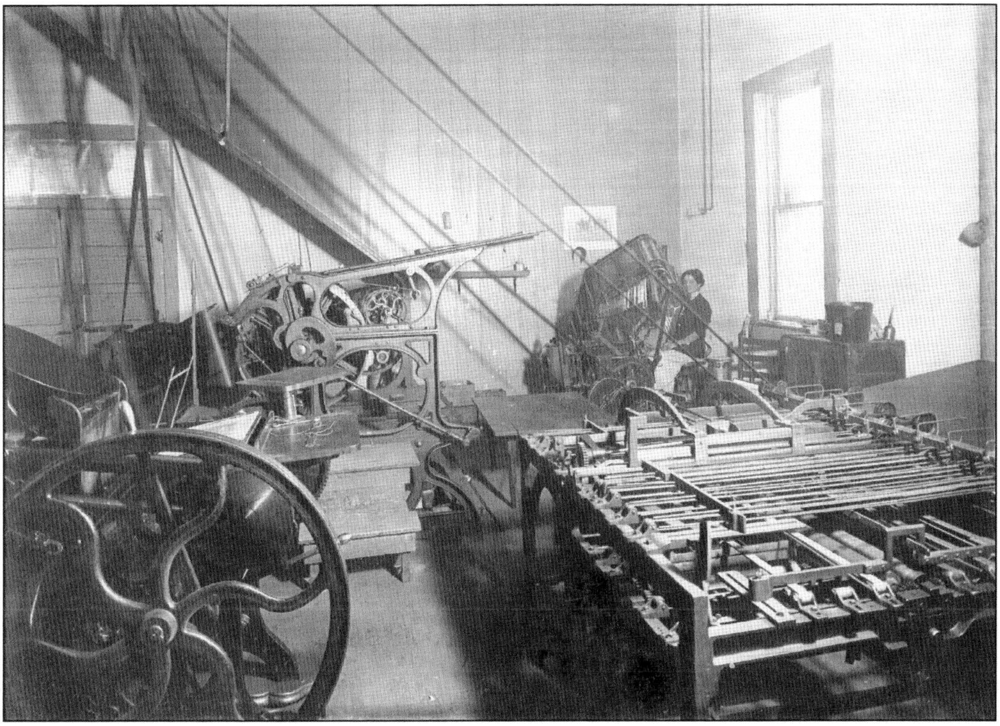

The *Uvalde Leader News* under the leadership of owner and publisher Harry Hornby Sr. had some of the best equipment available. The Babcock Cylinder Press above was a true workhorse in the printing room. Pictured at right around 1927, R.J. Jordan was the linotype operator. A linotype-typesetting machine produced an entire line of metal type at one time: a major improvement over manual typesetting. As editors, both Harry Hornby Sr. and his son, Harry Hornby Jr., viewed promotion of the town as their top priority. The elder Hornby was a contemporary and friend of John Nance Garner. The younger Hornby was good friends with Dolph Briscoe and helped promote his campaign for governor.

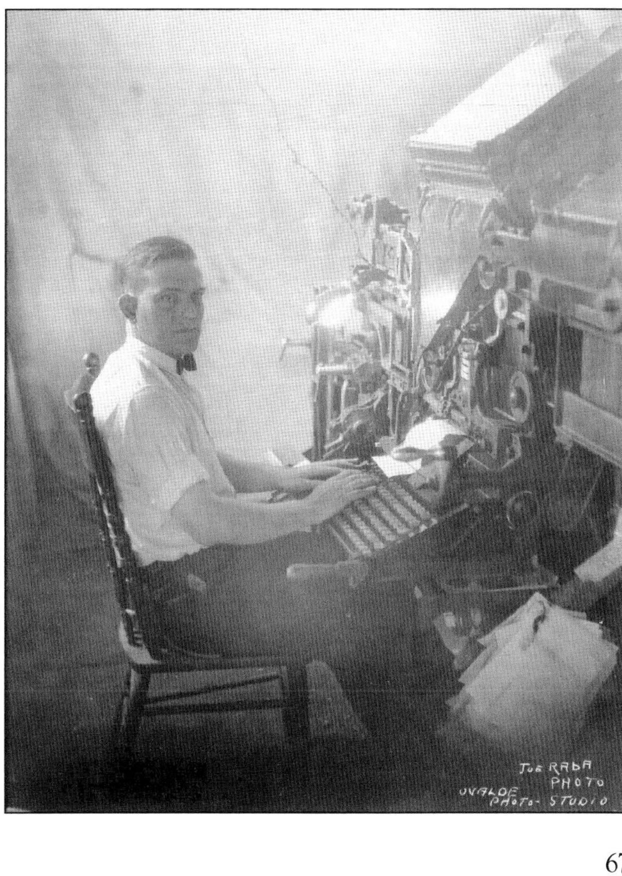

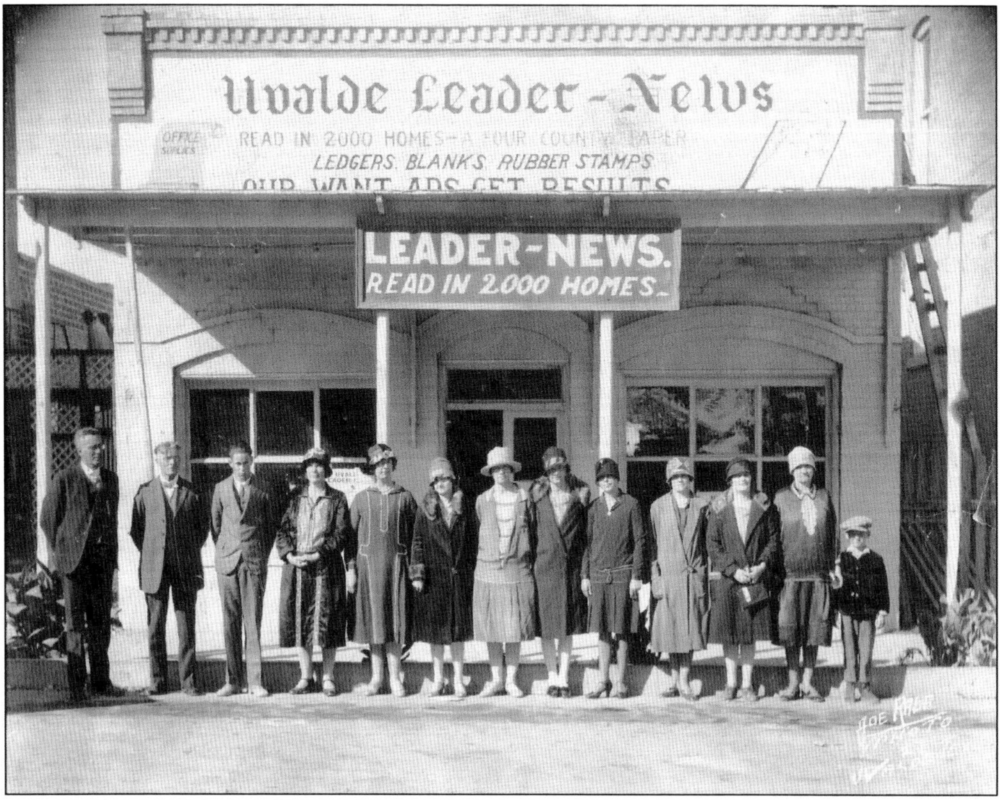

Another home of the *Uvalde Leader News* was on East North Street, next to the Kincaid Hotel. This photograph of the newspaper staff was taken in 1927. Publisher Harry P. Hornby Sr. is standing on the far left. As Uvalde grew, so did the *Leader News*, as evidenced by the hefty circulation advertisement on the front sign.

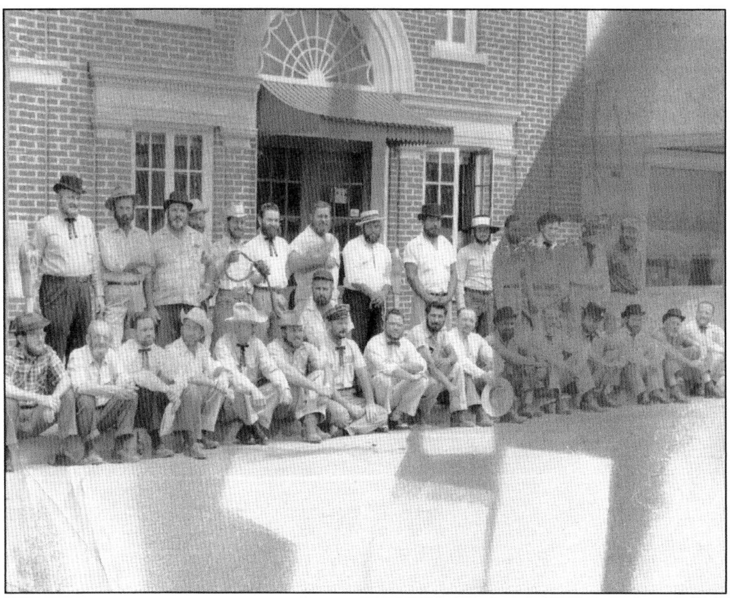

The Uvalde Centennial celebrations in 1956 were a festive occasion, with many events planned to honor Uvalde's past. One of the more entertaining contests to honor Uvalde's 100th year was the Beard Growing Contest held by the *Uvalde Leader News*. Even the owner and publisher, Harry P. Hornby Jr. (standing on left), got into the act and grew a beard

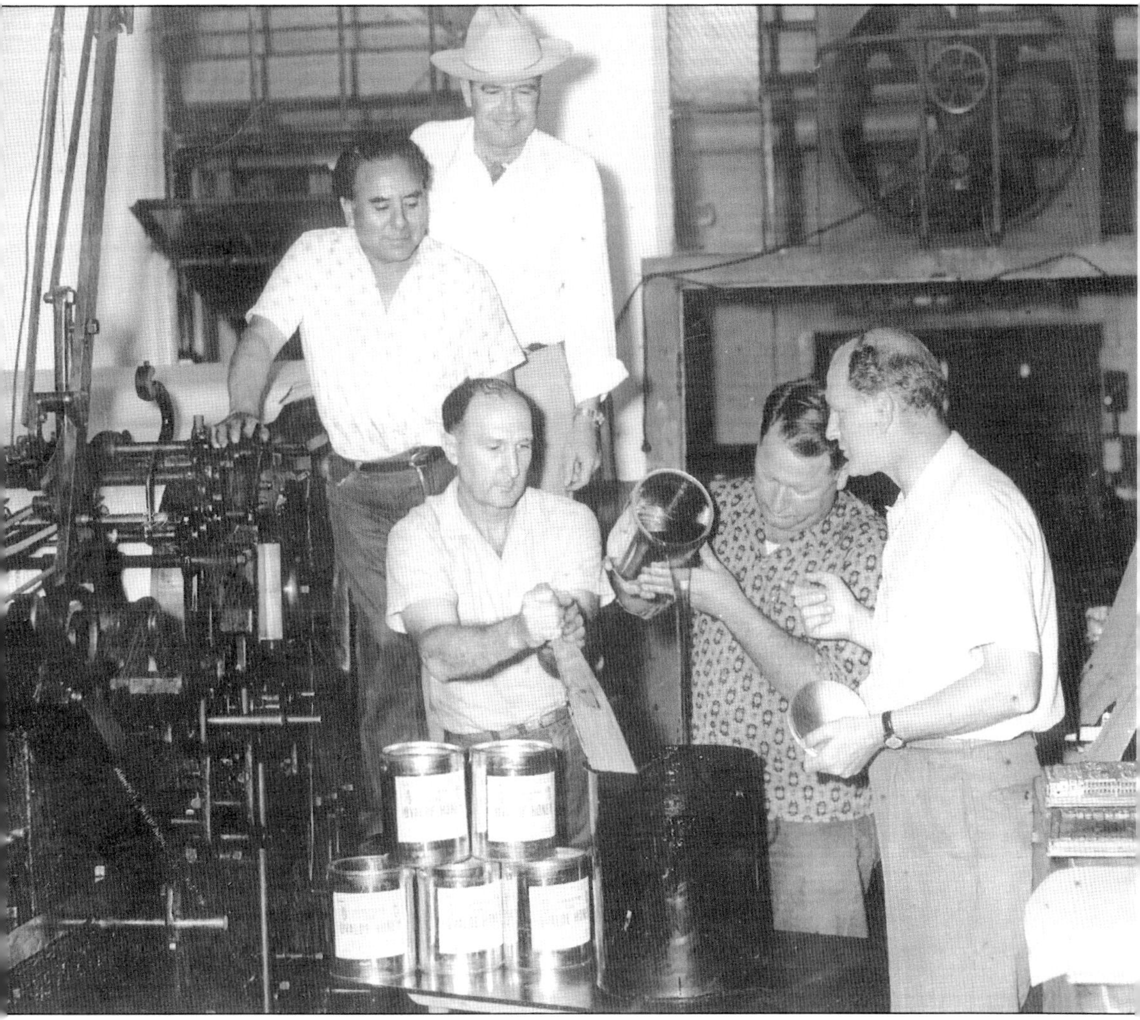

Each year in April, with the first monthly issue of the *Uvalde Leader News*, there will be hidden within the folds of the newspaper an April Fool's story. The story may be above or below the fold, and the author or authors surely had a very good time penning the tale. One year the story related a new find of an unlimited amount of water under the hills in North Uvalde County. In the 1950s, Dolph Briscoe Jr., Primo Uriegas, Ed Haby, Robert Peebles, and Frank Pinkens had an April Fool's story about Honey in the Ink at the *Uvalde Leader News*. The group did get the project started with cans of Uvalde honey being added to the ink for the presses. Unfortunately, the story must have ended up on the pressroom floor as it went unpublished.

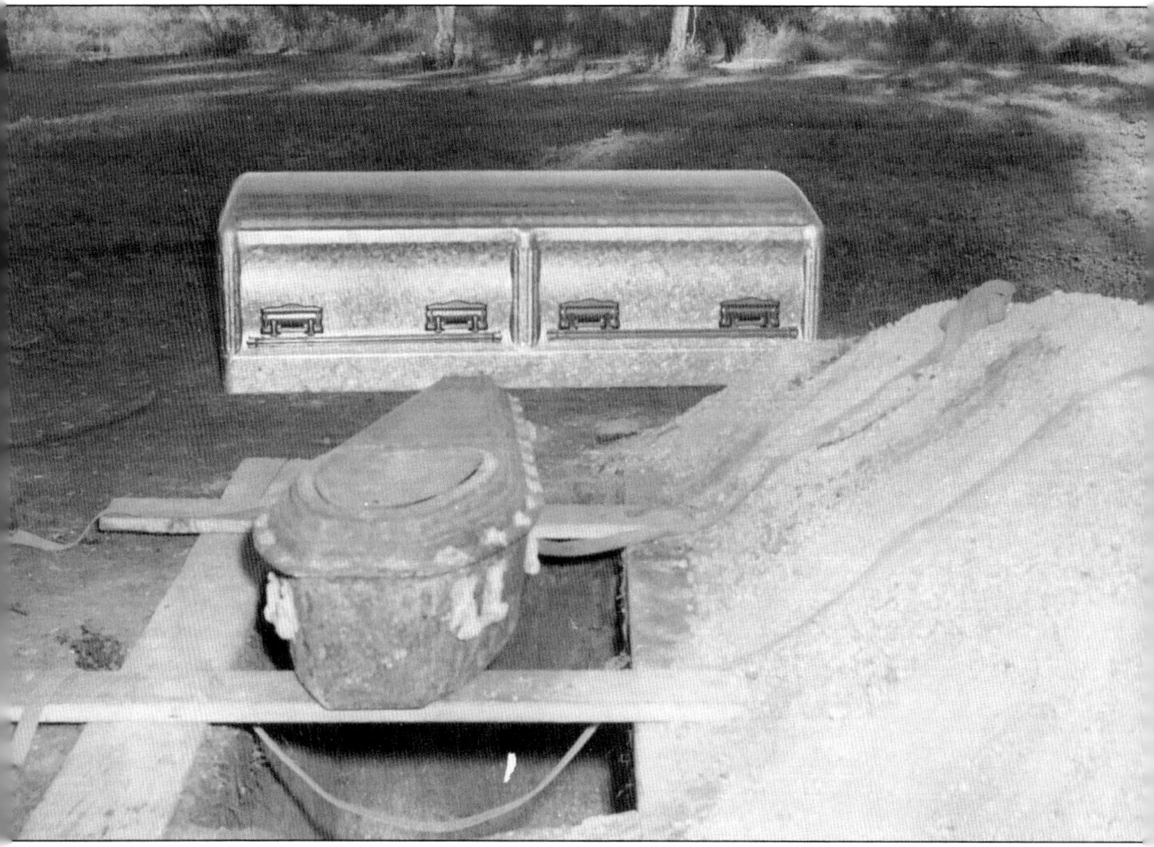

John King Fisher was a notorious gunslinger and outlaw who set up business along the Nueces Strip. The Strip was a lawless area and ideal for cattle rustling. As the frequency of King Fisher's crimes increased, so did their severity. Famed Texas Ranger Captain Leander McNelly arrested him several times for murder, as well as horse and cattle theft. A slick operator, Fisher was able to avoid conviction but chose to change his ways. He married in 1876, was appointed deputy sheriff of Uvalde County in 1881 and went from being an outlaw to respectable in a short period of time. In 1884, while on a business trip to San Antonio, he was shot and killed. He was buried at his ranch, clad in his famous chaps at 30 years old. Later, his body was moved from the original burial site to Pioneer Cemetery.

Two

Livestock, Wildlife, and Varmints

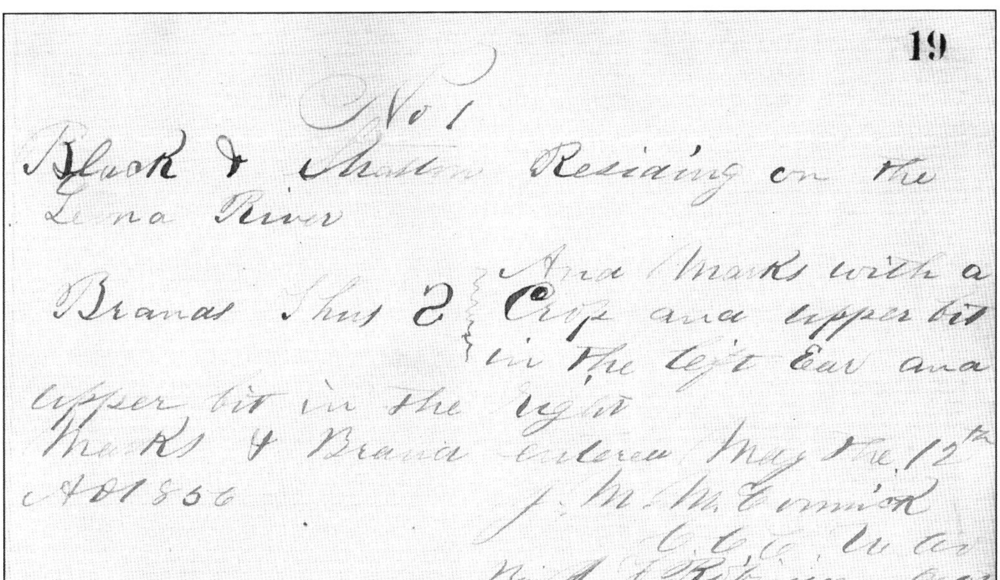

19

No 1

Black & Stratton Residing on the Leona River

Brands Thus S And Marks with a Crop and upper bit in the left Ear and upper bit in the right

Marks & Brand entered May the 12th AD 1856

J. M. McCormick C.C.C. U Co

By J. S. Robinson Dep

On May 12, 1856, the first brand, a backward "S" was entered in the Uvalde County Marks & Brands record book and issued to Black and Stratton, residing on the Leona River. Marks were used as well as brands to aid in owner identification of animals. Earmarks were used by nearly every rancher in the days of the open range. (Briscoe Center for American History.)

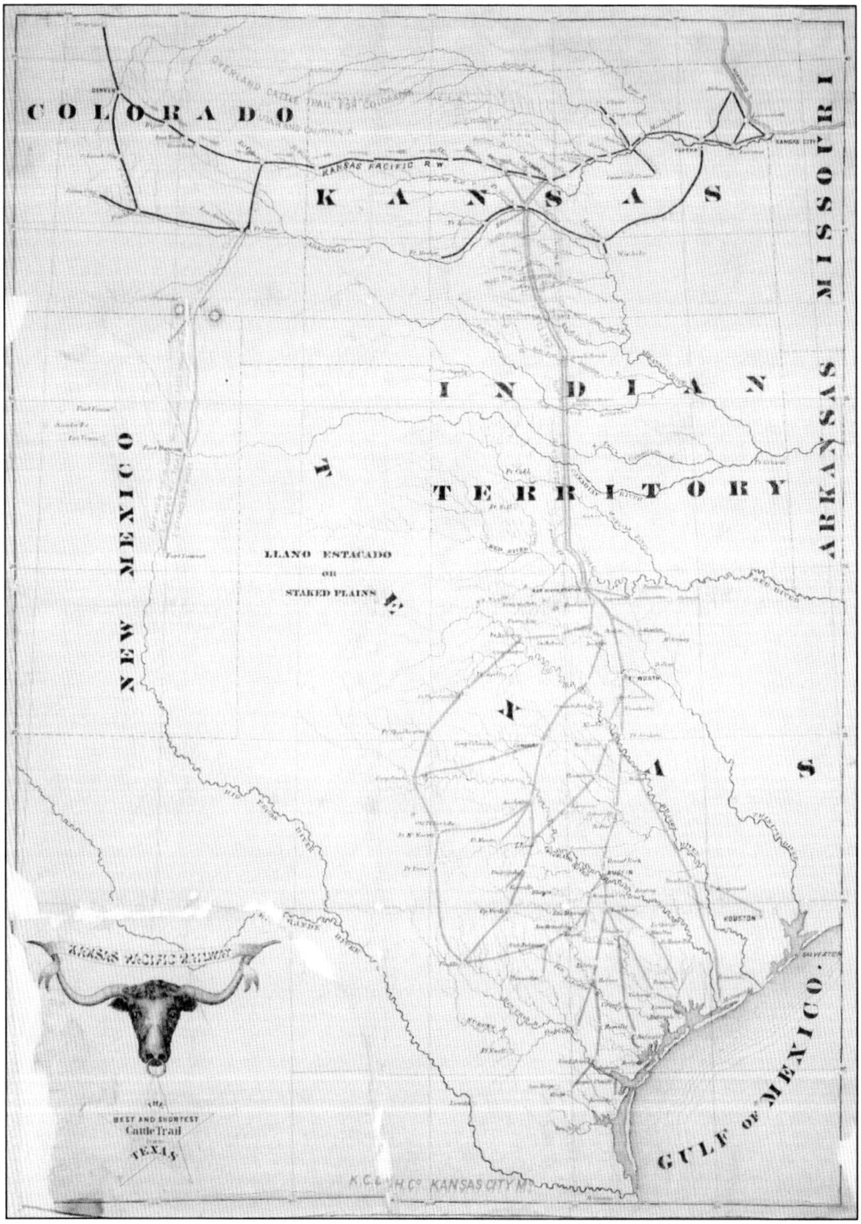

This rare Kansas Pacific Railway Map, "the Best and Shortest Cattle Trails from Texas," was published in 1875. At its zenith, between 1866 and 1890, trailing was the best way to get cattle to market from south and west Texas to the lucrative markets in Chicago and the Northeast. Due to the Civil War, these markets had been left with no cattle of their own to market, and a cow worth $2 in Texas was worth $40 in Kansas. Three trails started in Uvalde: a north-northwest trail to Camp Concho, a northeast trail to Fredericksburg and Llano, and an easterly trail to San Antonio and then north to Fort Worth. All three trails merged with other trails along the trip and then converged at Red River Station. From there the cattle were headed north across the Indian Territory to Kansas on what was known as the Ellsworth Cattle Trail. The Kansas destination was the Kansas Pacific Railway at Ellinwood, Russell, or Ellsworth, Kansas. (Briscoe Center for American History.)

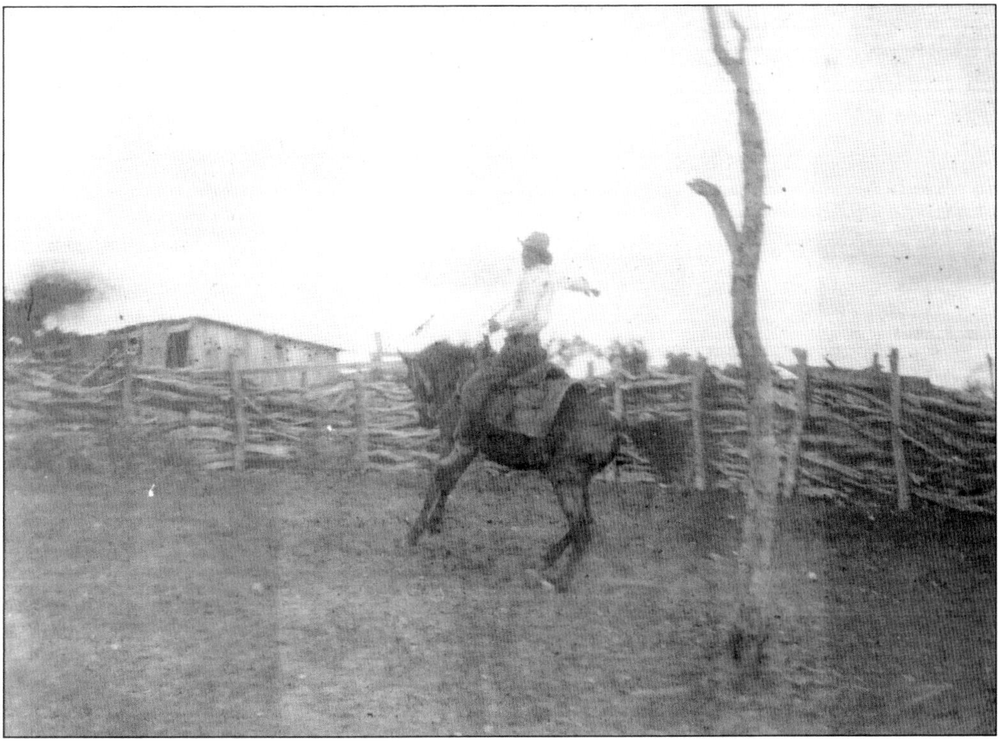

The horse was the engine for the cowboy prior to the advent of the pickup truck and motorized vehicles. In a country where getting to town could take a couple of days, being able to improvise and make do off the land was essential. Here a cowboy works the rough edge off his mount. Notice the tree snubbing post in the center of the pen. The fence, fashioned out of cedar logs and limbs, took advantage of a commodity, cedar, that was in abundant supply. Mule or ox-drawn covered wagons were the method of freight transportation prior to the automobile. They were essential in getting supplies to areas not served by the railroad.

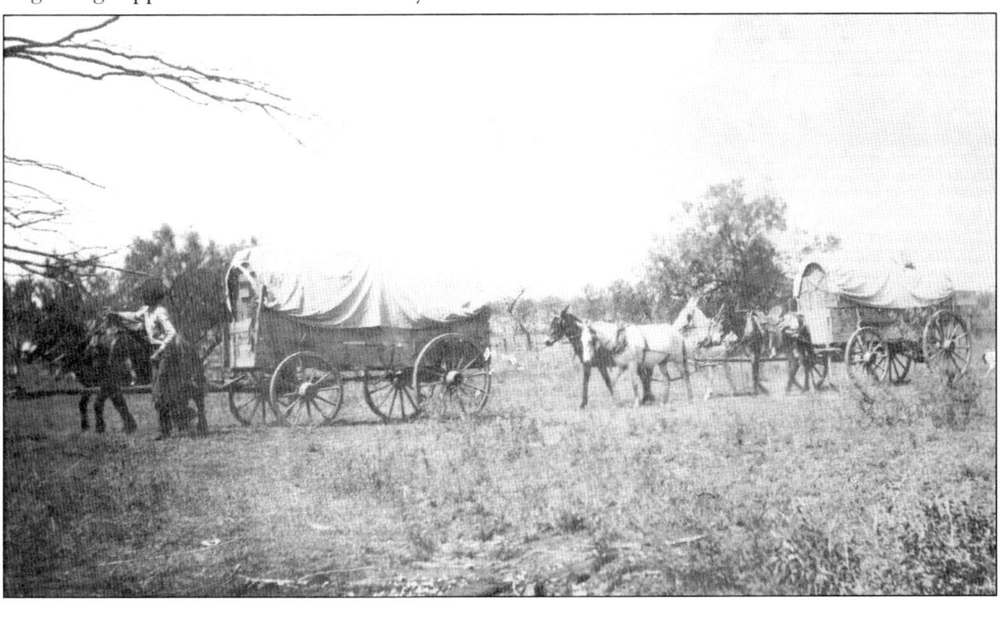

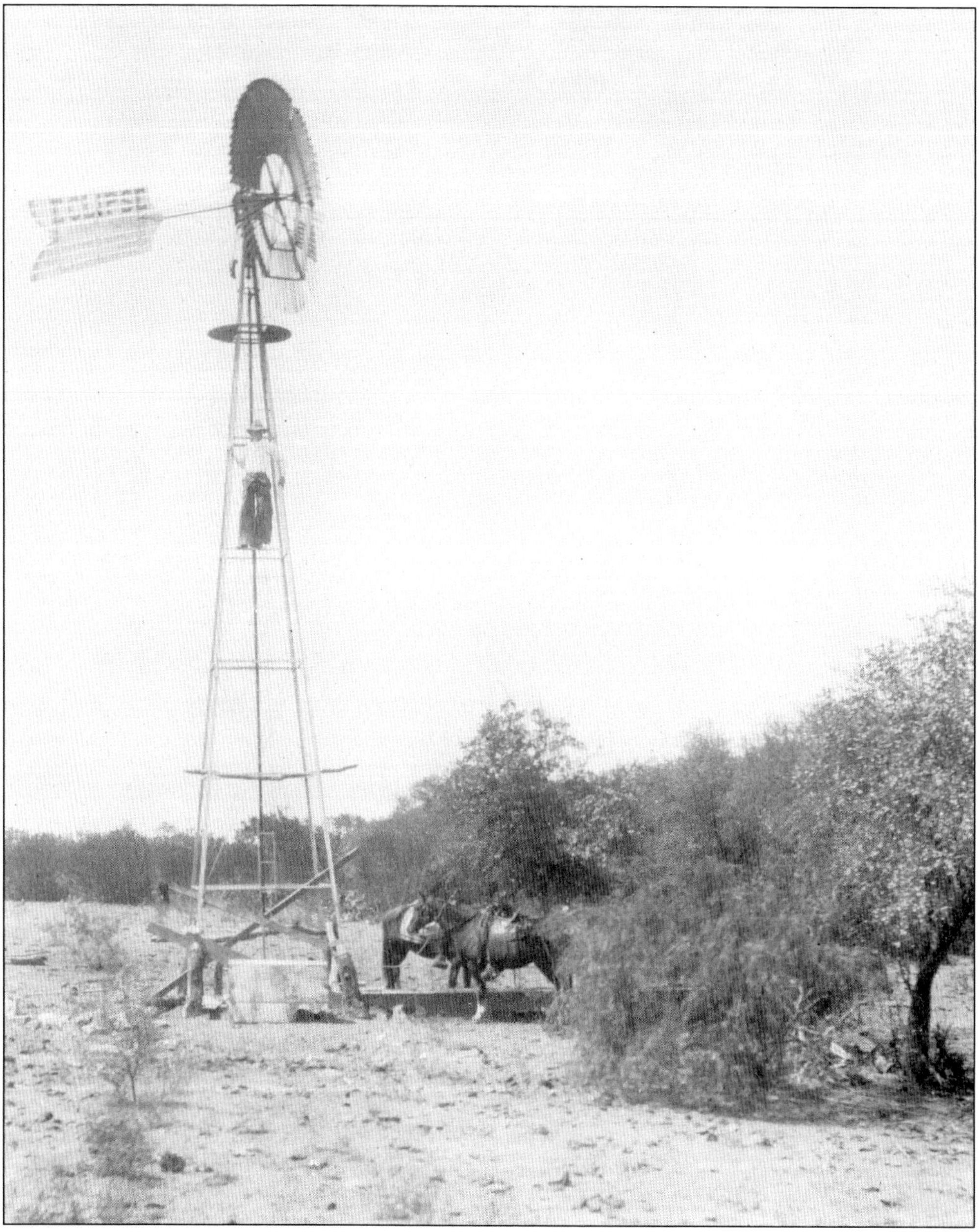

Prior to the introduction of windmills in the mid-1850s, land without a permanent source of water could not support a rancher or his stock. It was only after the advent of barbed wire in the late 1870s that windmills moved to the ranches. As new traps or pastures were fenced, a water source was needed. Ranchers hired two new hands—the driller and the windmiller. The driller went to each new pasture and drilled the well, usually with a horse-powered drilling rig. The windmiller followed and erected the windmill. A problem with the early rigs was the need for greasing every two weeks. This fell to the range rider, who would carry a can of grease around as he rode the heard. When he came upon a squeaky windmill, it was his job to climb the rig, mount the platform, and grease the wheel. Some of the dangers of the job were the height and the wasps that would nest under the windmill's platform.

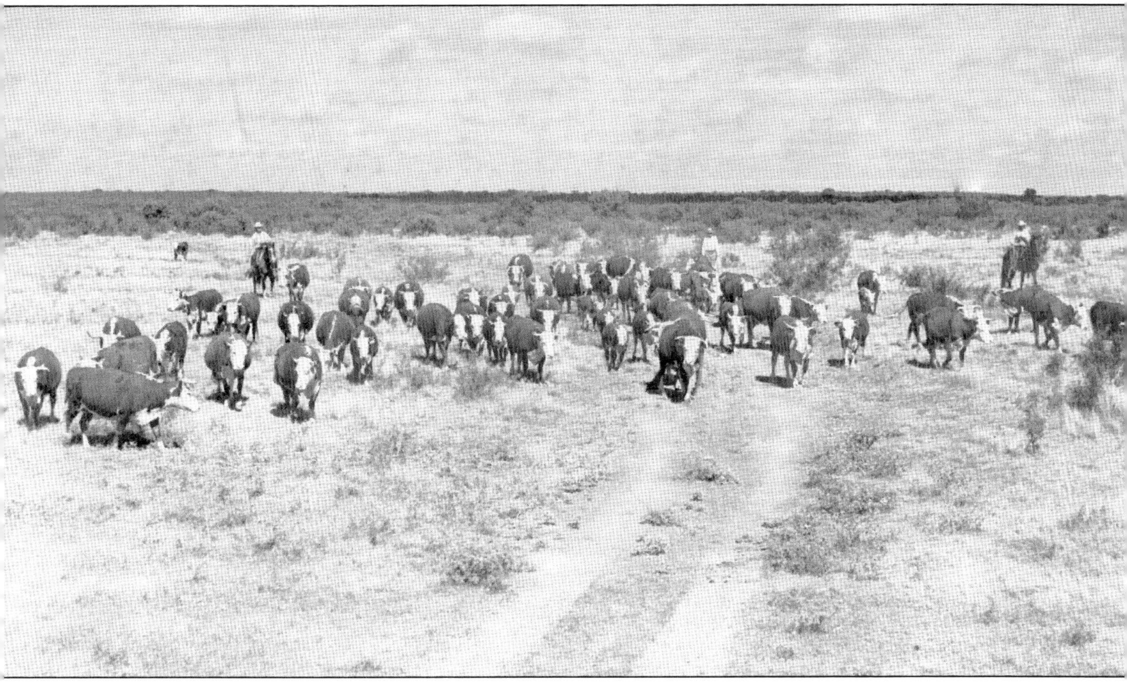

Originating in the Herefordshire area of West England, the Hereford breed of cattle made their first appearance in Texas around 1876. However, it was not until Charles Goodnight of the JA Ranch introduced Herefords to West Texas in 1883 that the landscape of cattle breeds started to change in Texas. With their introduction, Herefords were responsible for the disappearance of longhorn cattle as a major range breed. With their characteristic dark red to red-yellow color, white marked face, crest, dewlap, and underline, they proved adaptable to range conditions and flourished. Over time, Herefords proved to be hardy, prolific, and good foragers, and possessed fine beef qualities, making them ideal for Texas cattlemen. This 1940s gathering of Herefords was a typical scene around Uvalde with the strong grasses of the area being ideal for raising cattle. As the Hereford breed did well on Uvalde's grasses, so did the Uvalde ranchers.

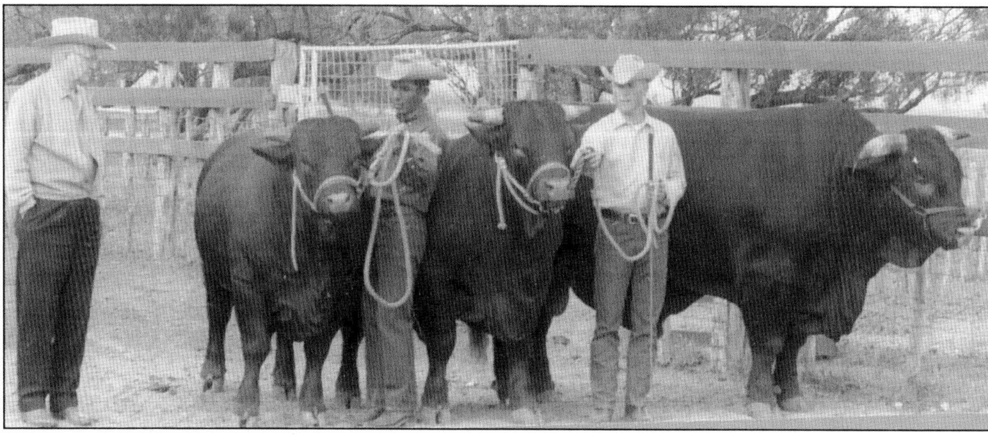

The Santa Gertrudis breed of cattle had its birthplace on the King Ranch around 1910. Derived from the cross breeding of Brahman and Shorthorn cattle, the result was the Santa Gertrudis. Deep red in color, with a deep and well-muscled body, the breed was designed to be adaptable to most climates, environments, and terrains. In addition, they were developed to thrive and gain weight on the native grasses of the South Texas brush county. The fine examples of Santa Gertrudis bulls above were photographed at the Marisol Ranch near Uvalde in the 1970s with owner C.A. McDaniel looking on. Below, even on fair grass or range conditions, this herd of Santa Gertrudis is in good condition.

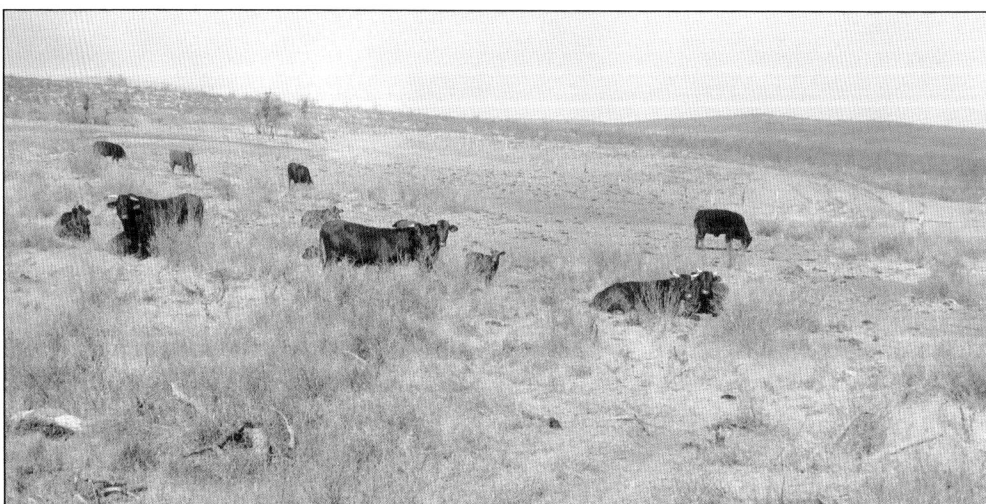

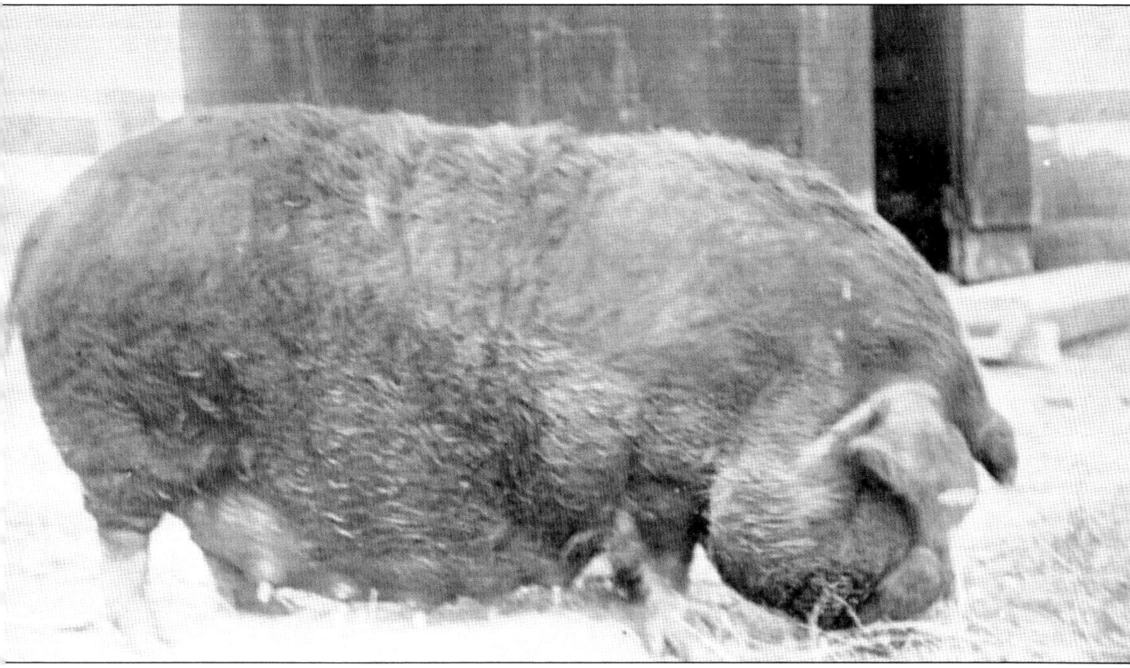

At the start of the 20th century, just as today, livestock had to be productive. In this case, productive translates into reproducing and raising their own young without any outside help from the stockman. A rancher was much more likely to keep a nanny goat (female) if she produced two to three kids (baby goats) each kidding versus only a single kid. This same philosophy held for other livestock. For example, Victoria, a sow (female hog), is nine years old in this September 15, 1913, photograph. Over Victoria's lifetime, she produced over $3,000 worth of offspring for her owner. $3,000 in 1913 roughly equates to over $63,000 today. This is one of the reasons Victoria remained in the hog pen. If she had not been such a good producer, she would have been sent to slaughter years before her ninth birthday.

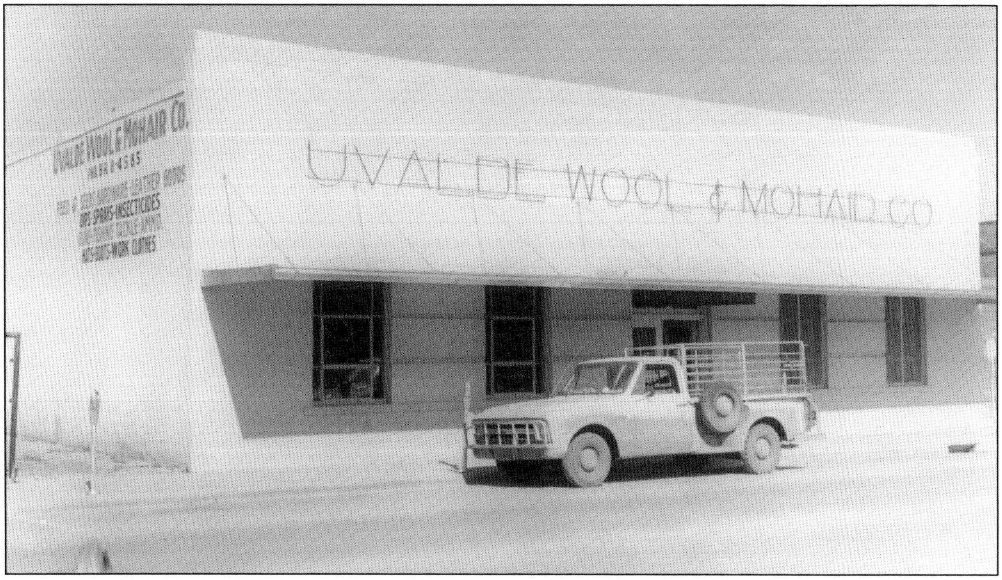

Dolph Briscoe Sr. owned a company called Uvalde Livestock and Loan Company. Many of his customers were in the sheep and goat business. During the Great Depression, the elder Briscoe did not care for the way his customer's wool and mohair was being handled. As a result, in 1933, he established the Uvalde Wool and Mohair Company. At peak times, the warehouse would handle 500,000 pounds of wool and an equal amount of mohair. This was a tremendous amount of wool and mohair and Briscoe was not the only game in town, with two other warehouses in business at that time. By 1973, Uvalde County ranked third in Texas counties in mohair production.

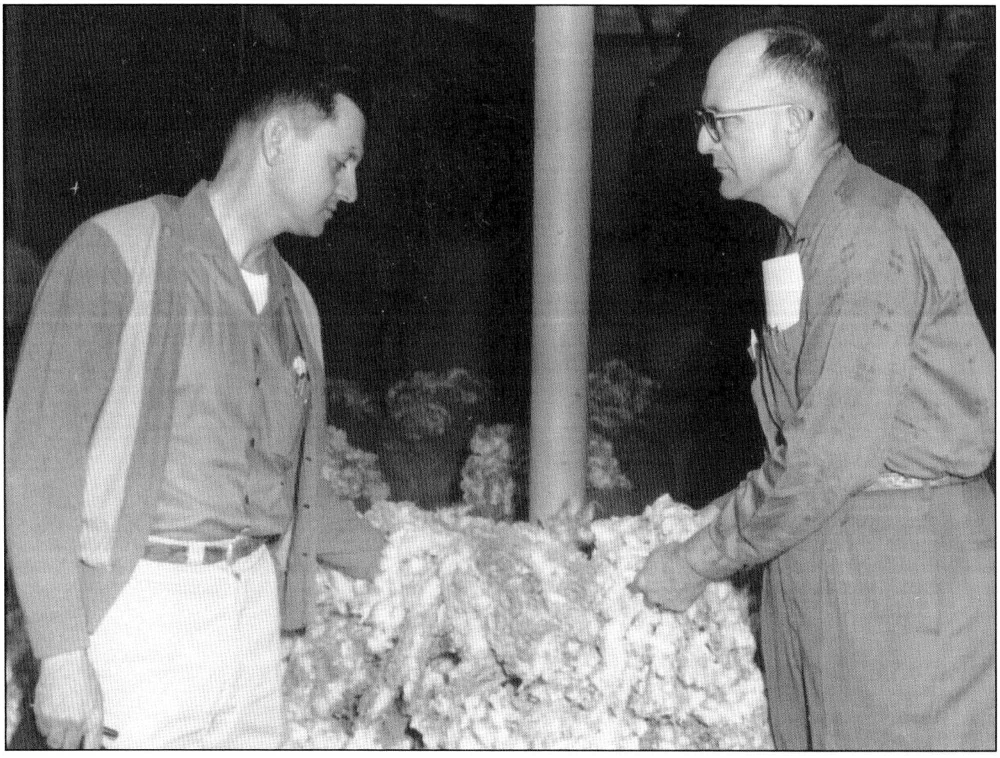

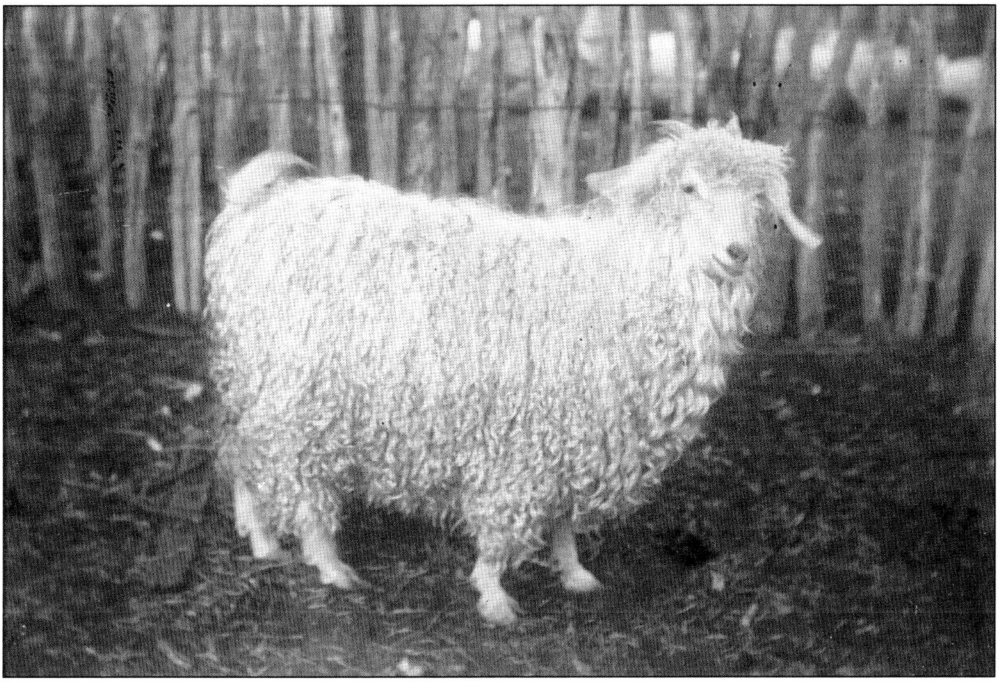

Goats were one of the many livestock species brought to Texas with the early settlers. The original goats were short coated and used primarily for milk and meat consumption. However, the area around Uvalde proved to be ideal for raising goats and by the end of the Civil War the Angora goat had been introduced. A goat of Turkish descent, it was known for its fine wool. Angoras thrived in the hilly brush country around Uvalde and mixed well with sheep and cattle for the best range utilization. By 1884, the Uvalde area had attracted a leading Angora breeder from California, William M. Landrum, who moved his operation to Uvalde County. By 1900, Texas was one of the leaders in Mohair production with 29 percent of the national total.

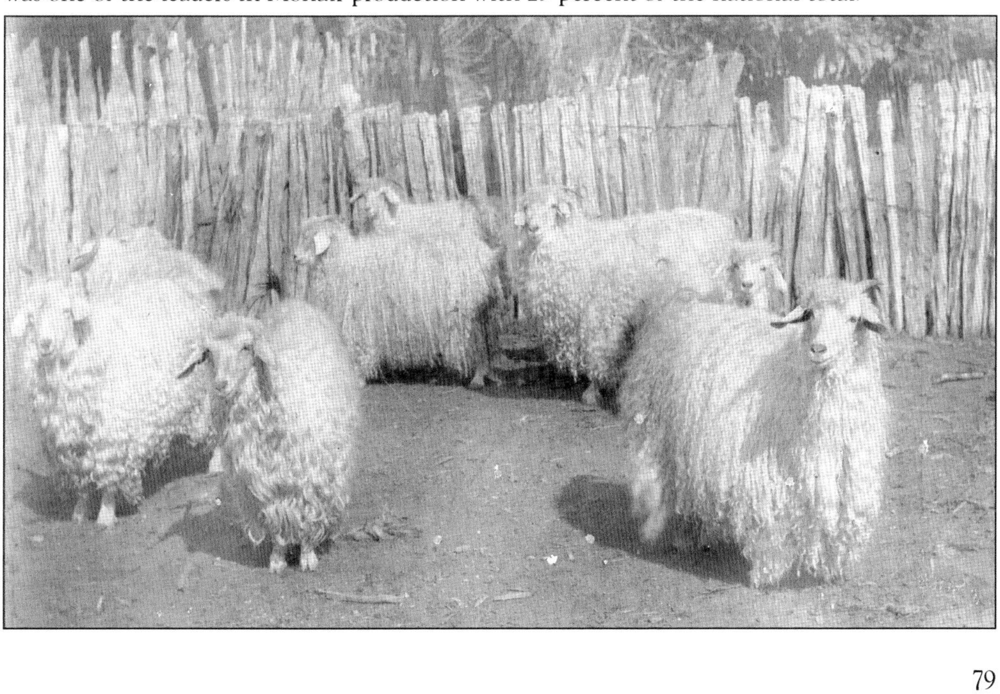

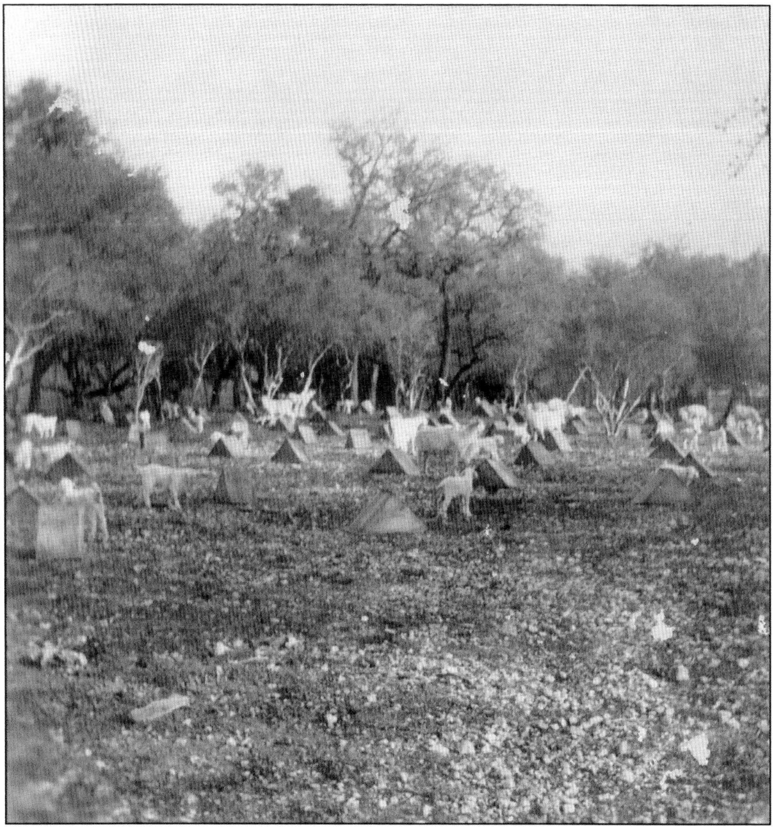

Coyotes, bobcats, and eagles could decimate a kid crop in a short time. Ranchers came up with different methods of keeping kids close to the home pasture until large enough to survive on the range. Some would use small huts, letting the nannies out to graze during the day while the kid was tethered at the hut.

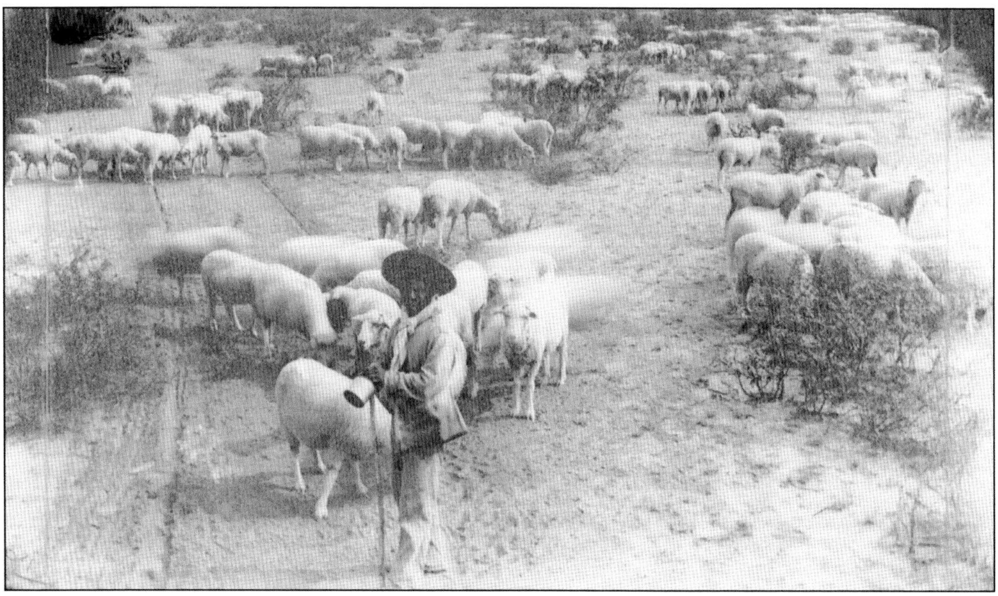

Shepherds were used with goat and sheep flocks up to the late 1890s. The shepherd's job was to keep the flock safe, help with lambing, and make sure lambs and goat kids did not get left behind to be bait for eagles and coyotes. With the advent of barbed wire and the decline in open range lands, the need for shepherds disappeared.

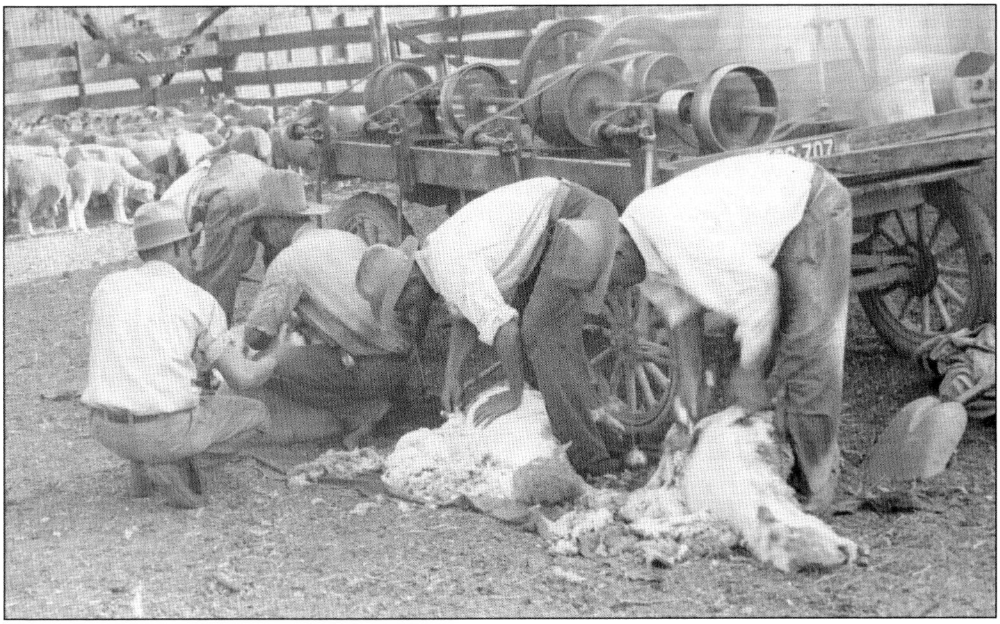

Usually each March and September, shearing crews would make their rounds from ranch to ranch. Here the sheep are being shorn on a tarp to help keep the fleece clean. Next the wool is graded, placed in woolsacks by grade, and then taken to the local wool warehouse.

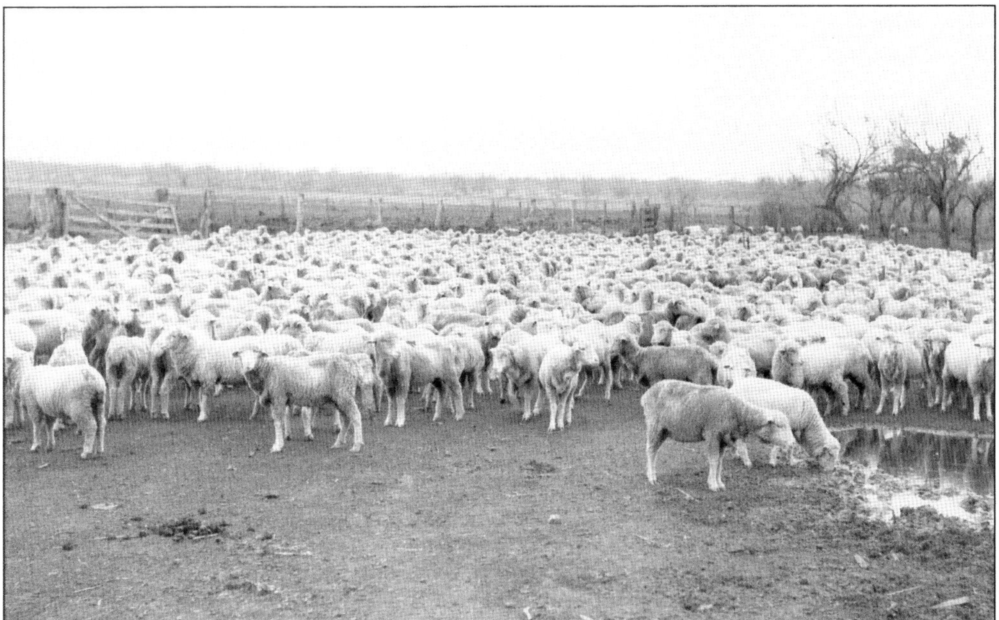

The sheep and goat industry around Uvalde helped diversify the agriculture economy. Goats and sheep have two distinct eating habits. Sheep are grazers and eat grass much like cattle and horses and thus compete for the same food crop. Goats are browsers and prefer their food source to be between 12 to 36 inches off the ground.

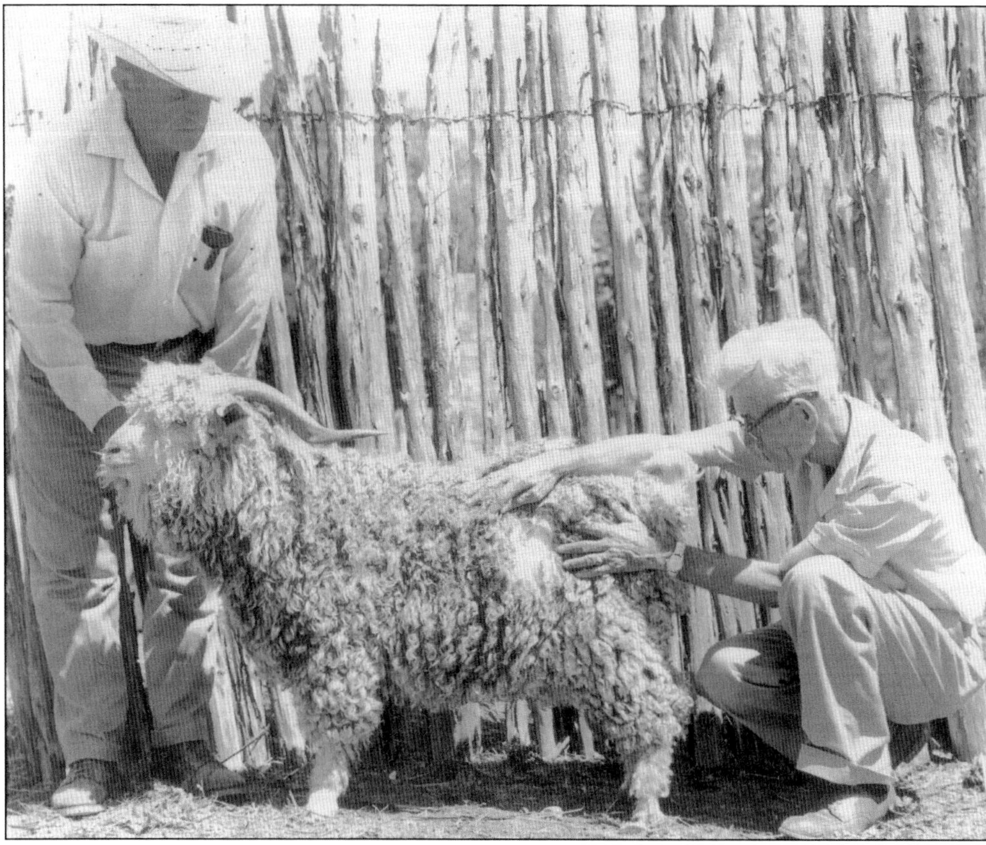

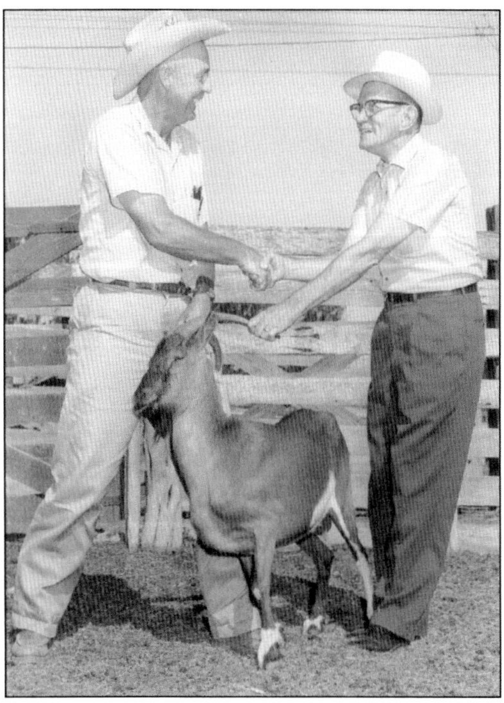

Grading mohair is a skill that is developed over the years from hands-on experience; here David Gulley is grading the mohair on an Angora billy (male goat). Mohair, the wool from angora goats, is graded for certain quality to determine its value.

The Spanish goat was a dual-purpose animal used for both meat and milk production. The Spanish goat was a mixture of different breeds that came to Texas with the Spaniards. Very sturdy and hearty with a short smooth coat in a variety of colors, Spanish goats were ideal for Uvalde's rough country.

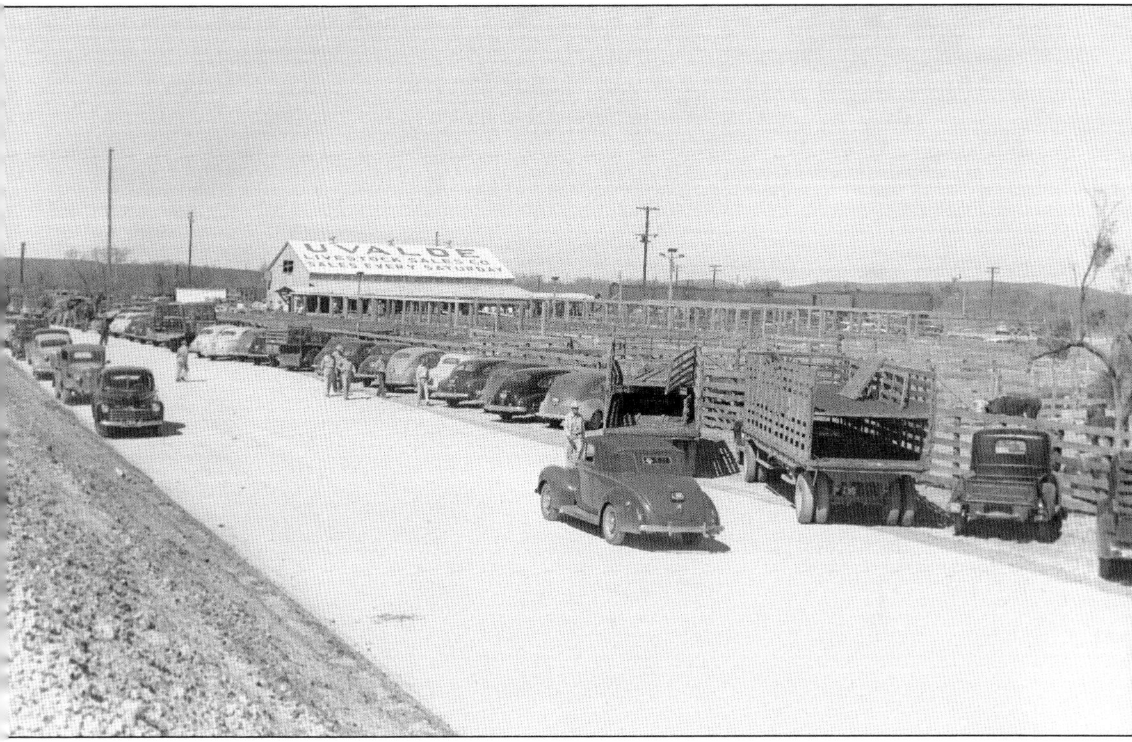

The heart of every rural agriculture community is the livestock auction barn, or sale barn. Providing a local selling point for cattle, sheep, goats, hogs, and horses, the sale barn serves as more than just a place of commerce. The weekly event is a social gathering place for many and trips to town are scheduled around it. While offering a convenient place for selling and buying livestock, the sale barn also attracts outside buyers from feed yards and ranchers from surrounding communities looking to buy and sell their livestock. The local sale barn helps stimulate the local economy and is vital to the lifeblood of the livestock industry. At the time this photograph was taken, the Uvalde Livestock Sales Company was located on North Getty Street next to the railroad tracks, with sales only on Saturday. Uvalde still has a weekly livestock sale with goats and sheep selling on Tuesday and cattle on Thursday.

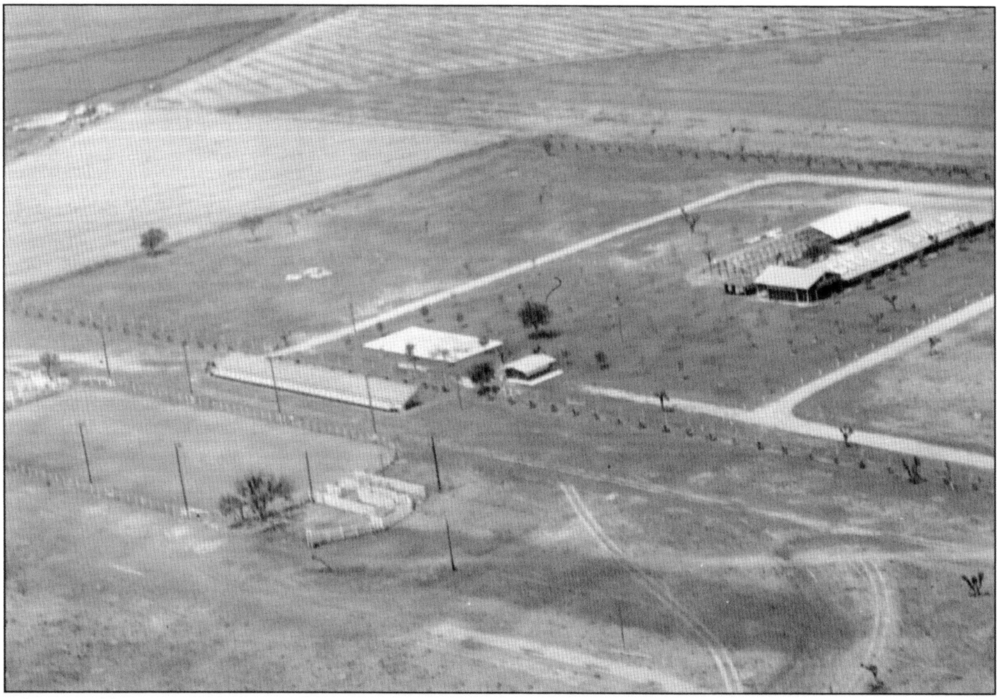

The Uvalde County Fairgrounds is located on US Highway 90 west of town and is home to the Uvalde County Junior Stock Show held each January. The fairgrounds sported a "quarter horse track," rodeo area, grandstand, livestock barn, and later, a multipurpose building.

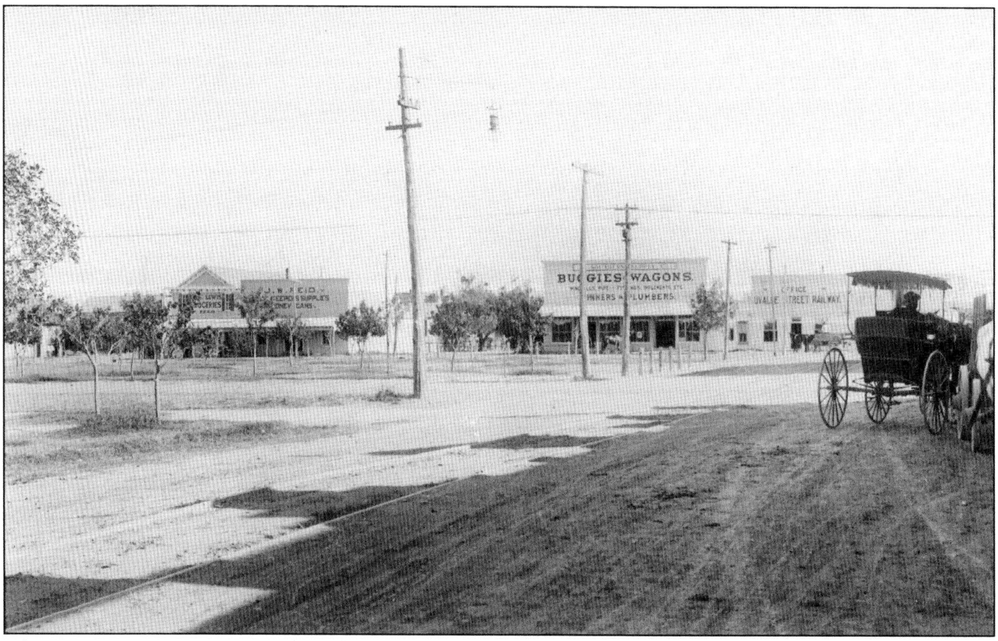

This view across Fountain Plaza looking south on West South Street shows a thriving town. To the left of the buggy store is J.W. Reid Bee Keeping Supplies and Honey Cans. Since most of Uvalde's honey was sold in tin cans and since the yearly amount produced was in the millions of pounds, Uvalde needed a store dedicated to bee keeping.

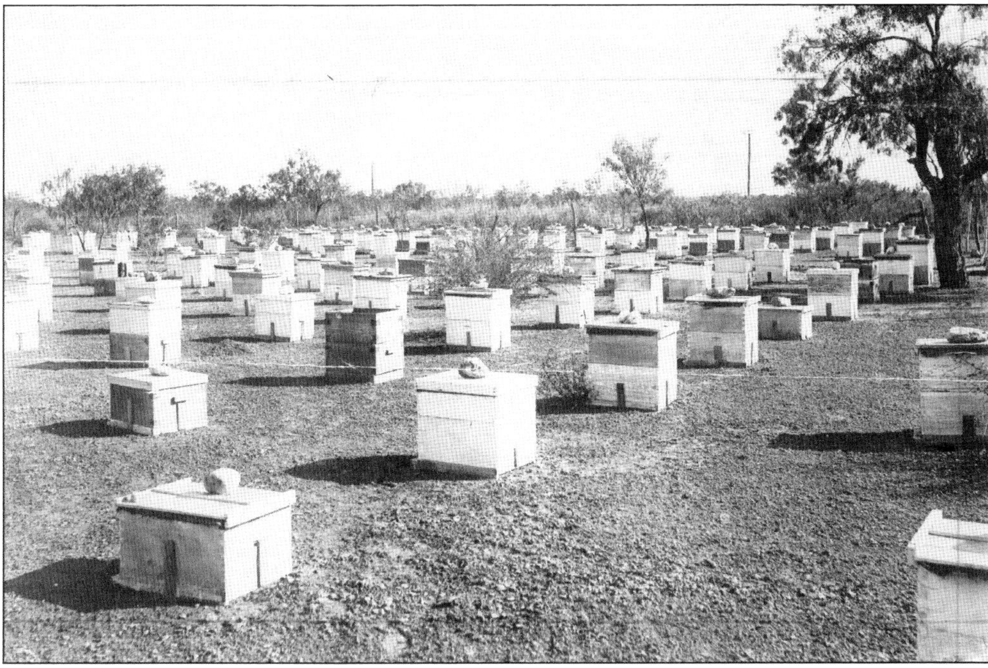

Turn-of-the-century Uvalde was well known for its production of the world's best honey. The average yield was between 1,000,000 to 1,500,000 pounds. However, 1903 proved to be a banner year for Uvalde honey producers, with more than 3,000,000 pounds marketed. The area around Uvalde is abundant with huajillo, catclaw, and other plants, most of which have many thorns. It is the nectar from the small, white, ball-shaped blossom of the huajillo bush and the catclaw bush that give Uvalde honey its pure, clear color and delicate flavor. In 1903, Uvalde honey sold for 9¢ to 10¢ per pound, and most was sold in buckets or cans with the honey still in the comb.

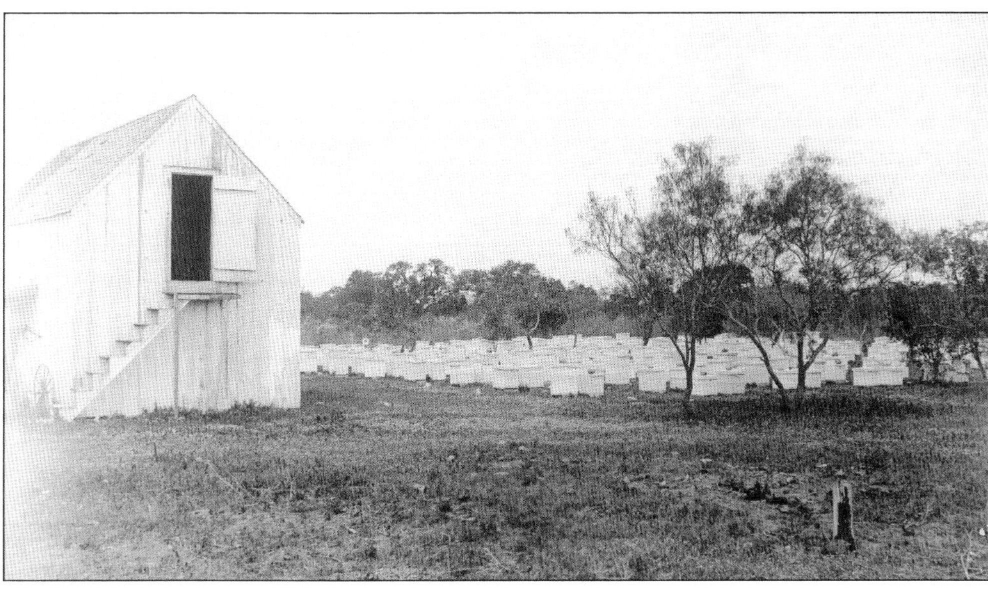

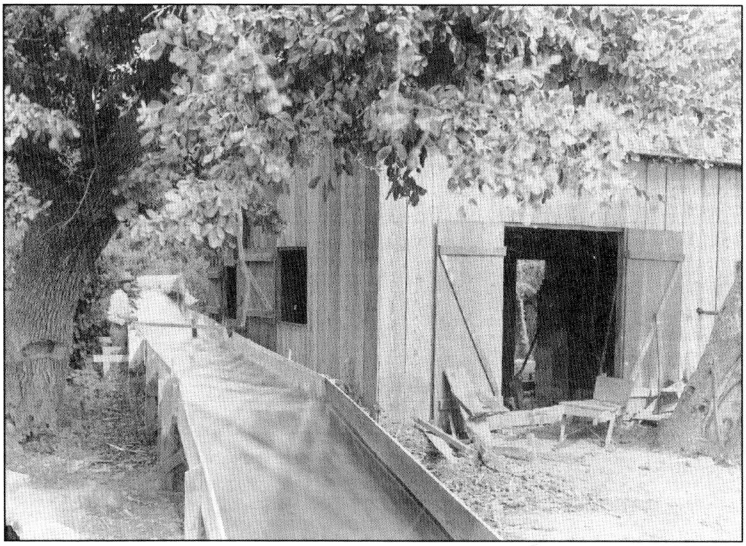

Water has always been a precious resource in the semi-arid countryside around Uvalde. Irrigation has allowed Uvalde County's fertile soils to produce a wide array of vegetables and grains. Around 1910 on the Lewis farm, an irrigation system was in place with this elevated water ramp system to route the water to the fields.

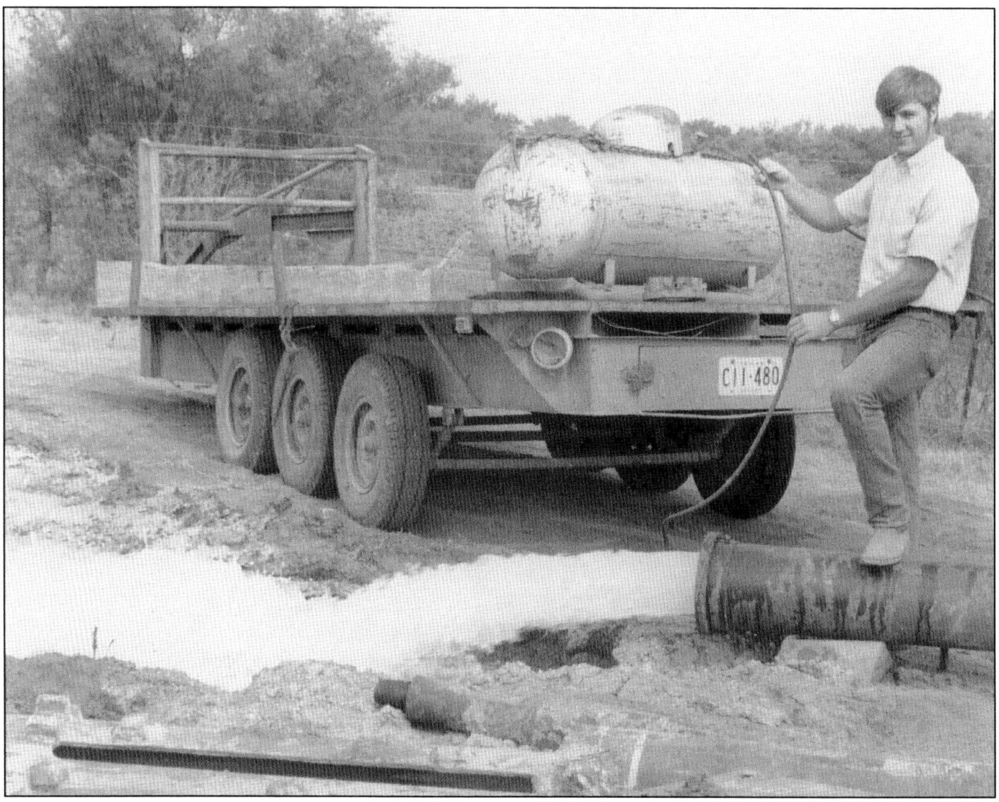

As irrigation methods improved, so did the acreage under production. This 1971 photograph shows Eddy Carnes at an irrigation well delivering water to the field. A third generation grower, Carnes is president of Winter Garden Produce, which grows and ships cabbage, carrots, and onions.

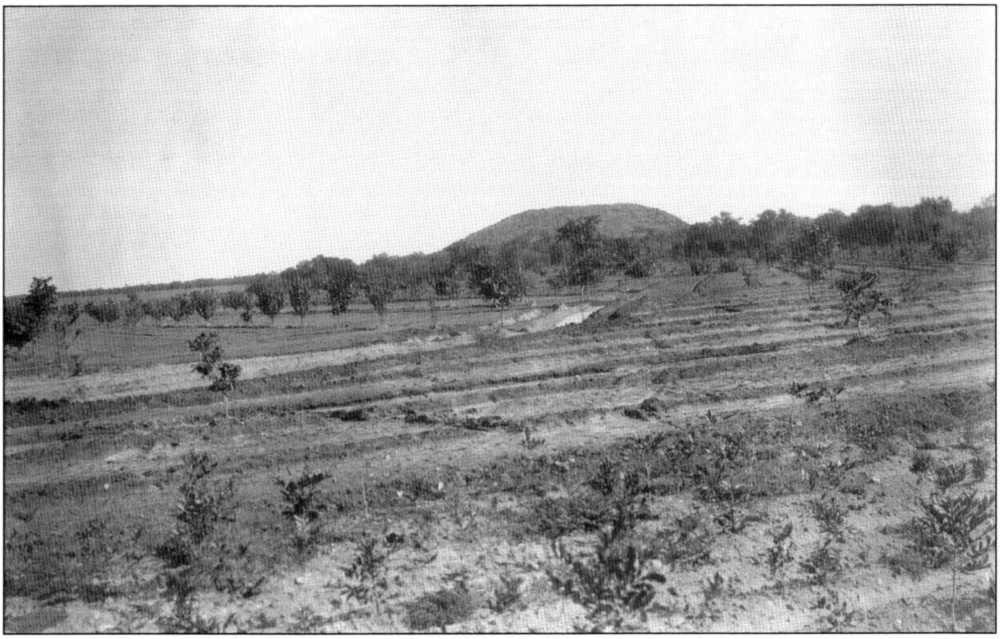

The Leona Ditch originated with a dam across the river and then a gravity-fed irrigation system to the fields. This 1920 photograph shows a pecan orchard with over 500 trees at the Leona Ditch Settlement. Mount Inge is in the background.

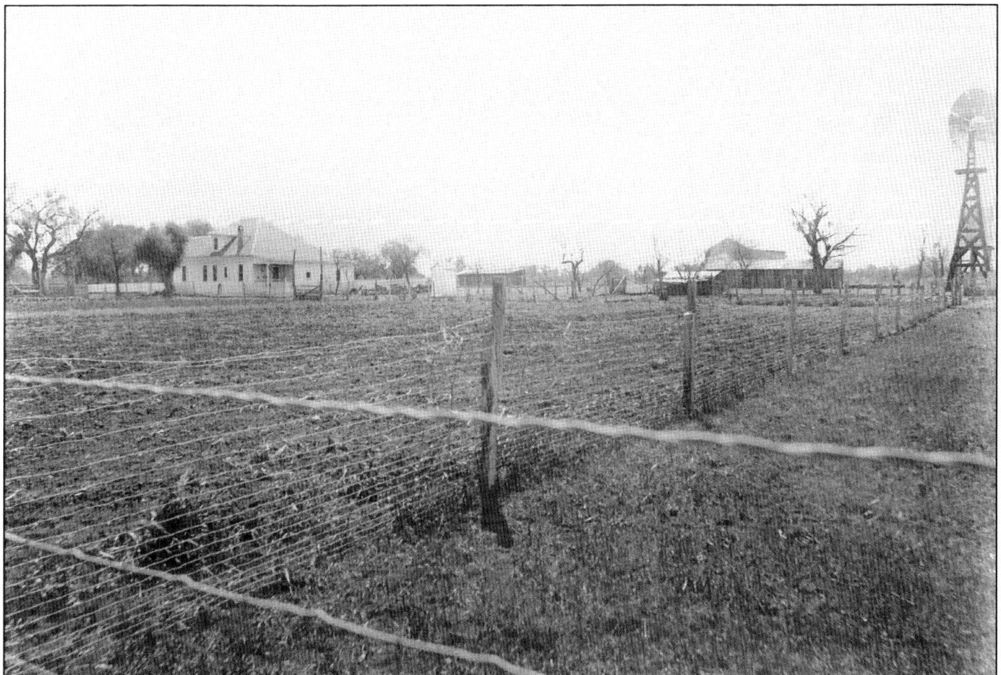

This Uvalde County farm scene was typical of Uvalde farmland in the early 1900s. The plowed field, separated from grazing area with the outbuilding for equipment, stock, chickens, and windmill are rarely viewed today. Note the net wire fence to keep varmints and young lambs and goat kids out of the row crop fields.

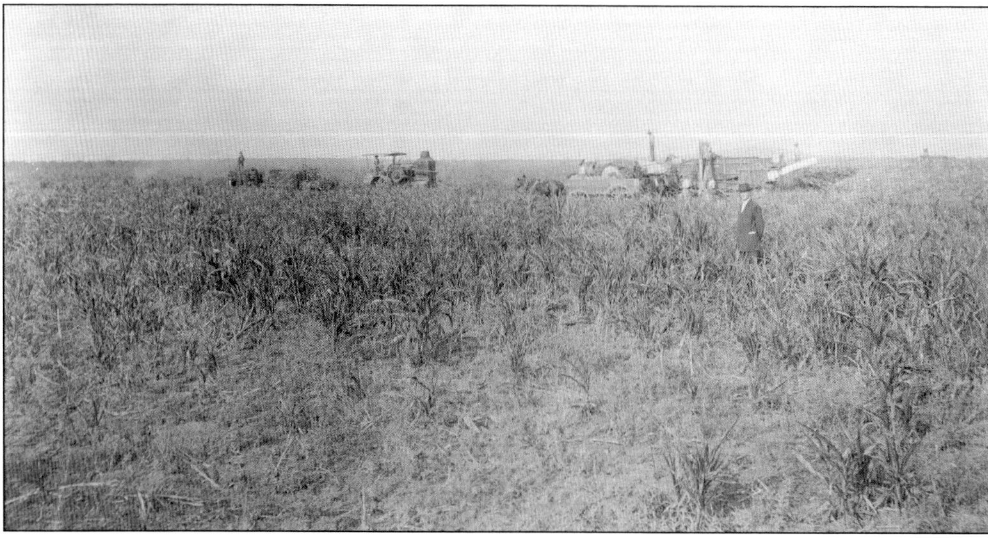

Agriculture has always been big business in Uvalde; not only from the produce angle, but also from the other jobs it creates. From farm supply stores to implement dealers, they are all Uvalde's agribusiness. Uvalde has also been home to seed contractors that raise crops for their seeds, which are then sold to the seed company for resale. Grains, when harvested, make their way to one of several grain elevators. Vegetable crops are taken to the processor and packer for shipment to stores across the state. All result in agribusiness dollars that stay in the community. As technology has improved, so has the agriculture production, as shown in this comparison of the corn harvest in the early 1900s (above) to the corn harvest of the 1970s (below).

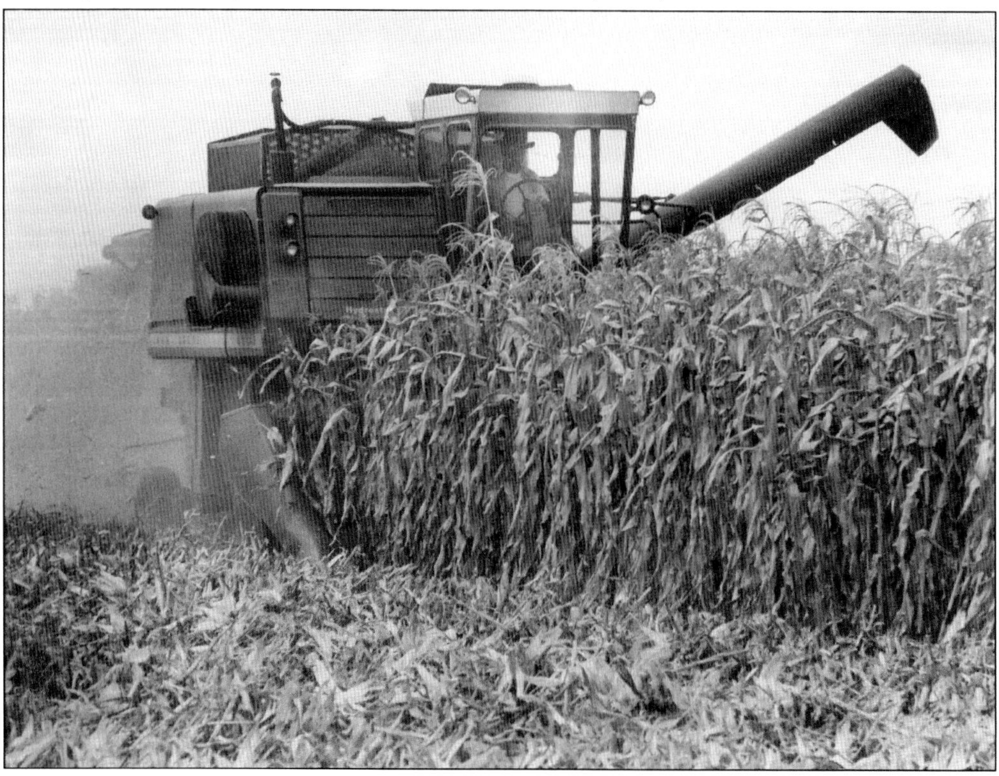

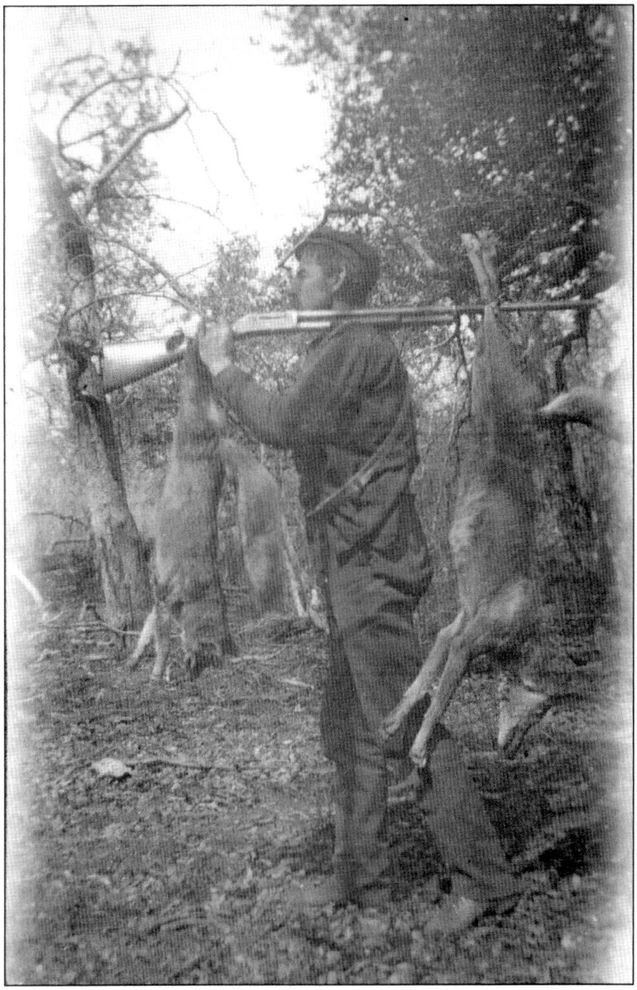

Not much is known about this 1902 photograph of a hunter with his kill slung over his shoulder. It was a successful hunt with both a fox and a coyote bagged. At the turn of the century, land owners depended upon their neighbors to help keep varmints under control. Today, with fewer ranchers, who mostly have "weekenders" for neighbors, the varmint population has soared. Below, photographed approximately 30 years later, this "home from the hunt" scene is still repeated every November in Uvalde. With three white tail bucks, three mallard ducks, and a stringer of bass, these proud hunters brought plenty of food home for the table.

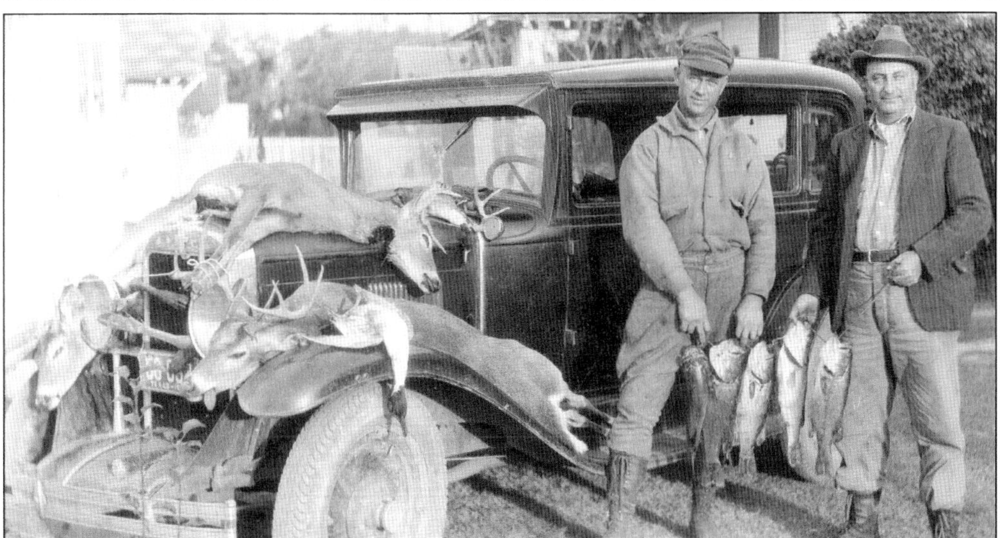

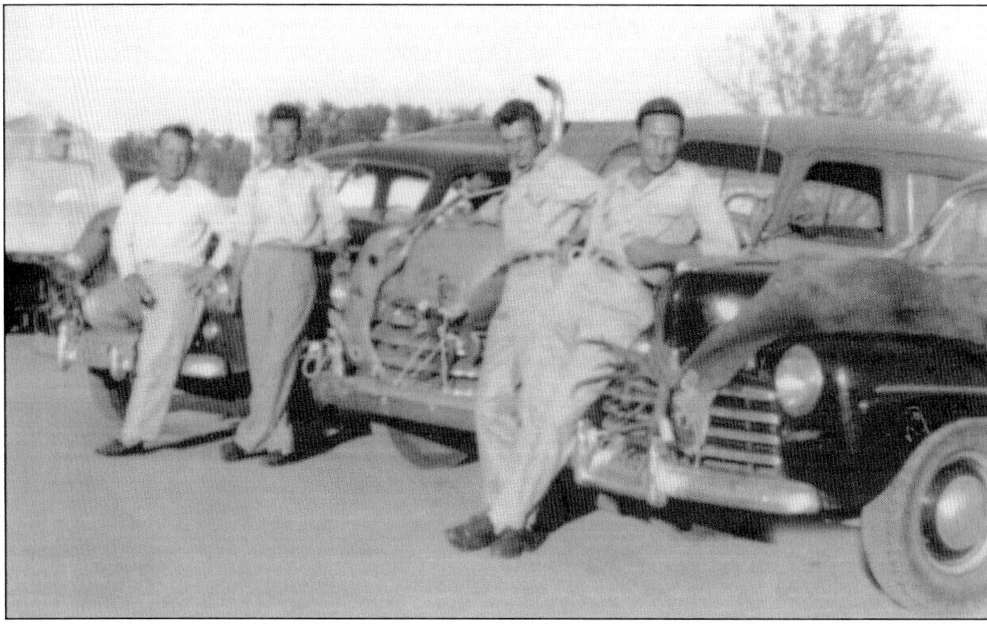

Hunting has always been a popular pastime around Uvalde. Hunters made the trip to Uvalde from all over the state and the country to bag their deer. Taken right after the break in the drought of the 1950s, this photograph shows Houston hunters Harold Bludworth, Jack Warriner, Danny Bludworth, and Billy Armstrong after a successful trip to the Marneldo Ranch in north central Uvalde County. (Bludworth family photographs.)

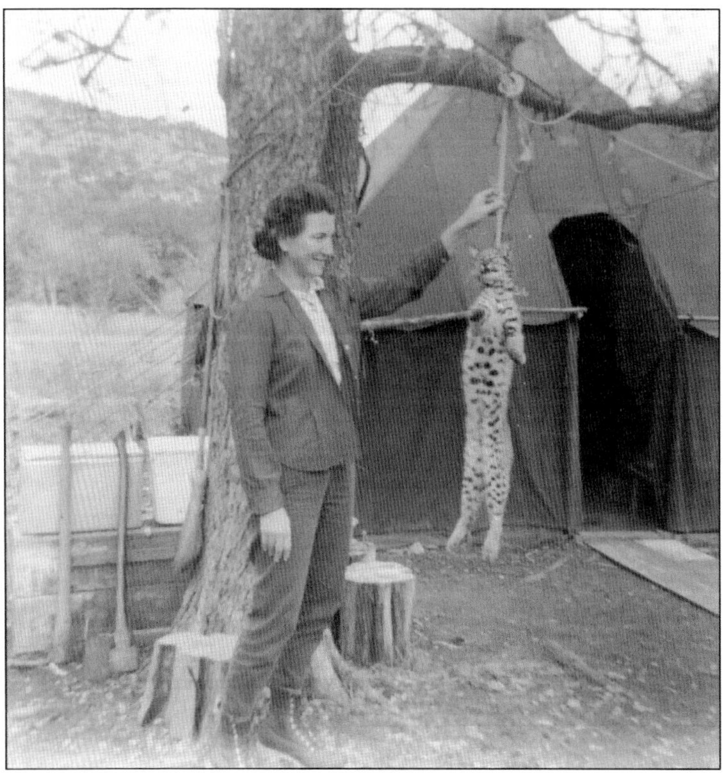

This 1959 deer camp hosted a lot of the comforts of home, including an army surplus tent with a wooden floor, wood burning stove, and small eating area. Quiet and skill were needed to take down a bobcat while hunting during the day. Betty Bludworth was the skillful hunter. (Bludworth family photographs.)

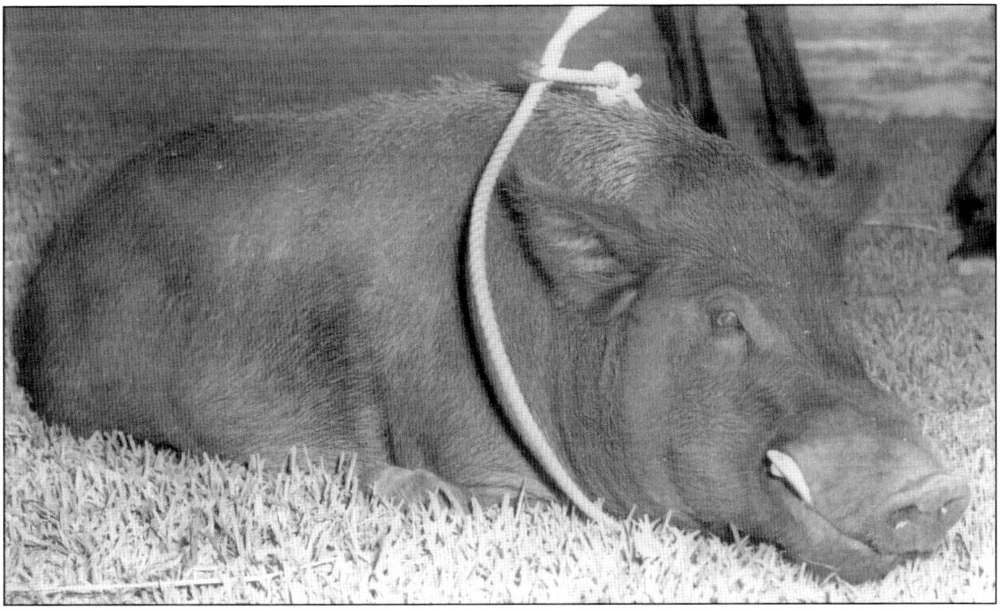

The feral pig is now present in all 254 counties in Texas. As more ranches died out and were sold to recreational owners from the large cities, the feral pig numbers became impossible to control. Combined with their "I will eat anything" appetite, nocturnal habit, astronomical reproduction rate, and offspring survival rate, they are a major consumer of fawn, kid, lamb, and turkey crops. George Brown (below, left) and Richard Stitts hunted pigs with dogs and by horseback in 1969. Today, the horse has given way to the four-wheeler or ATV. Trapping is another method of control used on the feral pig; however, they are intelligent animals and become trap shy if they ever escape a trap.

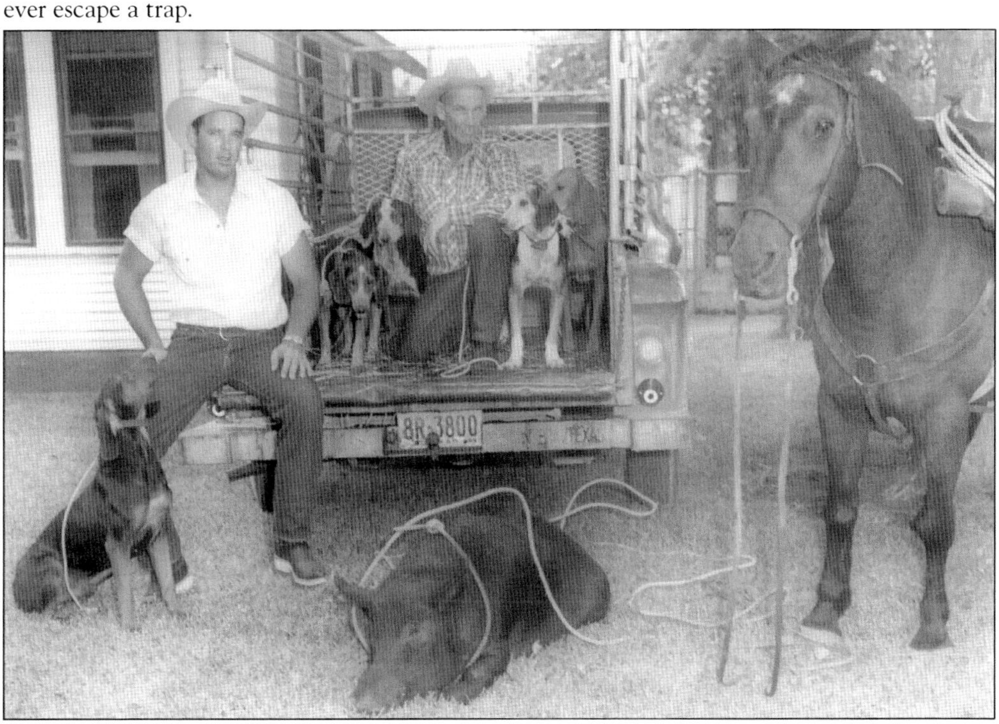

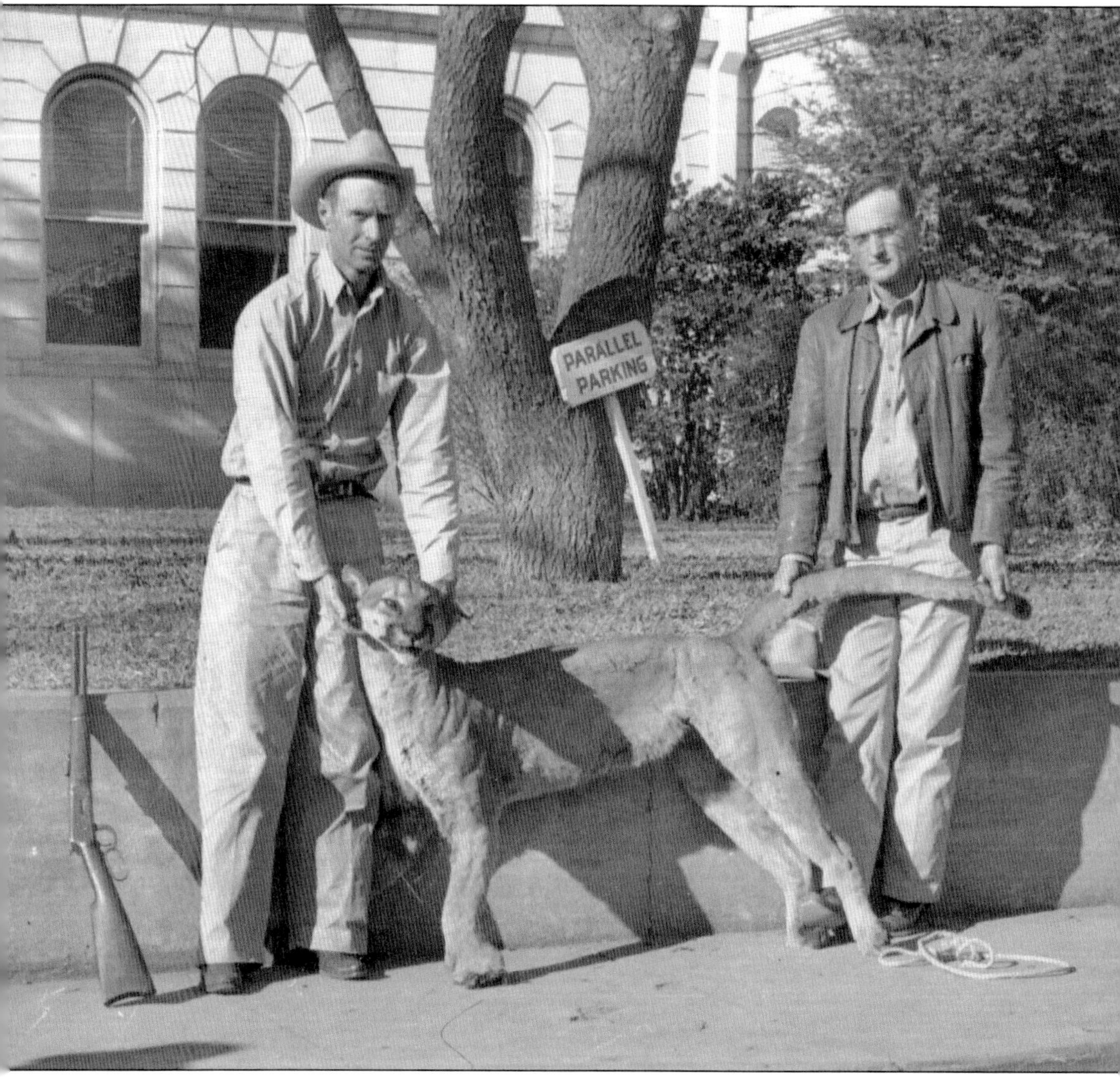

The mountain lion (*Puma concolor*) goes by many different names, such as cougar, puma, and panther. However, in the 1850s, they were quite common around what is present-day Uvalde. William Washington Arnett described numerous encounters with lions in 1852 while living near Fort Inge. In this undated photograph, deer tracker and trapper Richard Stitts (left) and an unidentified man have brought a captured (and dead) mountain lion to the *Uvalde Leader News* office for a photograph. While their main diet consists of white tail deer, mountain lions do prey on sheep, goats, and, to a lesser extent, cattle. Usually, the deer kills are single animal kills; however, it is not rare for a mountain lion to kill 30 sheep and lambs in one evening, but only feast on one or two animals. With a home range that covers 80 to 200 square miles in a remote and rugged habitat, they are most difficult to capture.

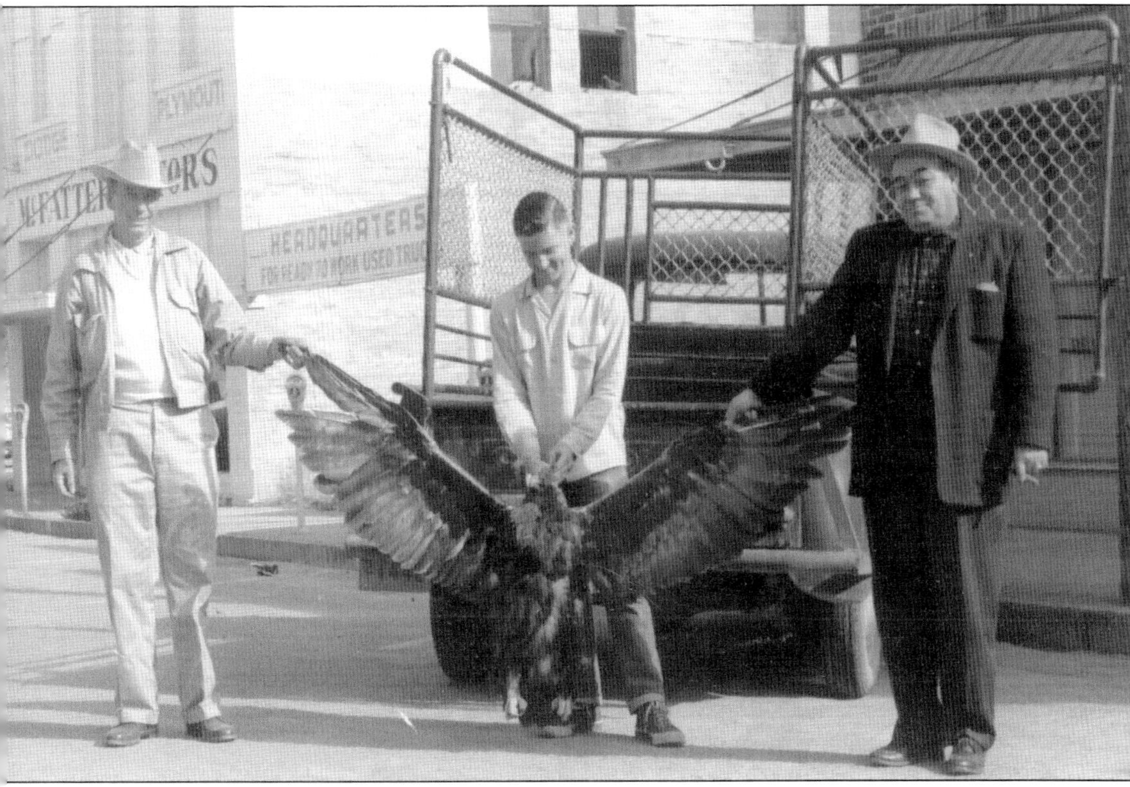

Golden eagles were given federal protection in 1962. Prior to that time, they were pursued by trappers and ranchers due to predation on lambs and goat kids. While scientific study has shown that eagles can take a great toll on livestock populations, much controversy and friction over these birds of prey remains between ranchers and conservationists. Golden eagles usually carry their prey back to their nests, and these nests can offer a good indication of a bird's diet. The Golden eagle will consume rabbits, squirrels, goats and lambs, and other mammals under 30 to 40 pounds. On occasion, Golden eagles, with their 6.5–7.5-foot wingspan, have been known to attack deer, pronghorns, coyotes, bobcats, and foxes. In this undated photograph taken on the Uvalde Plaza on East North Street, three hunters display a Golden eagle.

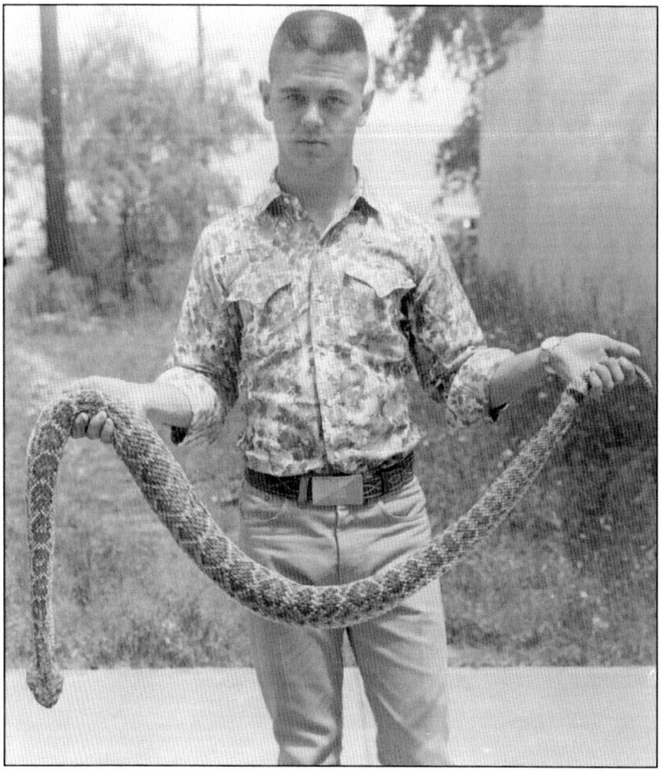

The western diamondback rattlesnake (*Crotalus atrox*) can be a daunting reptile when encountered. Once hearing their warning rattle, it is never forgotten. With a flat triangular head, diamond pattern on their back, black and white ringed tail, rattles, and a painful bite, the diamondback is very prevalent in the Uvalde area. With color to camouflage well in ground cover, the snake can be difficult to see in its natural environment. In Uvalde, when gardening, clearing brush, or any outdoor activity, people learn to watch where they step and be extremely careful when turning over hay bales, logs, or rocks.

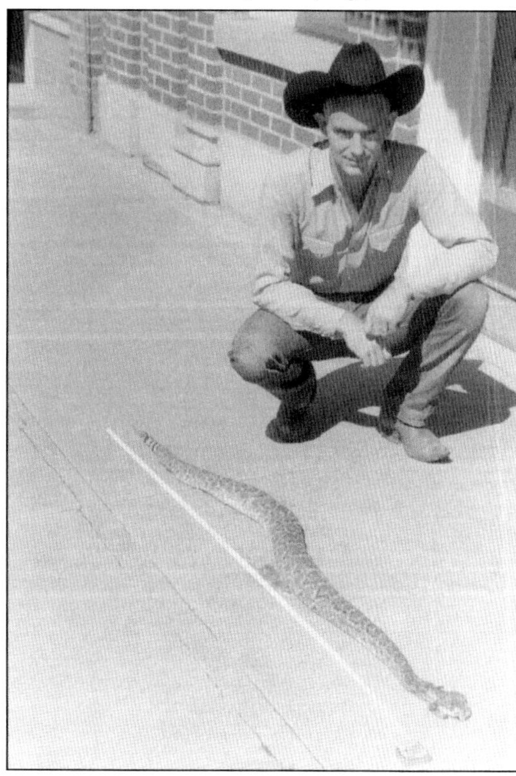

A member of the peccary family, the javelina, or collard peccary, is more closely related to the South American tapir than the pig. Found in the semiarid parts of the United States, it is at home in South Texas. Preferring a diet of prickly pear, which may provide up to half of its diet and almost all of its water requirements, this tough mammal was abundant in and around Uvalde up to the 1980s. While still found in the area, its number has been reduced with the invasion of the feral hog. During the depression of the 1880s, javelina hides brought 50¢ each. Thousands of javelinas were killed and the hides shipped from the Uvalde area, providing much needed income in lean times.

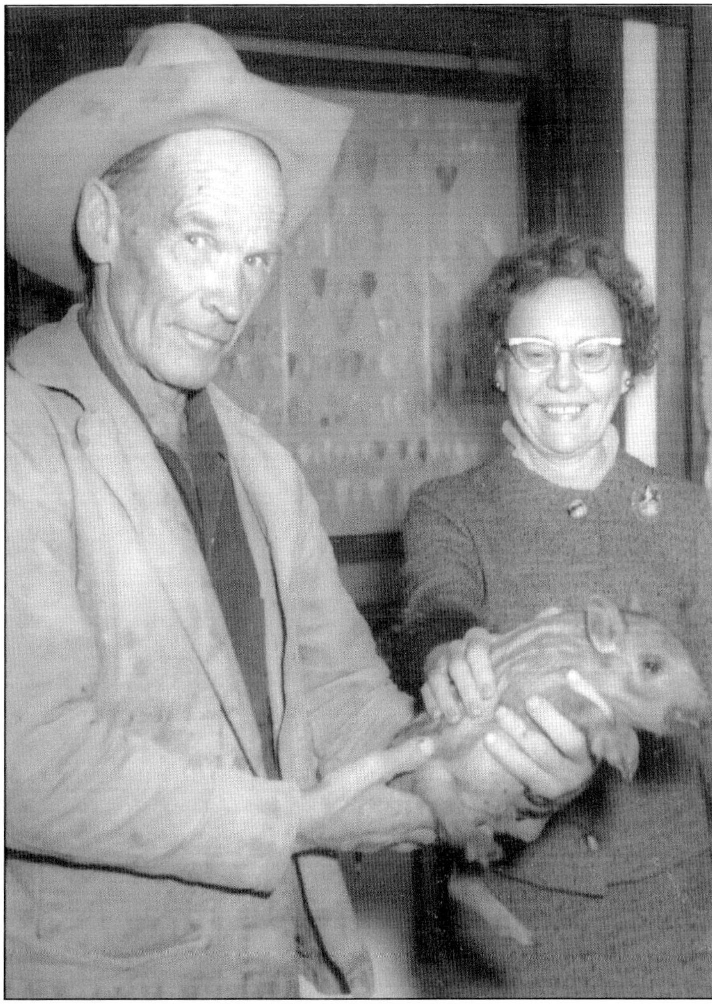

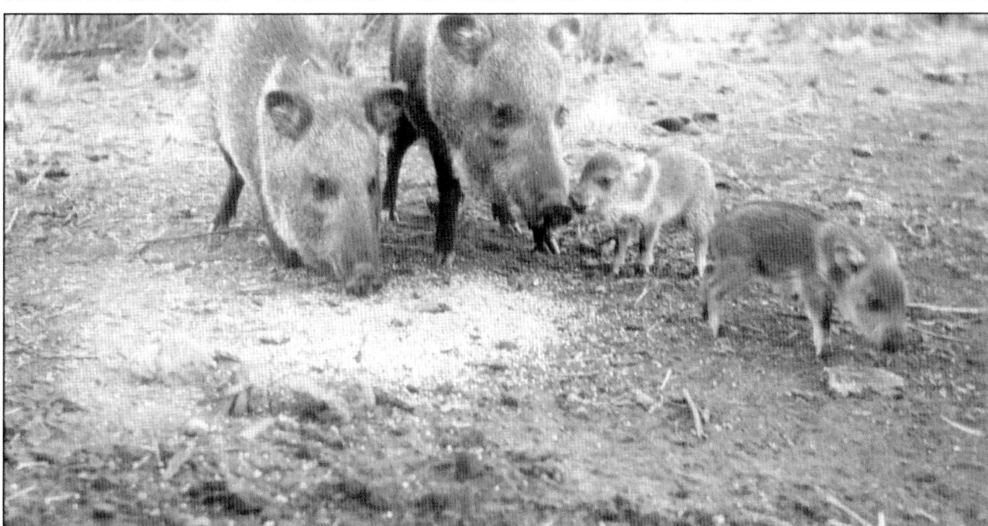

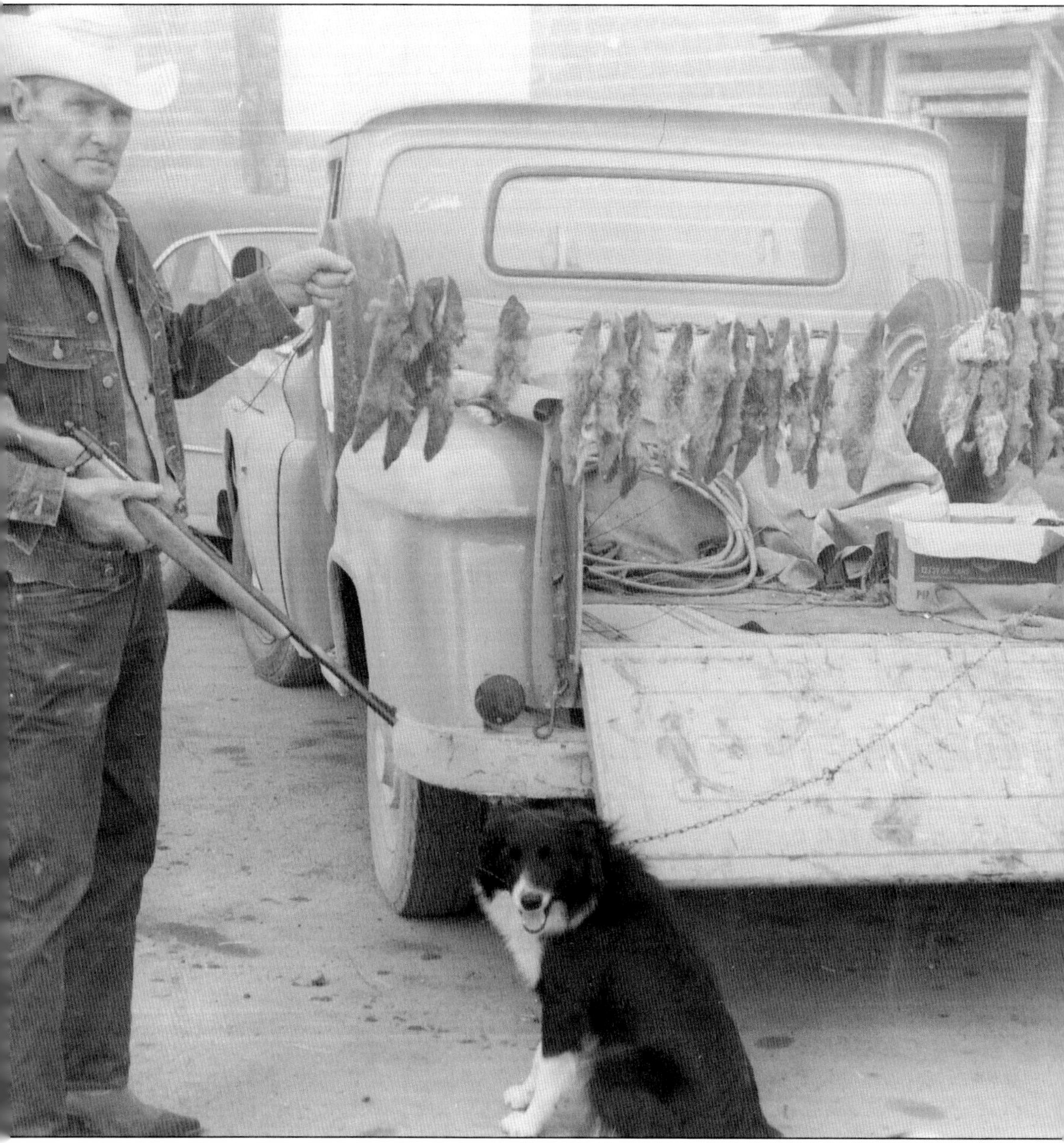

In the 1950s, a bounty was paid to trappers and hunters for certain varmint kills. Coyotes were a major menace to the sheep and goat industry. In most cases, neighbors, although several miles away, had the same coyote problem, and cooperation between ranchers in keeping predators under control was crucial to everyone's success. As family ranches have been sold off because there are no family members willing to take up ranching, predator control has become more difficult and raising livestock more challenging. At one time, Uvalde County paid a bounty of $5 per animal on coyote kills. In the 1950s, this was a good bit of money for a dead animal, since the going wage for a working cowboy was about $10 a day. To claim the bounty required proof of the coyote kill, and bringing the ears of the coyote did that. In the back of this pickup are approximately 40 coyote ears and one very happy Border collie. Nowadays, very few counties, if any, pay bounties for varmint kills.

Three

Sabinal Canyon, Concan, and Montell

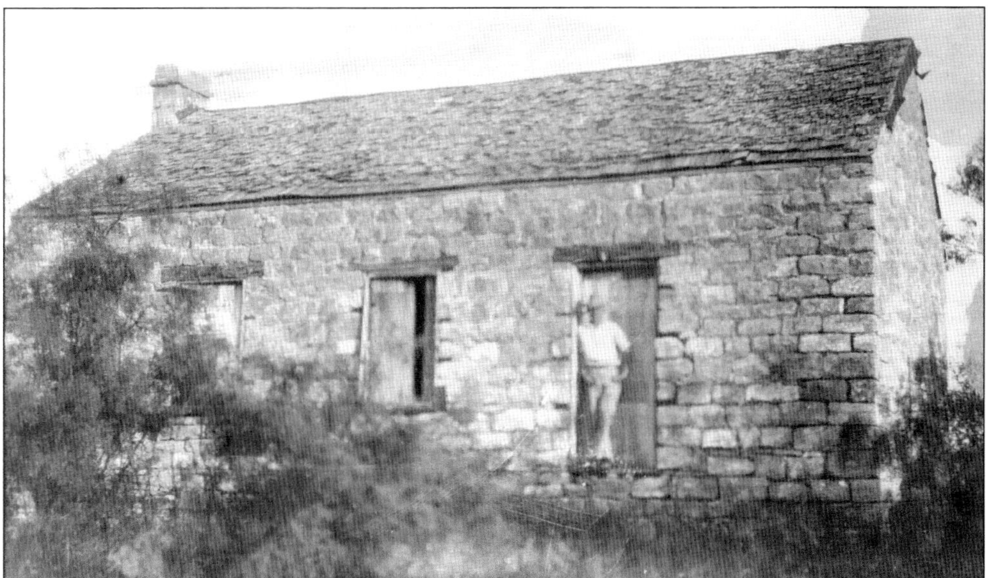

Camp Sabinal was established on the west bank of the Sabinal River on July 12, 1856. In 1874, Louis Peters built the Sabinal Store near the same location. A portion of the building still stands today, and a Texas Historical Commission marker on US Highway 90 west of the Sabinal River commemorates this location.

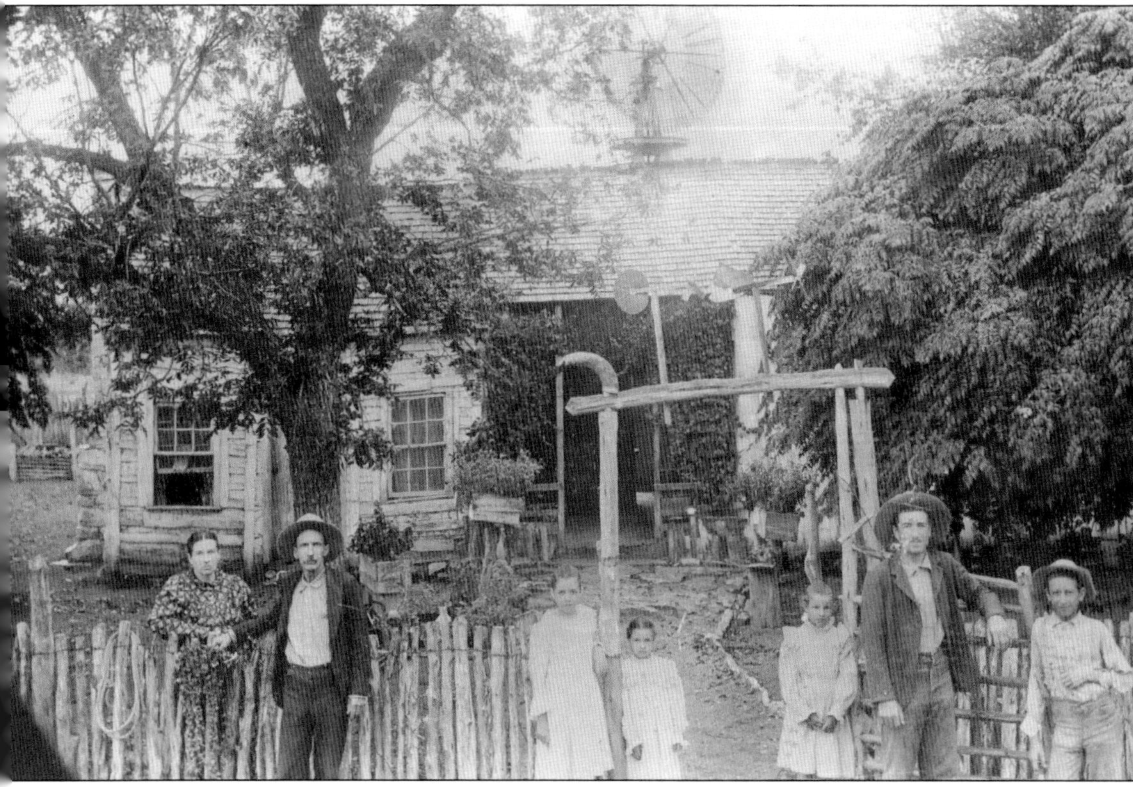

The Nueces Canyon northwest of Uvalde is beautiful but rough countryside. With spring fed rivers, creeks, and steep hillsides covered in juniper and hardwoods, the area drew new settlers. Alonzo Luce and his wife, Lena, moved to the canyon north of Montell in 1882. Originally from Lockhart, Lena was reluctant to leave her friends and family. Persuaded by her husband that they would return to Lockhart if she did not like the canyon, they moved to Montell and made their home on the banks of the Nueces River. The Luces never returned to live in Lockhart. A cattleman and horse trader, Alonzo Luce covered 13 states on horseback and drove cattle north to Medicine Lodge and Dodge City, Kansas. They raised seven children: Altah, Eloise, Lena May, Alonzo Baylor, and Roy are seen in this photograph taken in front of the log home. A typical "dog trot" design, with pecan and china berry trees in front, it is interesting to note the ram's horn and garden "whirly birds" over the front gate.

William Ware was born in Kentucky in 1801, but was always considered a true fighting Texan. He commanded a company at the siege of Bexar and took part in the Battle of San Jacinto. Following the independence of Texas, he moved around, and in August 1852, established Waresville, now Utopia, Texas, in north Uvalde County. At the time he settled in Uvalde County, his family was the only Anglo-American family between D'Hanis and the Rio Grande. Ware died in March 1853.

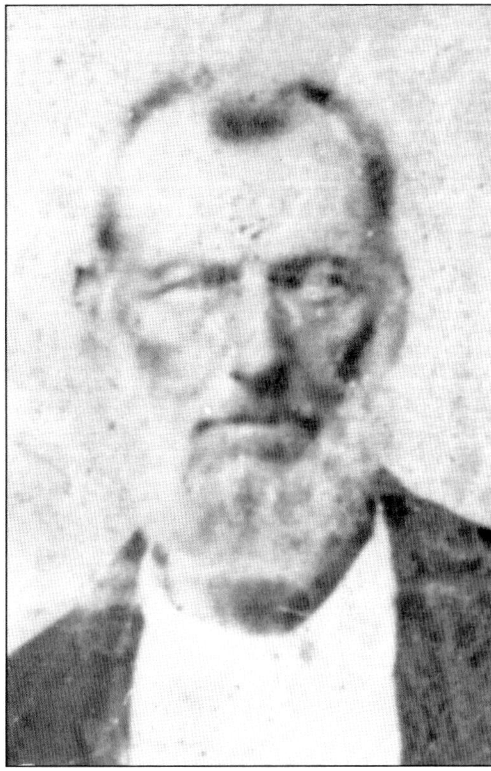

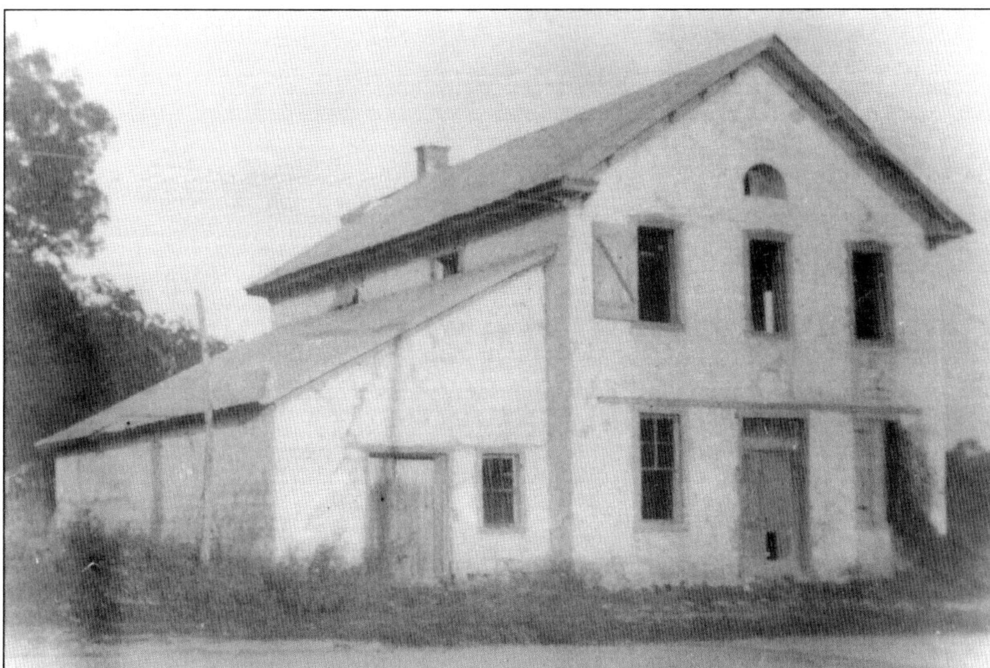

The Old Rock Store in Utopia was a multiuse establishment, with a store and post office on the ground floor. The stairway to the second floor was on the outside of the building. The second floor was used as a coffin store and a meeting location for the Masons.

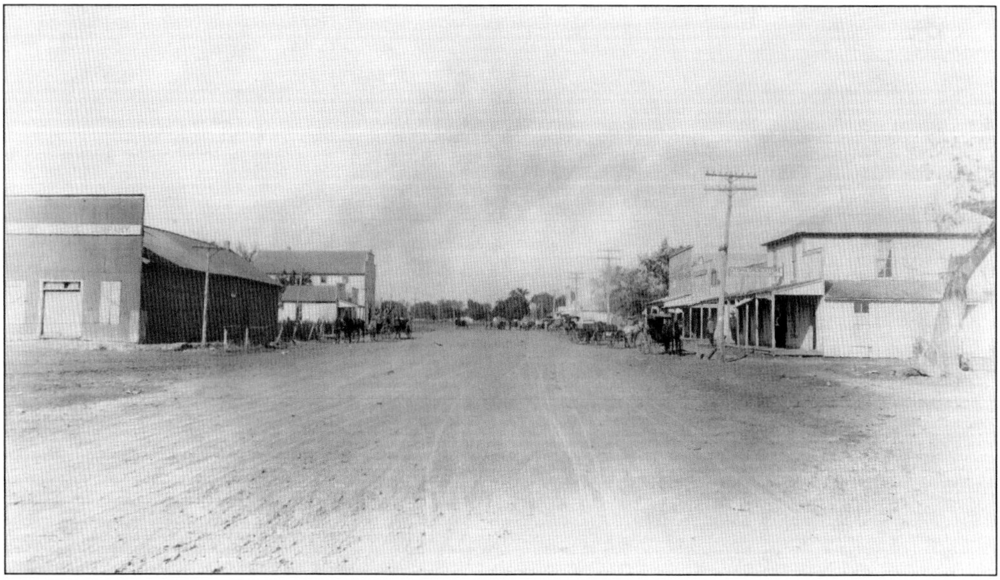

Utopia is a small north Uvalde County town on the banks of the beautiful Sabinal River, 21 miles north of Sabinal. Established in 1852, the community was plagued by marauding Indian tribes until well into the late 1880s. This Utopia street scene is undated, but today, a few of the original buildings can be seen on this same peaceful street.

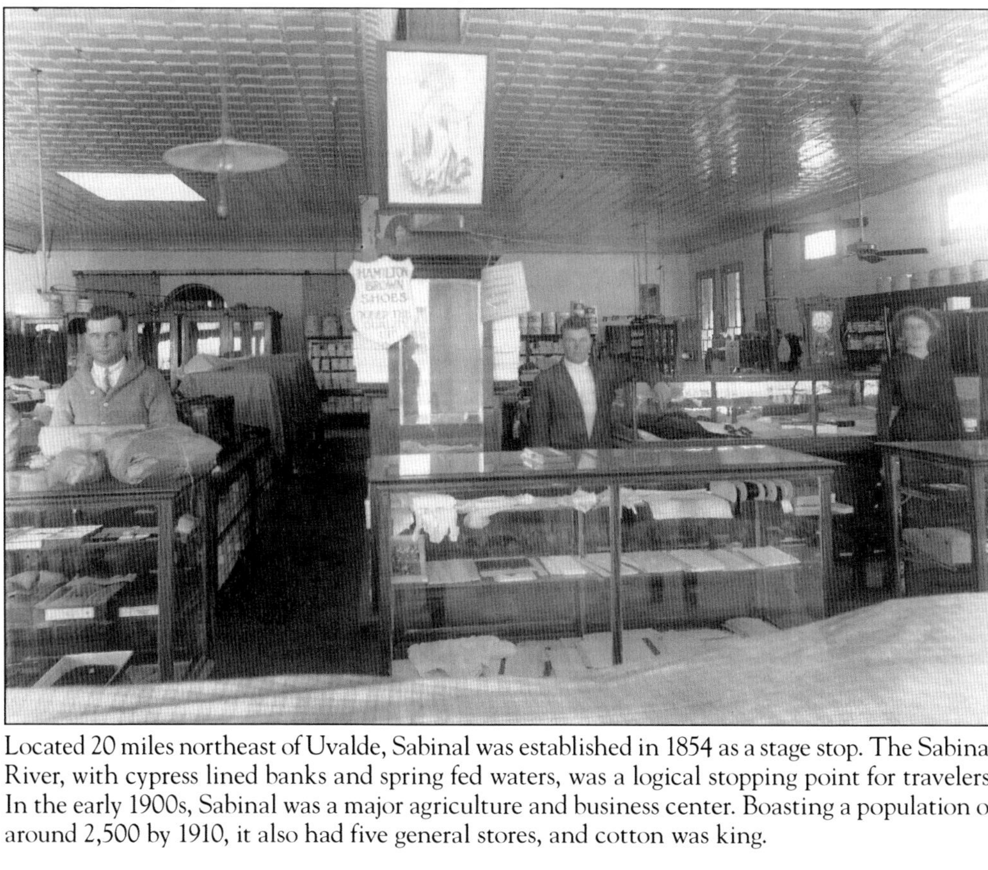

Located 20 miles northeast of Uvalde, Sabinal was established in 1854 as a stage stop. The Sabinal River, with cypress lined banks and spring fed waters, was a logical stopping point for travelers. In the early 1900s, Sabinal was a major agriculture and business center. Boasting a population of around 2,500 by 1910, it also had five general stores, and cotton was king.

Uvalde is peppered with limestone caves. Some are open holes in the ground that may drop down 20 or more feet before opening into a cavernous room and then continue for miles underground. Near Concan on the Annandale Ranch, the bats put on a twice-daily show with one of the largest concentrations of bats in flight as they leave and return to the cave.

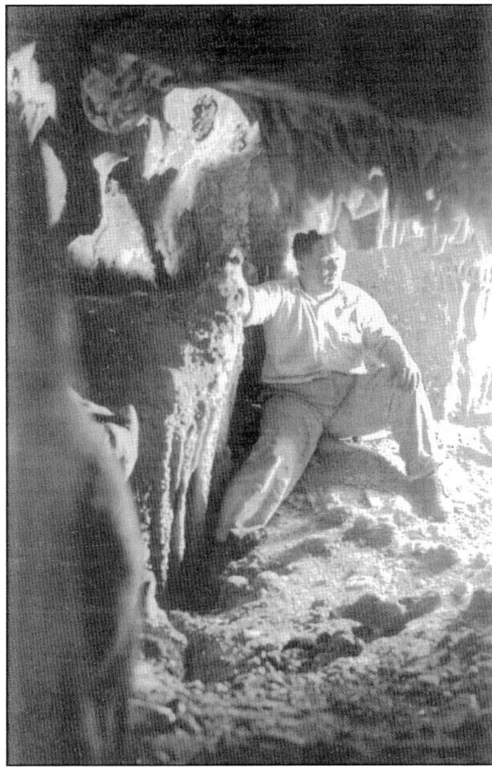

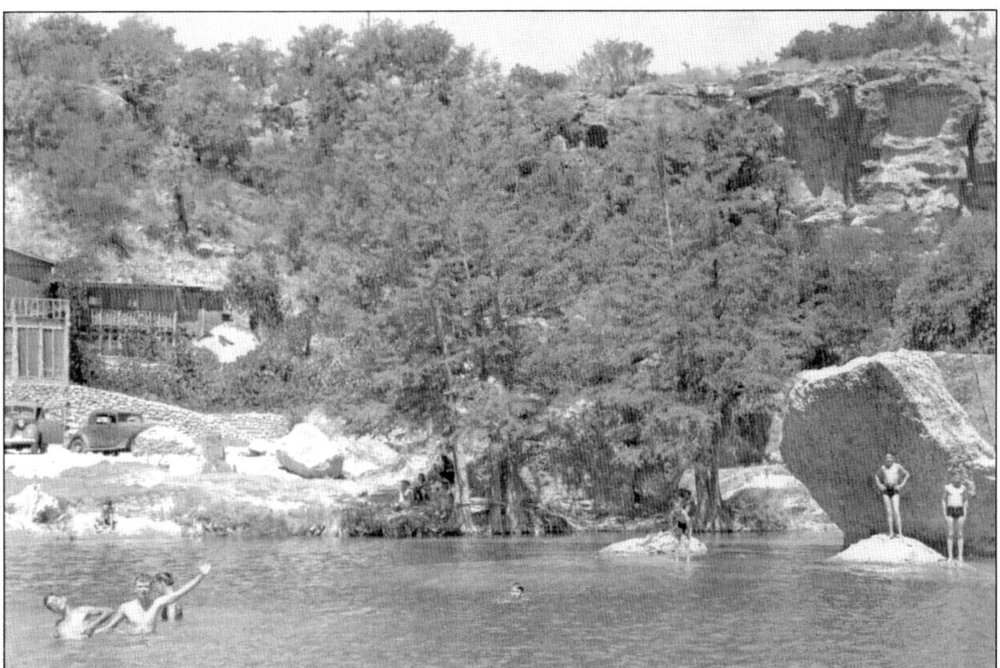

The beautiful Frio River at Concan, north of Uvalde, has been drawing locals and out-of-towners for years to the crystal-clear, cool waters of this beautiful river. The swimming hole at Neal's Cabins with a rope swing was a crowd favorite.

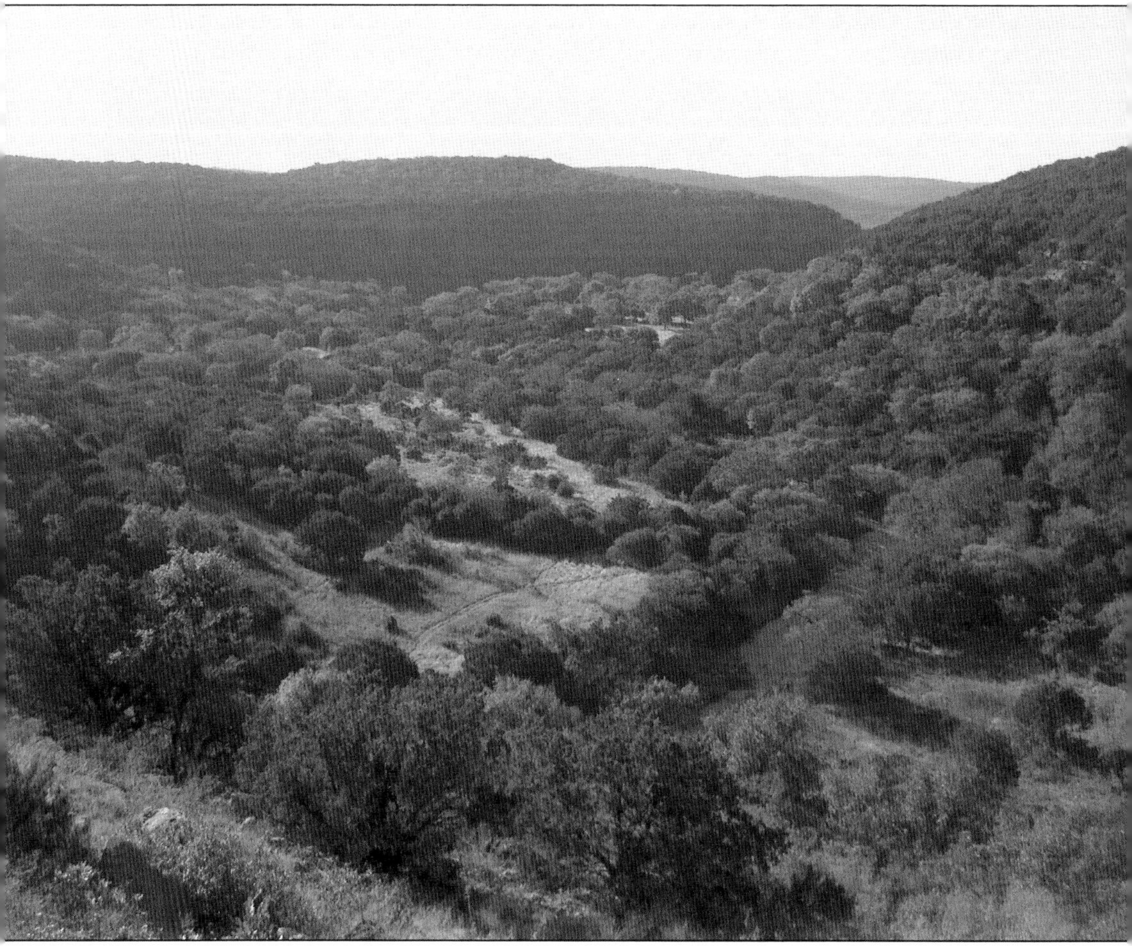

The topography of north Uvalde County is much different than the fertile, brushy plains of the southern section of the county. With steep draws, rough limestone outcrops, and elevations from 700 to 2,000 feet above sea level, the area is not suited for much more than raising goats. Goats were one of the major livestock raised in this area. The land is too rough to be preferred by cattle, which performed much better in the flat, rich brush county to the south. For the first settlers, life was hard. Not only was the land difficult to work and navigate, the Indians were a persistent threat. Settlers stayed as they had good water from the springs, abundant wild game, and a preferred habitat for goats. Today, very few of the original ranches are still intact. Most property owners in this area live in the large metropolitan areas of San Antonio, Dallas, and Houston and use the area mainly for weekend recreation and hunting. (Jody Williford.)

Four

Cactus Jack and Dolph Briscoe

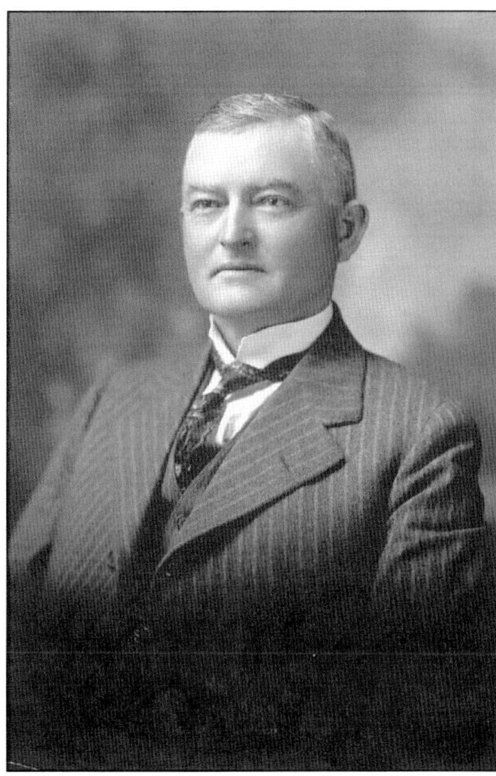

John Nance Garner was born in Blossom Prairie, Texas, in 1868. Suffering from consumption, he moved to Uvalde for the drier climate in 1893. He became a circuit-riding judge, and the days and nights spent traveling the area seemed to improve his health. He received the nicknamed "Cactus Jack" while in the Texas legislature because he wanted the prickly pear blossom to be the state flower. (Briscoe Center for American History.)

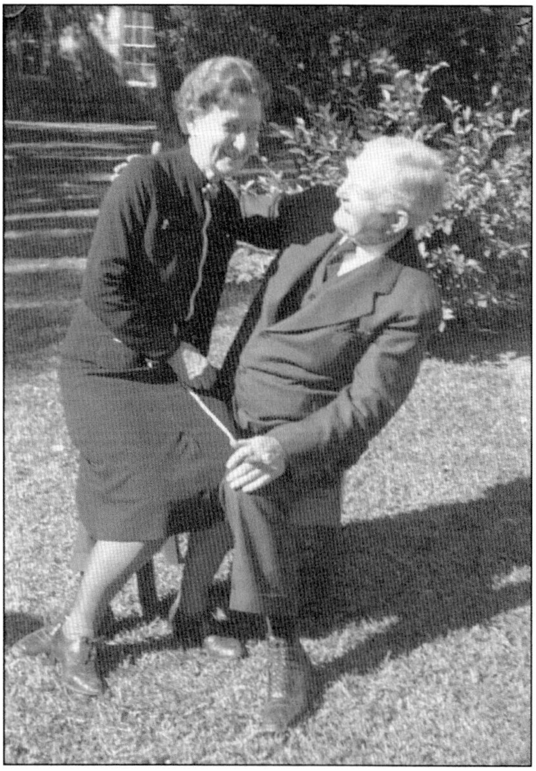

Fondly known as "Ettie," Mariette Rheiner Garner was a devoted partner to her husband, Vice Pres. John Nance Garner. The daughter of a wealthy Sabinal ranching family, she met her future husband on the train from Sabinal to San Antonio in the early 1890s. Garner was interested in meeting the lady who vocally opposed his run for county judge. The future Mrs. Garner could be quite outspoken; she did not think "his whisky drinking, poker playing ways" were proper for the county judgeship. Garner always credited Ettie with his success. On the lawn of the Garner home or in the office, the Garners enjoyed each other's company. (Briscoe Center for American History.)

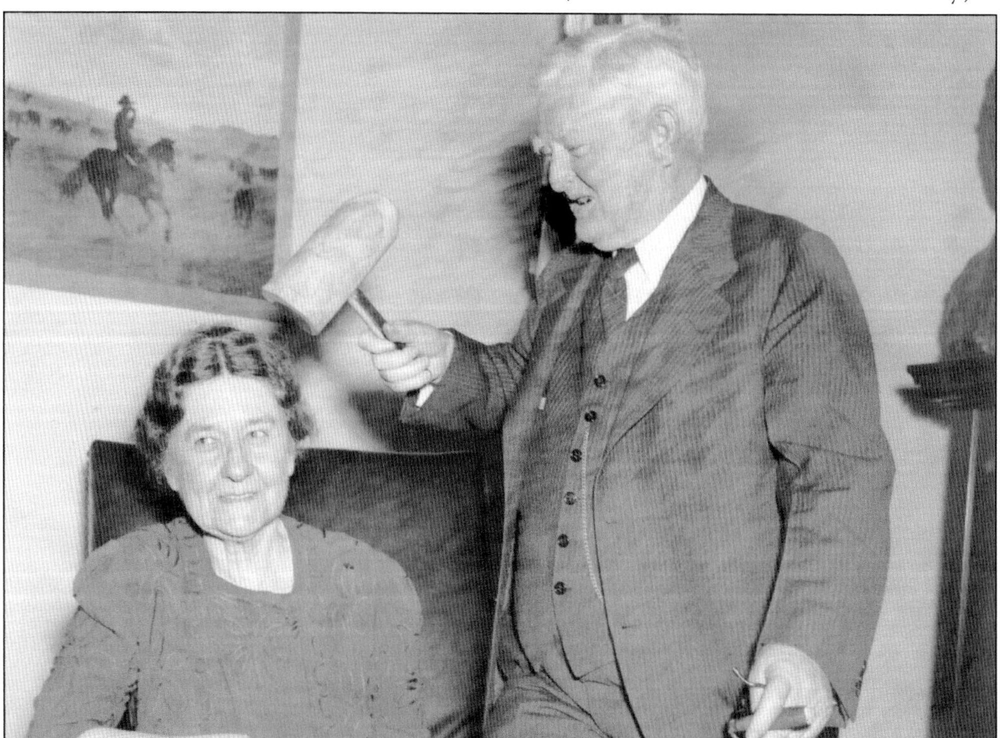

John Nance Garner loved to fish and hunt. When he was vice president, the press would often report that he had returned to Uvalde for a short vacation to hunt and fish. Here he is with Aubrey Meacham and Bob Smith after a fishing trip on the Leona River. They have a nice stringer of fish and a turtle.

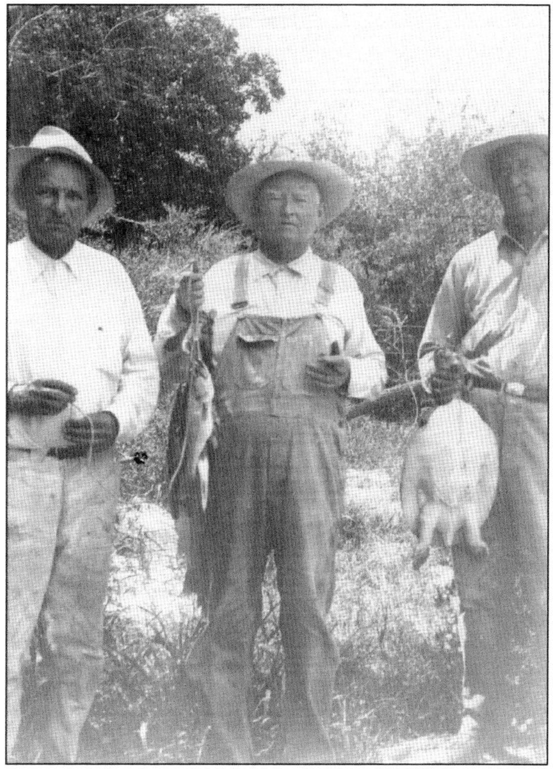

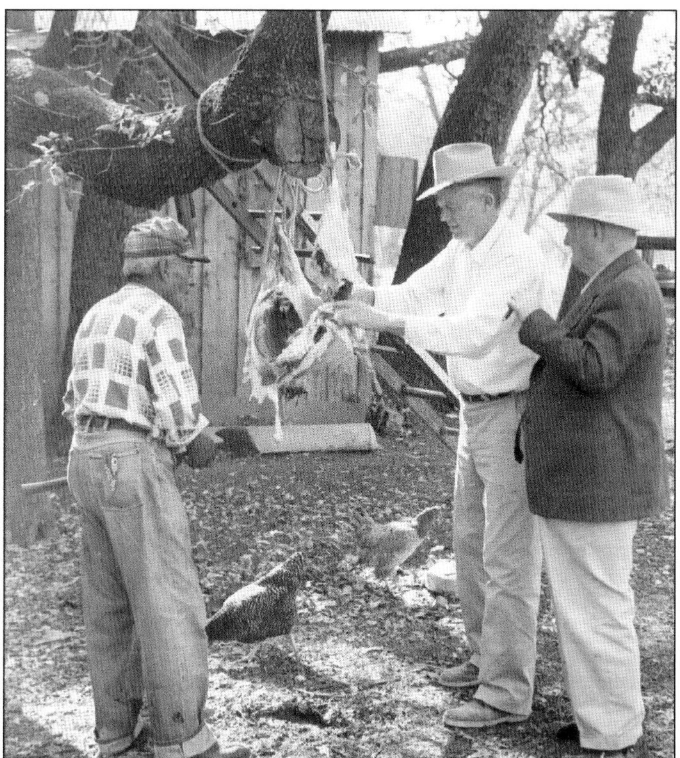

Not only did John Nance Garner love to deer hunt, but he also enjoyed a good venison meal on occasion. Here his longtime employee Lucas Zamora and friend Acree Carlisle are butchering a deer while the vice president looks on and probably offers advise.

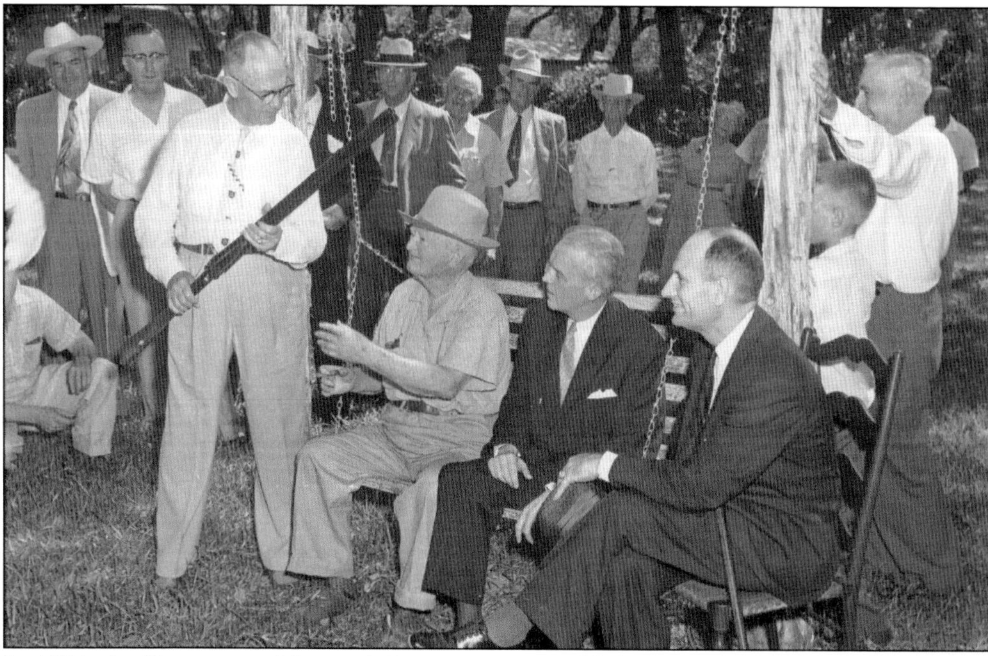

In 1954, the Democratic National Committee visited John Nance Garner in Uvalde. Paul Butler, the committee chair, is presenting an elephant gun to John Nance Garner. Looking on in amazement is John Connally and US representative Jack Brooks. One must wonder if it is four-legged or two-legged elephants that they are hunting.

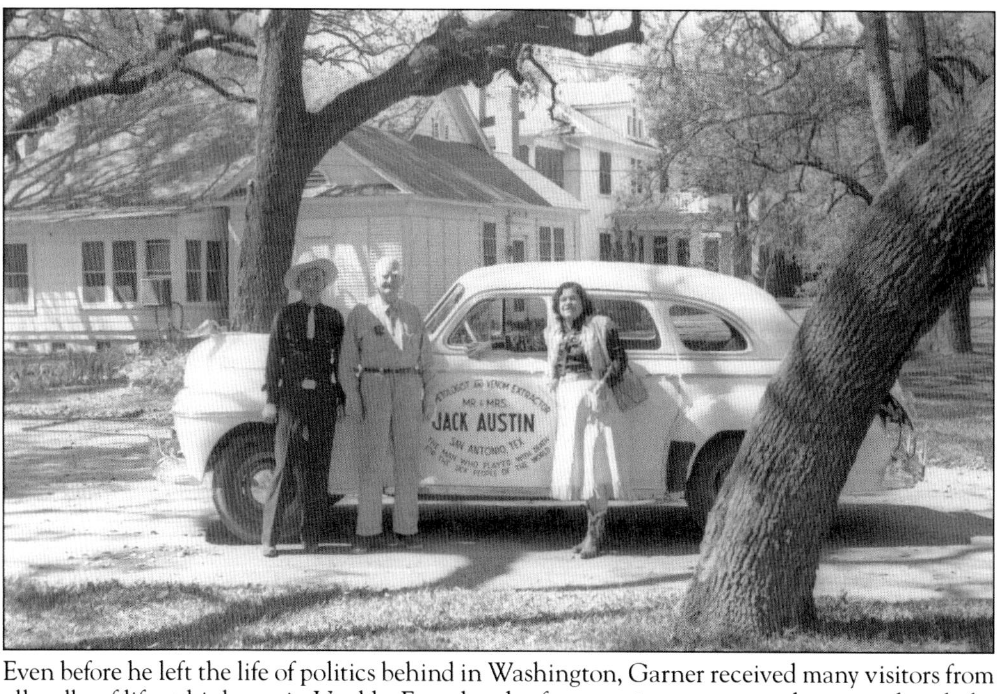

Even before he left the life of politics behind in Washington, Garner received many visitors from all walks of life at his home in Uvalde. From heads of state to just someone who wanted to shake the hand of the vice president, he always obliged. Here he is with Mr. and Mrs. Jack Austin, a snake charmer and venom extractor out of San Antonio.

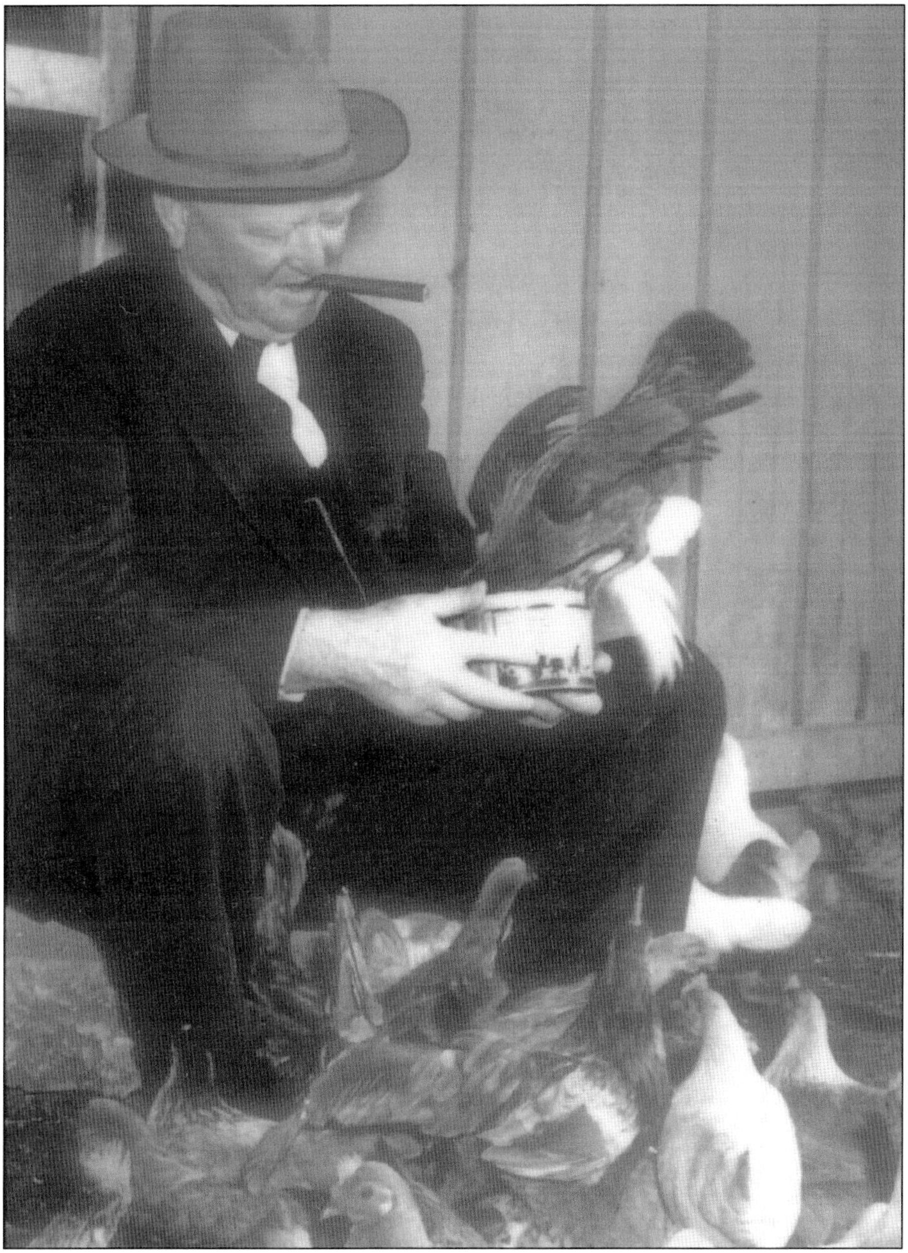

John Nance Garner spent 38 years in Washington, DC, representing south and southwest Texas as congressman, speaker of the house, and vice president. When the Garners first went to Washington, they lived in boardinghouses. Later in his career, they stayed in hotels. While he attended many black-tie events and state dinners, Uvalde was his only home. Garner always looked forward to returning to Uvalde, his friends, and the district he represented. He would often sit out in his front yard just enjoying the day and talking to those who passed by. One of his favorite pastimes was caring for his flock of bantam chickens. Today, at the John Nance Garner Museum, chickens freely roam the neighborhood. Whether they are the descendants of Garner's chickens, no one really knows. However, if Garner visited today, he would be pleased to see them. (Briscoe Center for American History.)

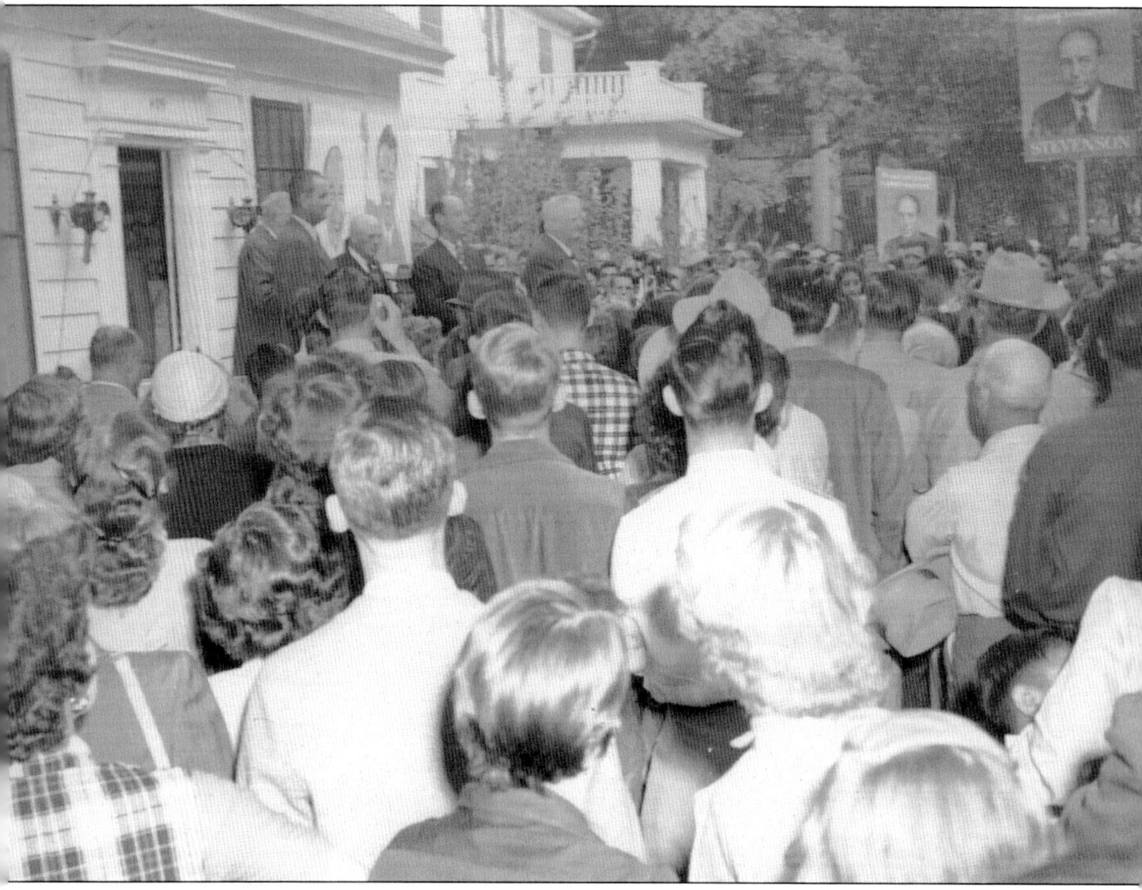

Uvalde in the 1950s did not have the population of the metropolitan cities of Dallas or Houston; however, it did have one major advantage over them—it was the home of John Nance Garner. In both the 1952 and 1956 presidential campaigns, Adlai Stevenson made stops in Uvalde to receive the endorsement of the elder statesman from the Democratic Party. This 1950s "Stevenson For President" rally was held on the front lawn of Tully Garner's home. Tully was the only son of John and Ettie Garner, and his home was next door to the elder Garners' home. At the podium are major political figures of the time with senator and future president Lyndon Johnson next to the then current Speaker of the House Sam Rayburn, with Adlai Stevenson and John Nance Garner standing before the crowd of well wishers.

With a sharp pocketknife, John Nance Garner would sit for hours in his front yard and peel pecans. The Garner property at 333 North Park had numerous pecan trees that produced a bumper crop of pecans each fall. Garner was generous with his pecans, always offering them to visitors and often sending them to presidents and heads-of-state.

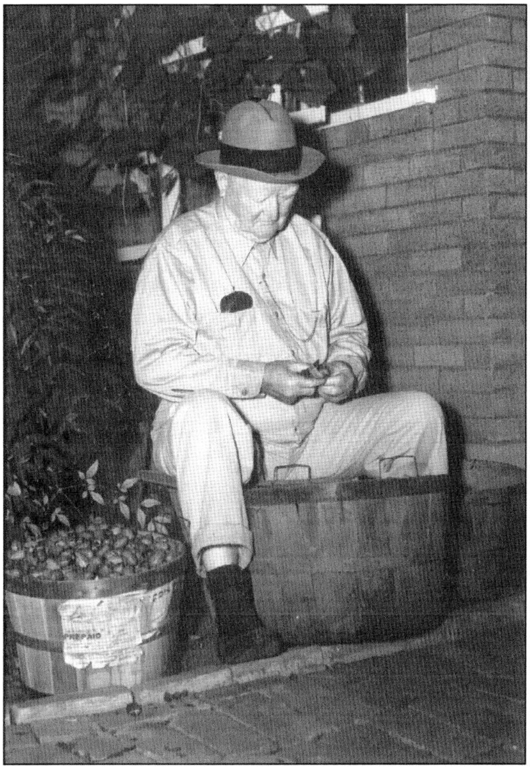

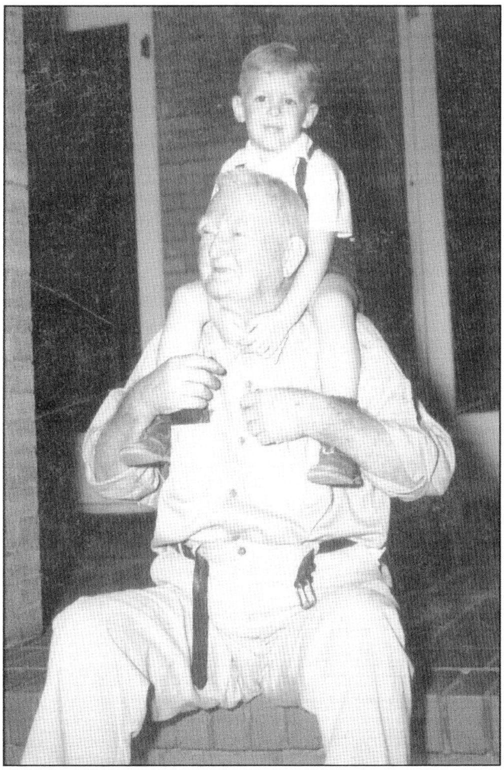

Here John Nance Garner is enjoying life in retirement and his great-grandson John Currie Jr. The Garner clan was small, with John and Ettie Garner having only one son, Tully. When Tully married, he and his wife, Ann, had one daughter, Genevieve.

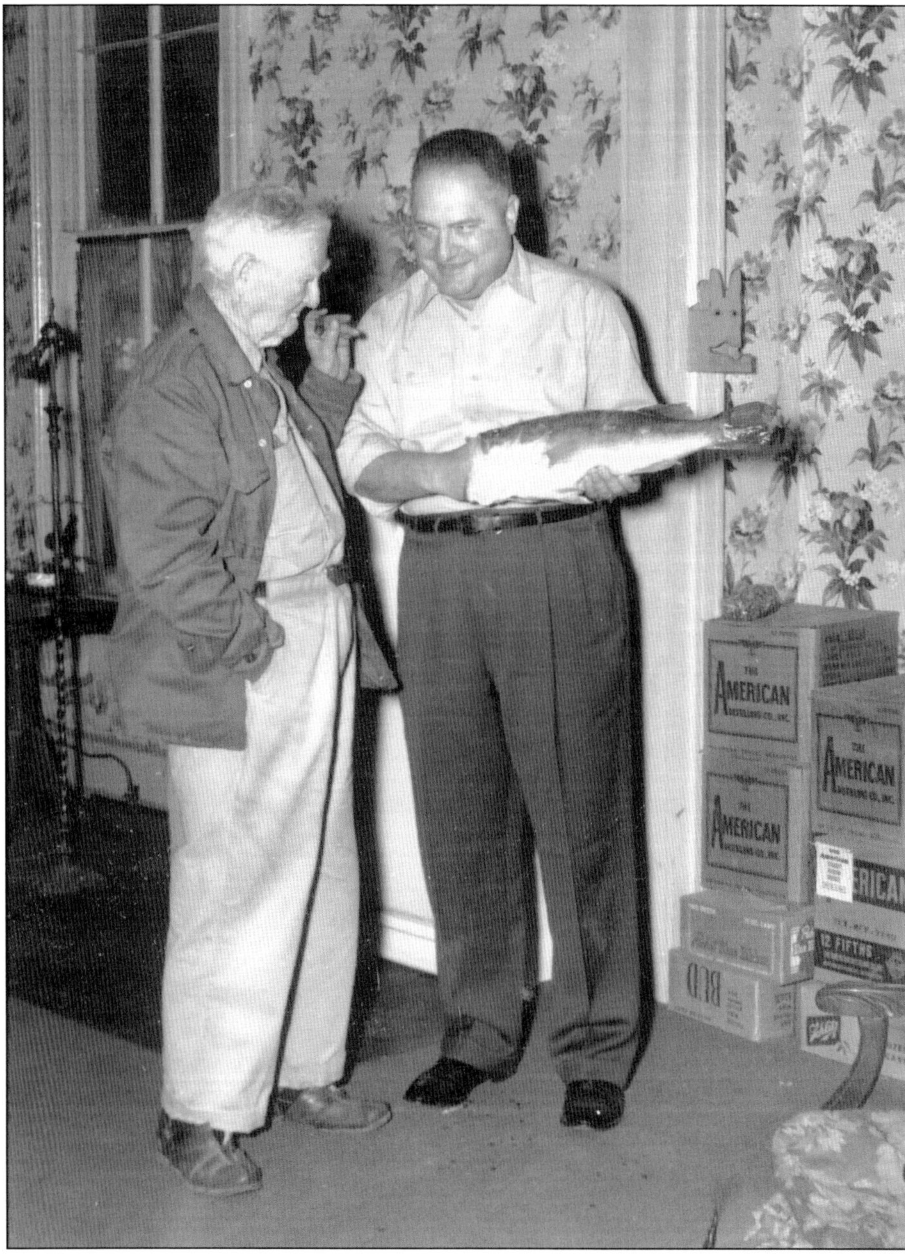

In his younger days, John Nance Garner spent many an hour fishing the rivers and streams around his beloved Uvalde. As he neared the last decade of his life, the fishing trips dwindled in number, but his love for a good fish story continued. By the smile on his face, the elder statesman is appreciating the catch being shown to him by newspaper editor Harry Hornby Jr. It is interesting to note that Garner made sure to have plenty of refreshments for his guests. On the right are three cases of beer—Schlitz, Pabst Blue Ribbon, and Budweiser—plus four cases of bourbon whiskey from the American Distilling Company. On top of the cases is a bag of shelled pecans. It was no secret that Garner liked to strike a blow for liberty every evening with a shot of good whiskey, a habit he started while in Congress when he and fellow congressmen would escape to the Capitol basement and have a bit of branch water and whiskey.

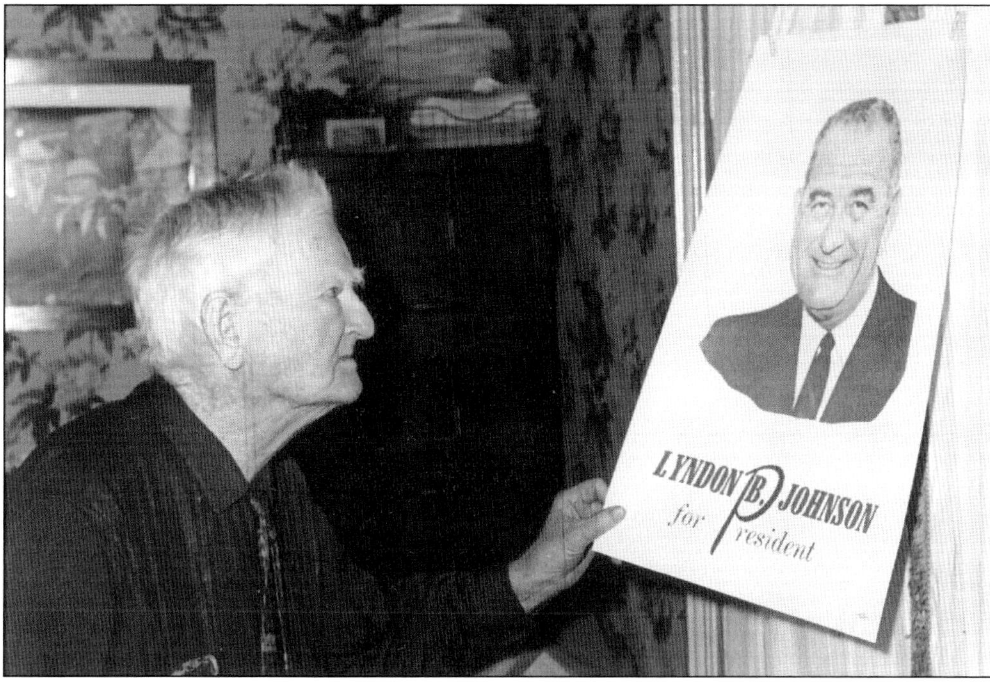

Lyndon Johnson was often a visitor at the Garner home prior to his unexpected rise to the presidency. John Nance Garner, ever true to the Democratic Party, was a staunch Johnson supporter not only verbally, but also in his home and on his car. This photograph was taken during the presidential campaign of 1964.

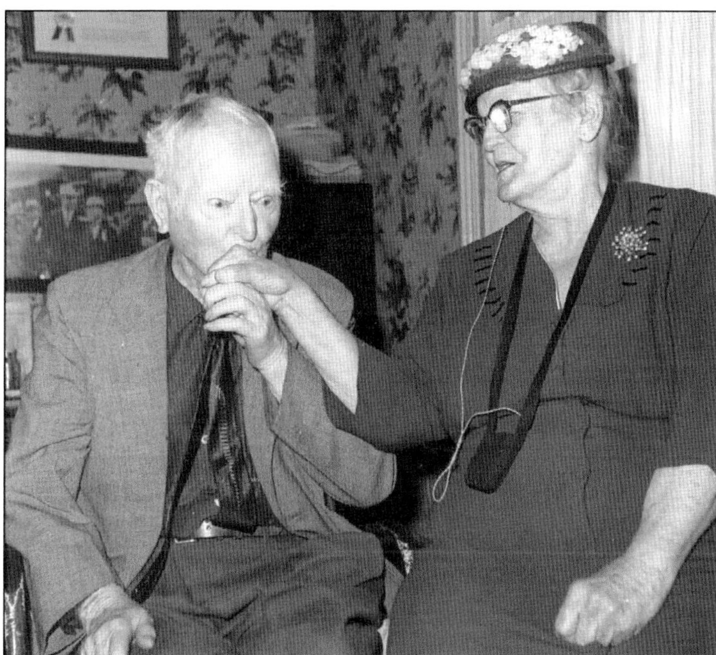

John Nance Garner was loved by his constituents and knew how to charm them to get their vote. Garner was a bit old-fashioned in that he never discussed politics with women. However, small talk and pleasantries were his style, and thus, he was able to gather the votes of men and women.

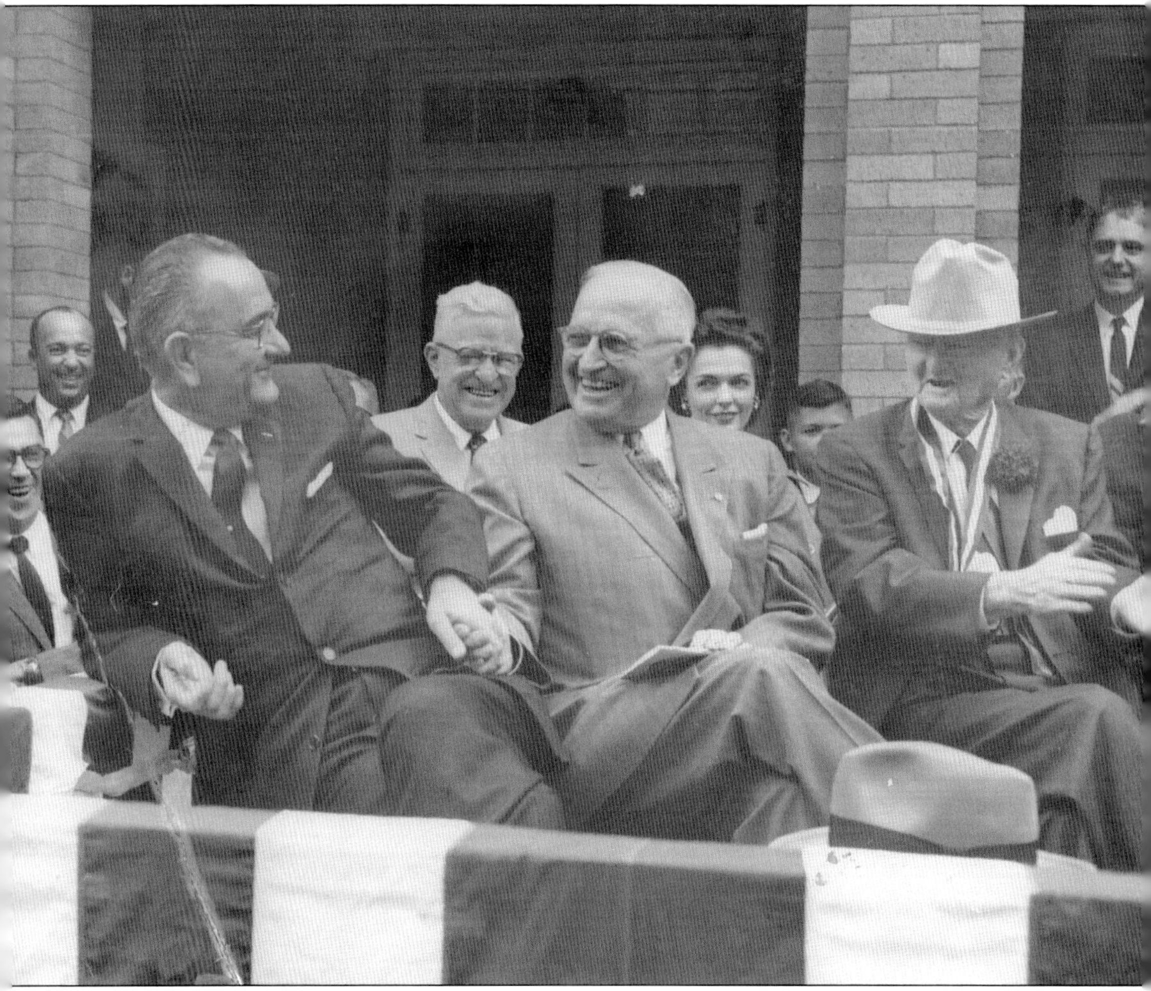

Just what is everyone laughing about? Sadly, we will never know. While undated, this photograph was most likely taken on John Nance Garner's 90th birthday as the guest list included those famous in the Democratic Party. On the left is Texas senator Lyndon B. Johnson, who, within a few short years, would become president of the United States after the assassination of Pres. John F. Kennedy. Next is former president Harry Truman, a good friend of Garner. Behind Truman are Garner's only son, Tully Garner, and his only granddaughter, Genevieve Currie. It was not only the famous who visited Garner. He spent many a day shelling pecans next to the front sidewalk at his home and talking to everyone who passed by. It is not unusual today to have visitors to the Garner Museum recall visiting with Garner in the front yard or on the porch of his home.

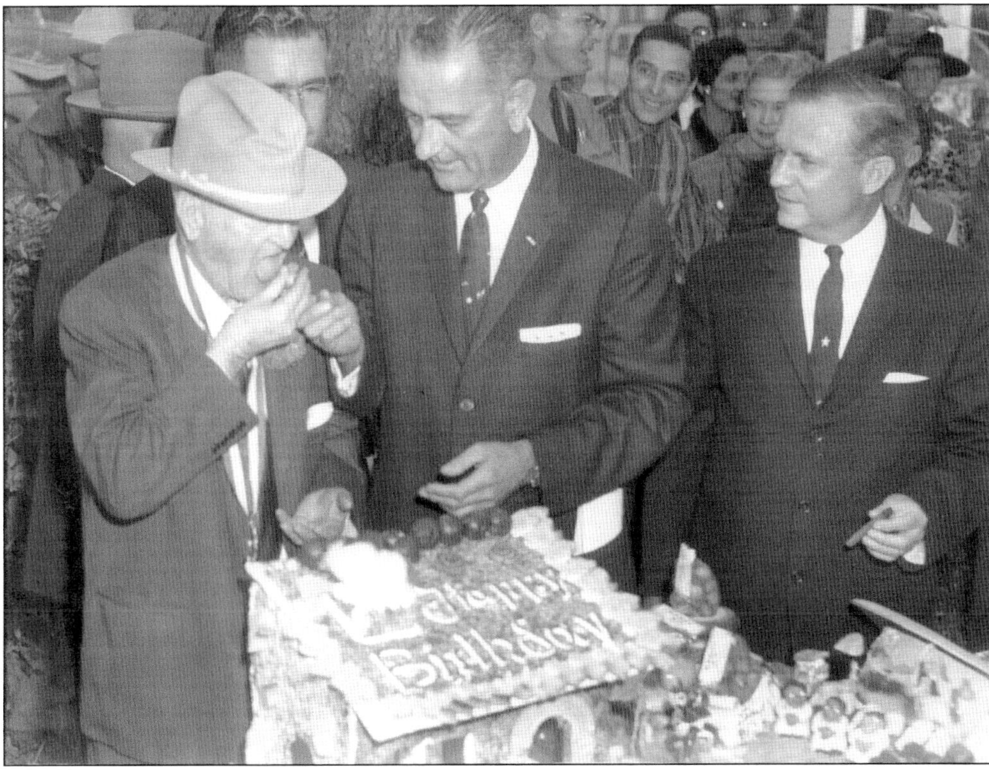

The guest list at John Nance Garner's 90th birthday party was a who's-who of the Democratic Party. The birthday cake was designed as a replica of Garner's birthplace in Blossom Prairie, Texas. Sen. Lyndon Johnson is helping Garner with the cake while Dolph Briscoe and Gov. Price Daniel look on.

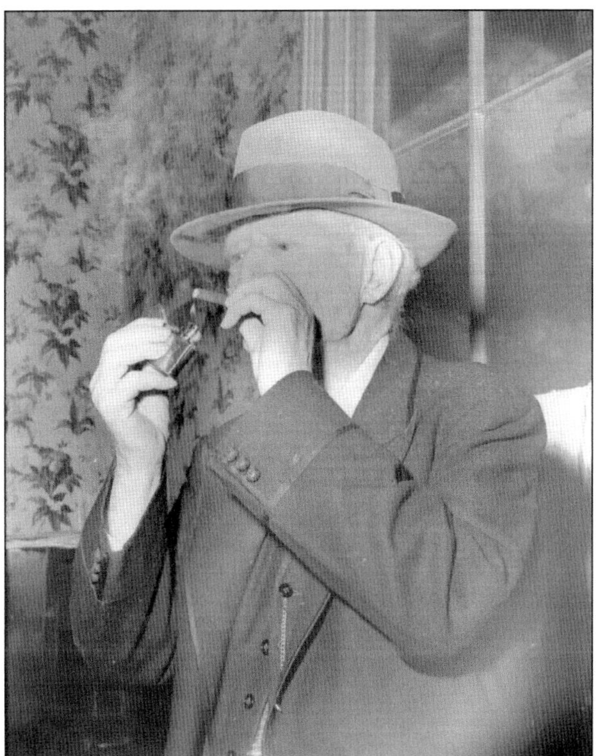

If there was one description about John Nance Garner that could be made, it was that he was seldom, if ever, without his cigar. He did not favor fancy Cuban cigars, but usually smoked a La Rica Hoja, a cigar made in Mexico.

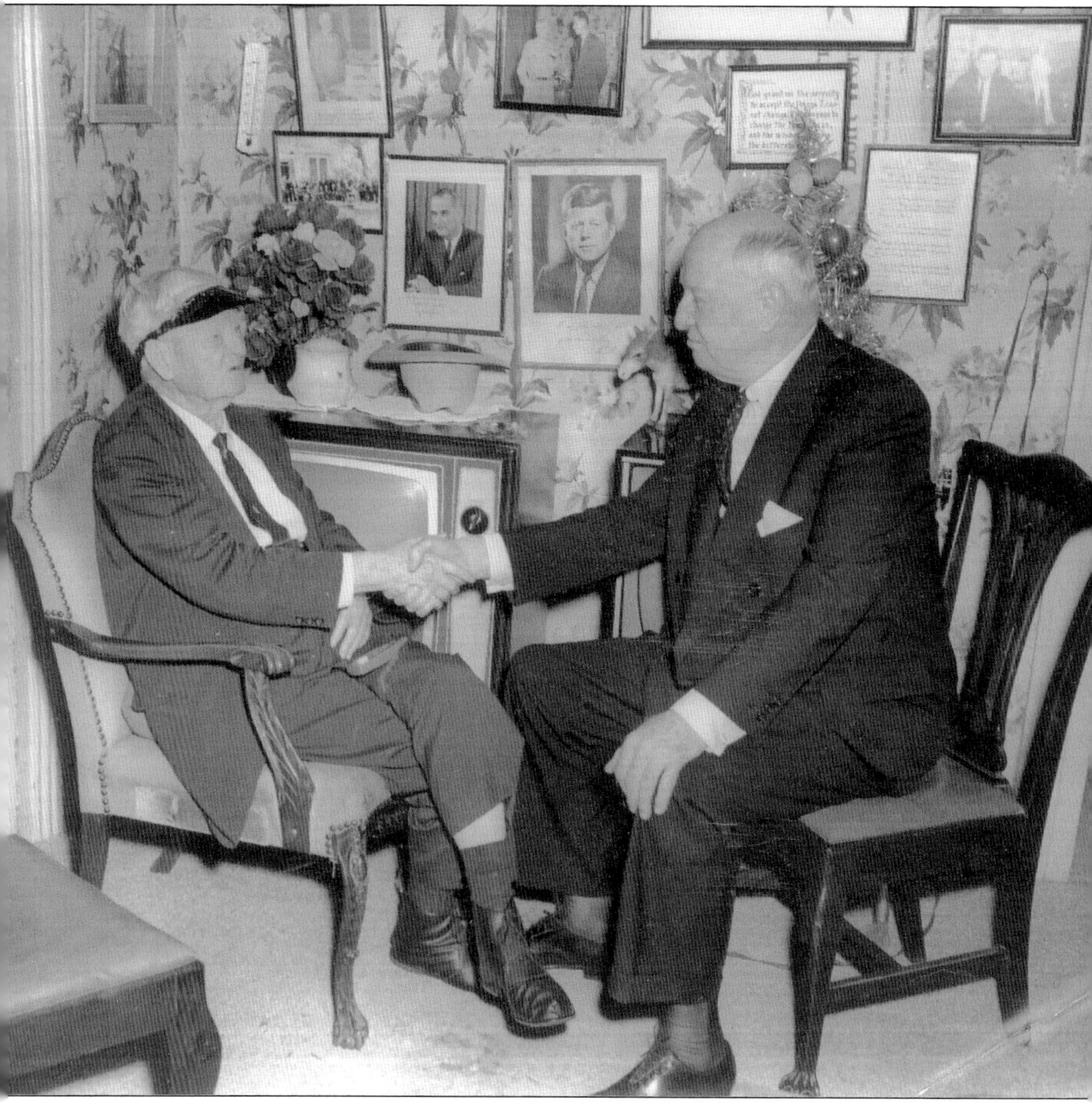

John Nance Garner is visiting with James Farley, an old friend from his time on the campaign trail, with his running mate, Franklin Roosevelt. The walls are a congressional history exhibit unto themselves, with autographed photographs of presidents Truman, Johnson, and Kennedy. The two televisions were a Garner trademark, as he liked to watch simultaneous newscasts and baseball games. An avid cigar smoker, Garner smoked cigars into his 90s. He liked to use the most common matches of the time, which were "strike anywhere" matches. Garner's chair was one his late wife, Ettie, had adapted for him to make striking matches easier by nailing a piece of sandpaper to it. This way, she was able to save her furniture, walls, flooring, or whatever else Garner decided to use to strike a match. The sandpaper is attached to the side of the chair just behind the edge of Garner's jacket.

Even 25 years after leaving Washington, DC, the passing of Vice President Garner made national headlines. Attending for President Johnson was his vice president Hubert Humphrey; on the right is the US senator from Texas, Ralph W. Yarborough.

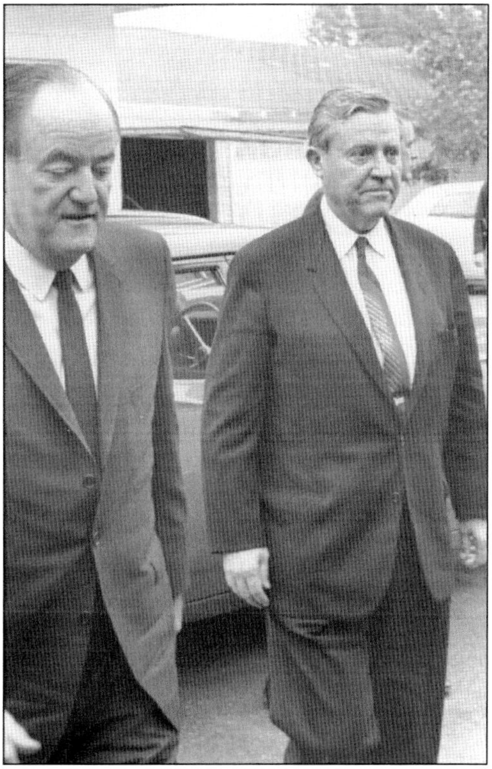

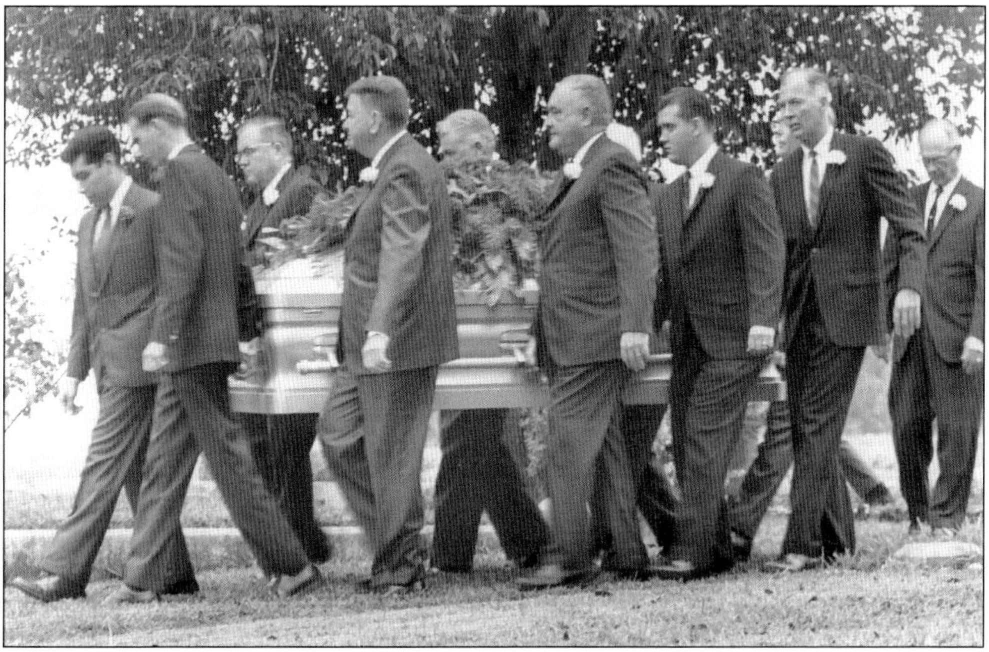

The nation mourned the passing of John Nance Garner on November 7, 1967, fifteen days shy of his 99th birthday. The pallbearers that day included many of his friends from Uvalde, such as Ross Brumfield, Bob Wellborn, Harry Hornby Jr., Dolph Briscoe, great-grandson John Currie, Don Large, Acree Carlisle, Judge D.W. Suttle, J.H. Ashby, and Dr. Hershall LaForge.

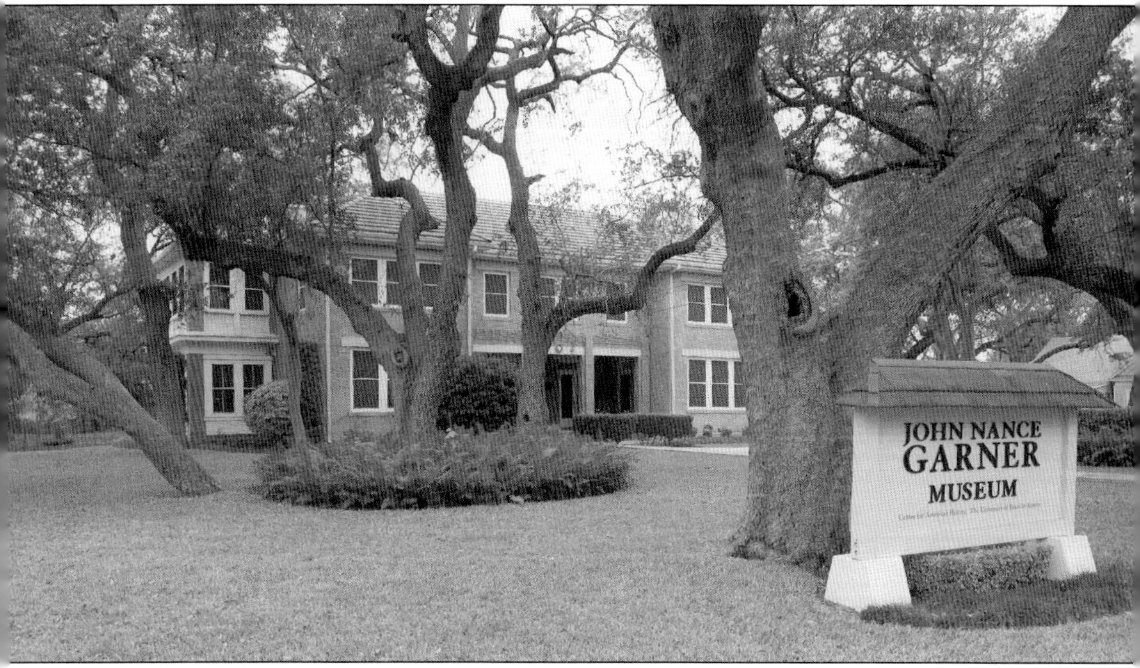

The John Nance Garner home was designed by Texas State Architect Atlee B. Ayers and built in 1921. Garner tired of Ayers's letters requesting their construction material preferences when designing the home and quickly directed him to his wife, stating, "Whatever Mrs. Garner wants is fine with me." This is the home where John and Ettie Garner lived, worked, and raised a family. Although Garner served 38 years in Washington, they never owned a home there. In 1952, Garner and his only son, Tully, donated the home to the City of Uvalde in memory of Ettie Rheiner Garner. Since that time, the home has been a social gathering place, library, and museum. A National Historic Landmark, the City of Uvalde donated the museum to the Briscoe Center for American History at the University of Texas at Austin in 1999, and it now houses the permanent John Nance and Ettie Garner exhibit. (Briscoe Center for American History.)

Dolph Briscoe Jr. was born in this little frame house on Leona Street on April 23, 1923. About two years later, the family built a two-story frame house across the street, where he lived and played as a child. (Family of Dolph Briscoe.)

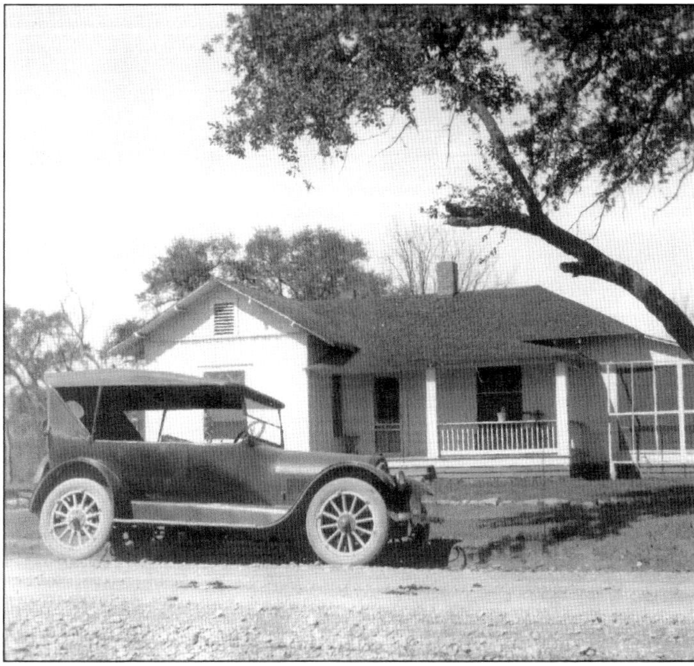

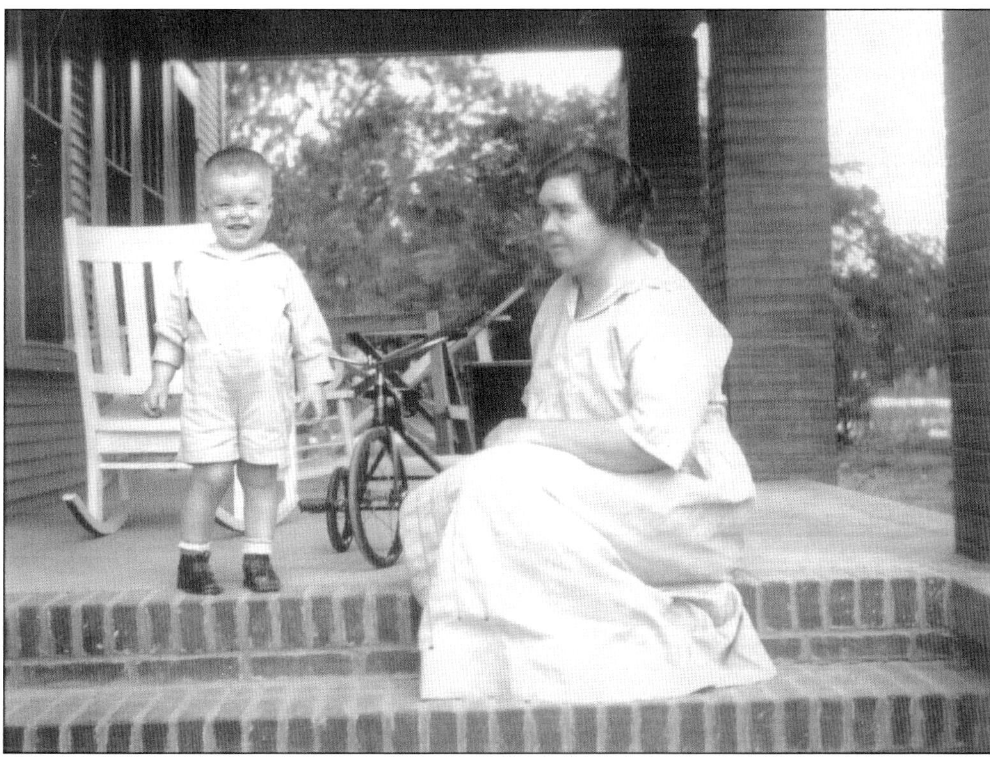

Young Dolph Briscoe is pictured here on the porch of the family house on High Street with his mother, Georgie Briscoe. Georgie, a southern lady from Fort Bend County, Texas, was devoted to her husband and only child. She offered them her love and full support in all aspects of their lives. (Family of Dolph Briscoe.)

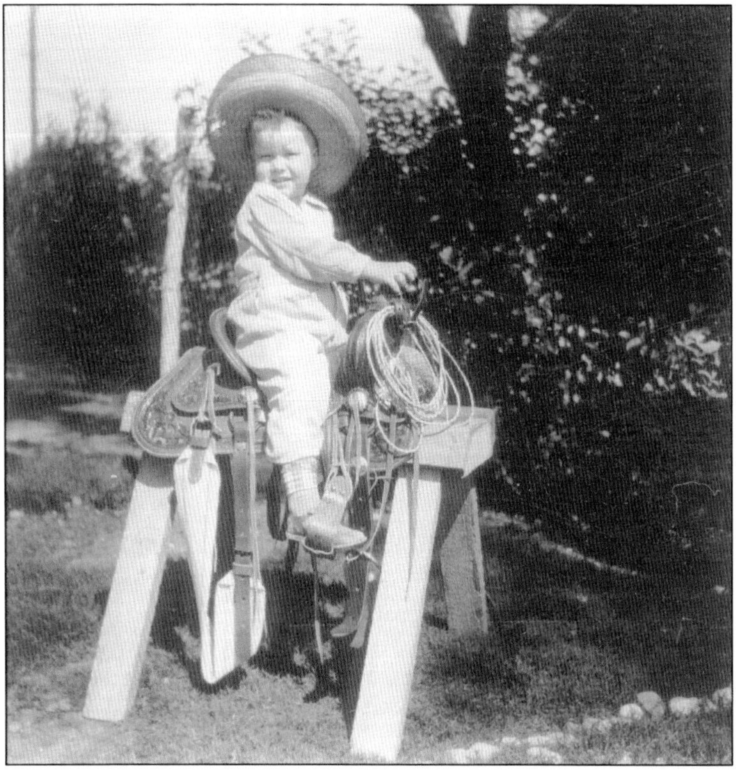

Dolph Briscoe Jr.—future cowboy, businessman, and governor of Texas—had a love for the land, and being a cowboy started at a very young age. This photograph, taken when he was a toddler, has him already in the saddle. Note how the stirrups had to be altered so they could actually be used, and that his saddle came complete with a lariat. (Family of Dolph Briscoe.)

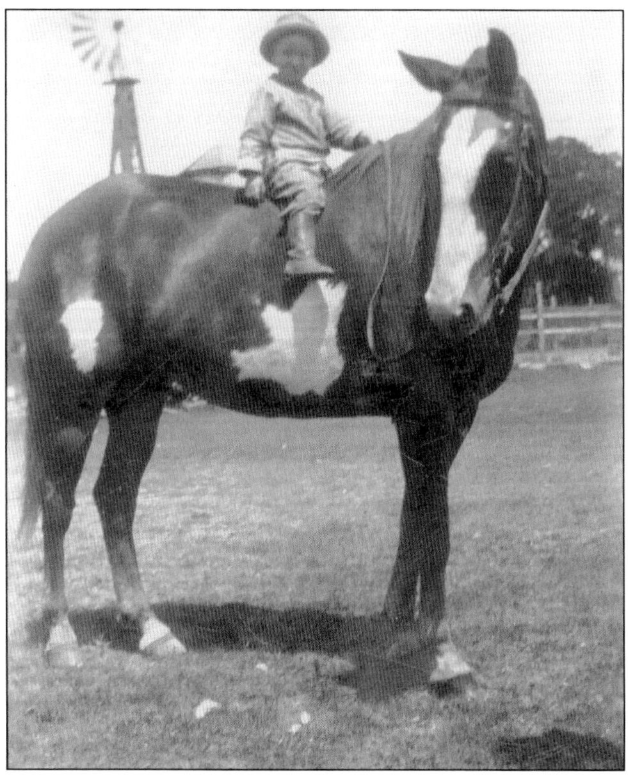

As a child, Dolph Briscoe spent many a weekend and summer with his family on their ranches. Riding horseback at a young age just went with life on a ranch and with a father who was involved in the cattle business. (Family of Dolph Briscoe.)

Dolph Briscoe learned to ride a horse at a very young age, and when he was on his father's ranch, he liked to help work livestock. His early love of the land and livestock reinforced his inspiration to be a rancher. Here he is with his father Dolph Briscoe Sr. (Family of Dolph Briscoe.)

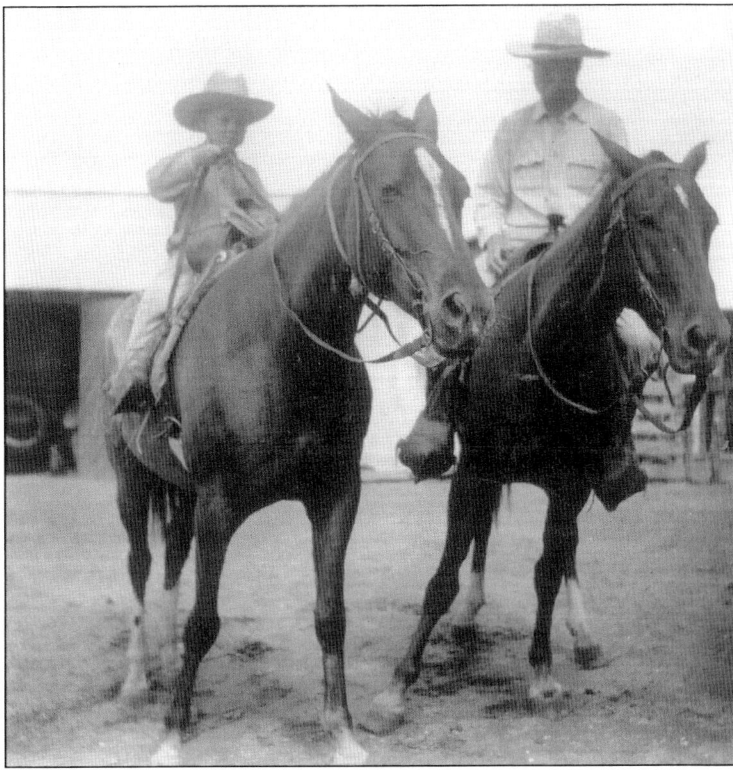

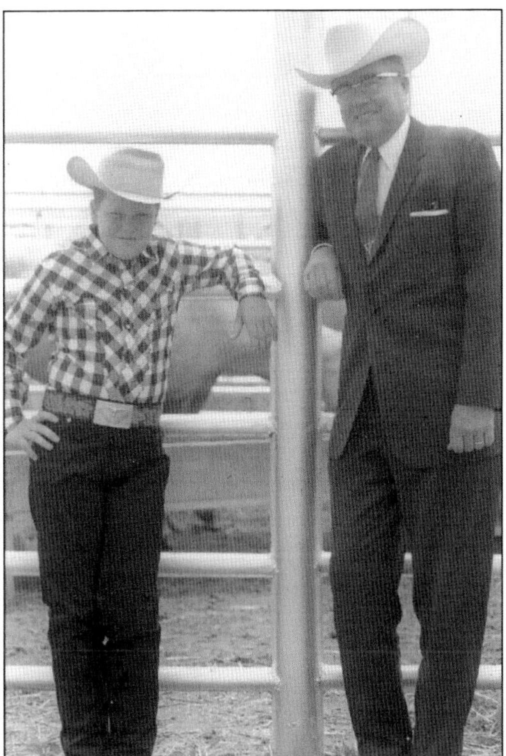

Dolph Briscoe and his wife, Janey, had three children, Chip, Janey, and Cele, and all are involved in ranching in some way. Here the senior Briscoe is pictured with his son Chip, whose love of ranching is just as strong as his father's.

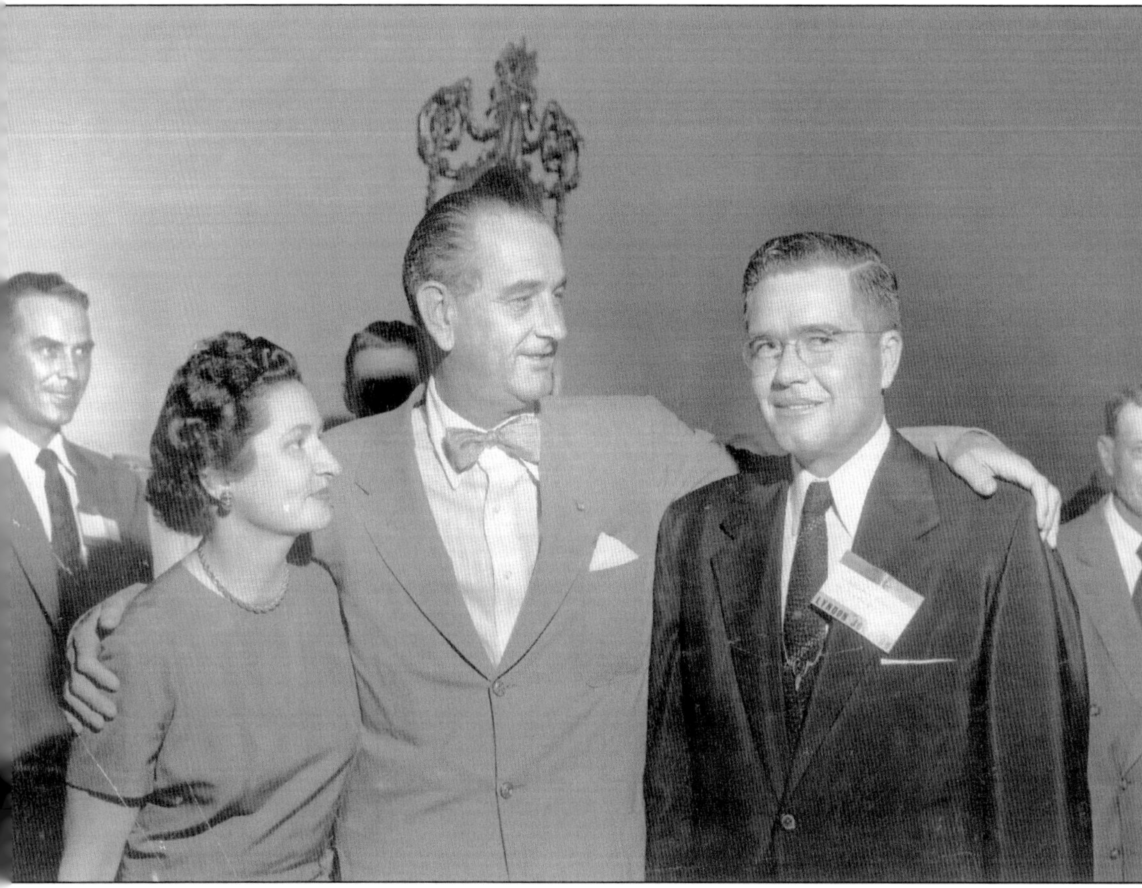

Lyndon Johnson (center, with Lady Bird Johnson on the left) was always on the campaign trail, even in non-election years. Dolph Briscoe (right) first met Johnson in 1952, when he made a campaign swing through Uvalde County and Briscoe was summoned to the airport to pick up the senator. Not up for reelection until 1954, Johnson still insisted they visit the coffee shop at the Kincaid Hotel where he stopped at every table, shook every hand, and listened to the concerns of the citizenry. The next stop was the *Uvalde Leader News* office for an interview with the editor Harry Hornby. Following the interview, Dolph and Janey Briscoe took Johnson to their home on the Dry Rio Frio. According to Briscoe, as Johnson visited, he never stopped talking, or listening to how people felt on a wide range of issues.

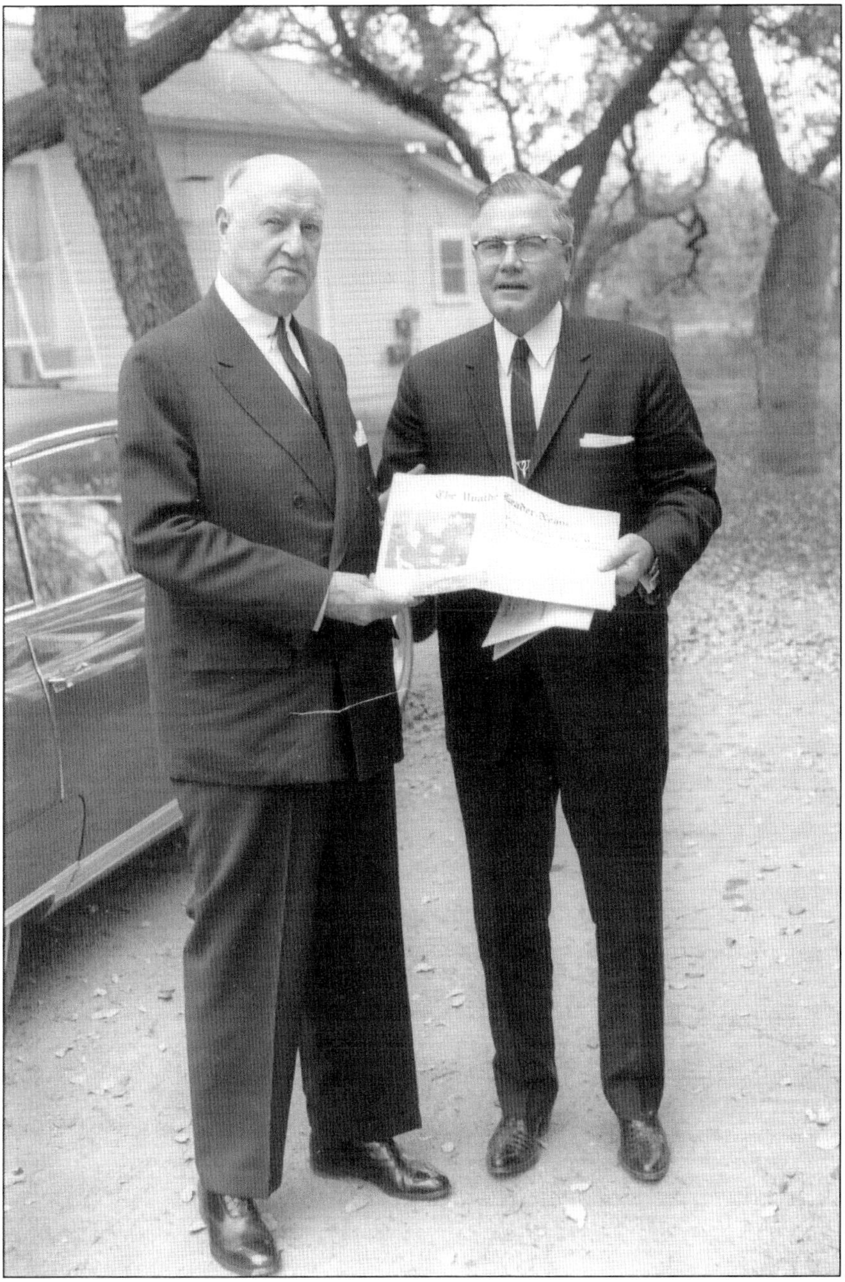

In the 1932 presidential election, James A. Farley, Franklin D. Roosevelt's friend and campaign manager, helped the Roosevelt/Garner ticket win the election. Thankful for the victory and aware of Farley's management skills, President Roosevelt appointed him as the 53rd postmaster general. Also a very good friend to Vice President Garner, Farley supported the New Deal, and approved the construction of new post offices as a means to facilitate New Deal policies. In this 1963 photograph, Farley and Dolph Briscoe are reviewing a headlines in the *Uvalde Leader News:* "Post Office Will Move to Temporary Location." This was in reference to the upcoming renovations planned for the current post office. This photograph was taken next to the small house that John Nance Garner called home after he donated the "big house" to the City of Uvalde.

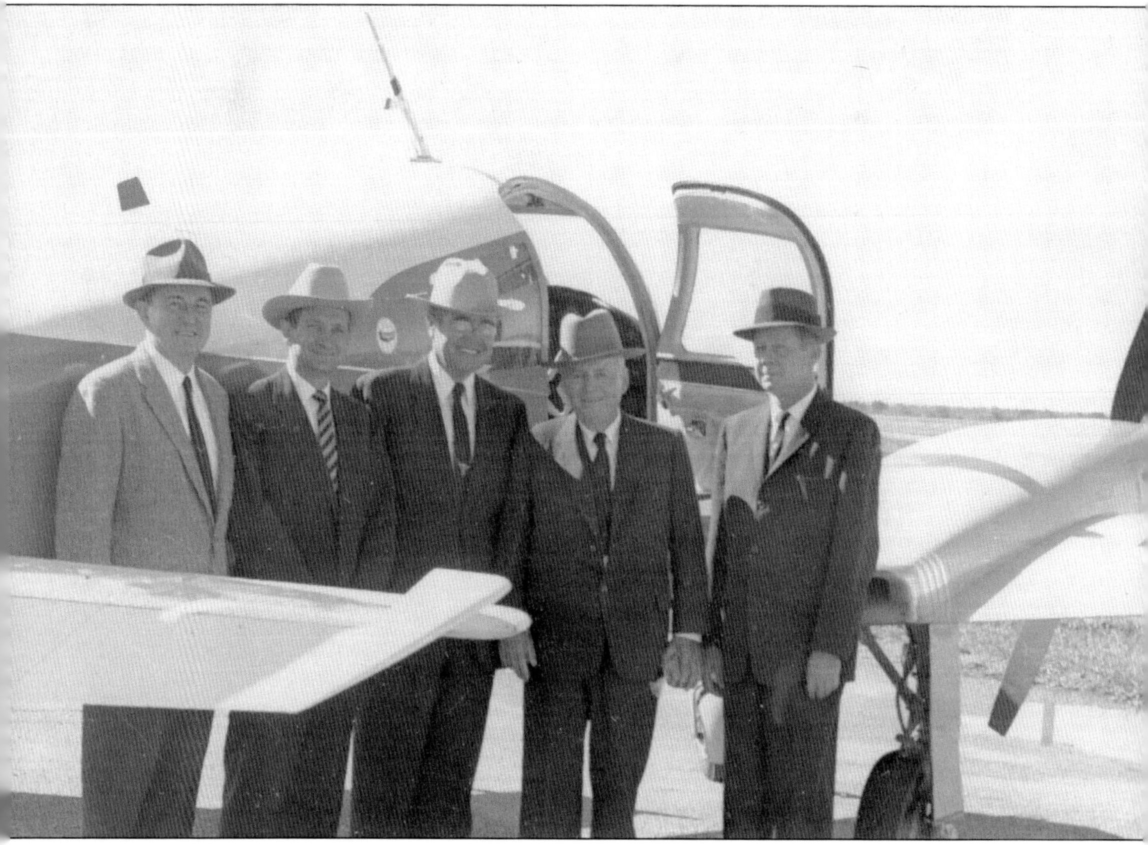

Dolph Briscoe often hosted a number of dignitaries when they visited Uvalde. This 1950s photograph at the Uvalde airport shows Uvalde attorney William Kessler Sr., US representative Jack Brooks, Dolph Briscoe, Speaker of the House Sam Rayburn, and Uvalde mayor Melvin Rowland. "Mr. Sam," as Rayburn was called, may have been in town for Garner's 90th birthday party or possibly for a fishing trip on the Briscoe Ranch. When Briscoe invited Mr. Sam to the 90th birthday party for Garner, he was hesitant to attend. He finally committed to the event and only promised to come if he did not have to spend time alone with Garner. It seemed that Garner could complain a bit harshly about the job Rayburn was doing as speaker of the house, and Rayburn did not want to have to listen to the insults.

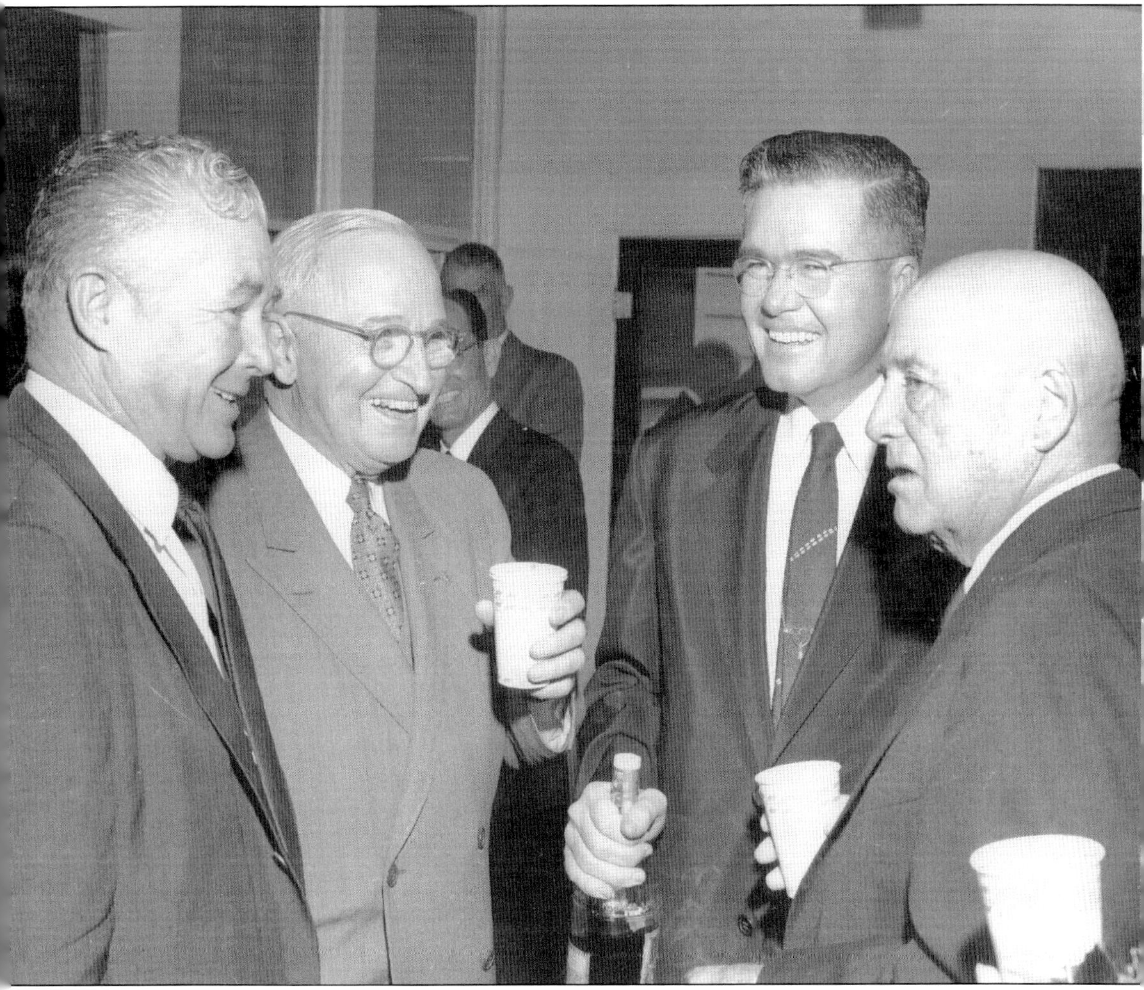

In 1923, Dolph Briscoe's father went into the cattle business with soon-to-be governor Ross Sterling. This was a business relationship that lasted many years, and in 1932, the Briscoes traveled to Austin to stay with the governor and his wife, Maud Sterling, in the governor's mansion. Sleeping in the bed of Sam Houston was the highlight of the trip for the younger Briscoe and paved the way for future political ambitions. Later, when he first ran for the state legislature, he was not completely sure it was what he wanted to do. However, his wife, Janey, thinking the decision had been made, filed for his candidacy and thus made his first step into Texas politics. Whenever Speaker of the House Sam Rayburn came to Uvalde, he had Dolph Briscoe pick him up at the airport and escort him on his visit. Here an unidentified man is joining in with Harry Truman, Dolph Briscoe, and Sam Rayburn at a Uvalde reception.

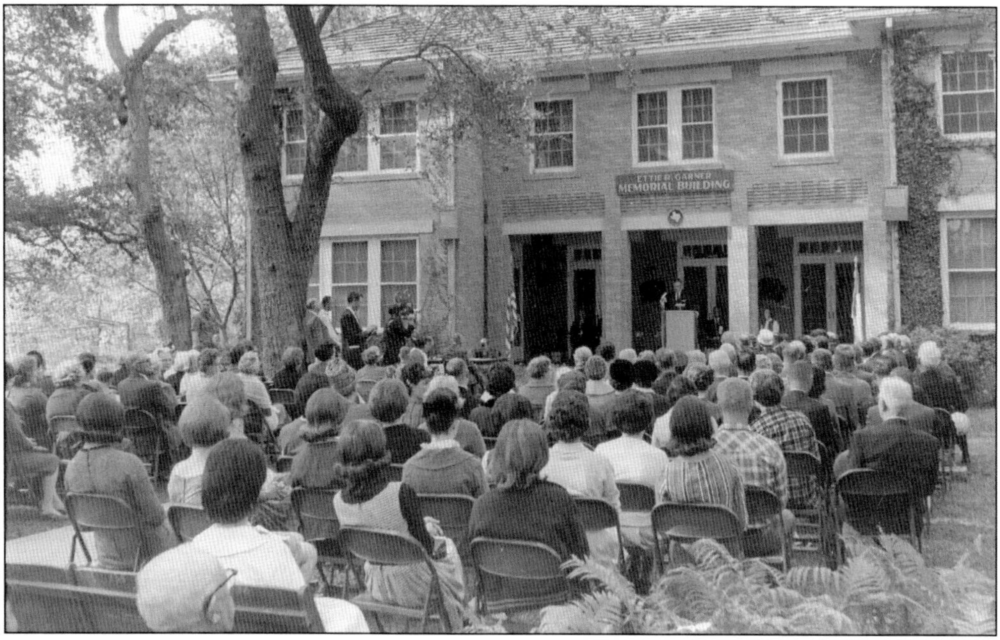

As a child, Dolph Briscoe used to roller-skate on the front porch of the Garner home. It was appropriate that he selected that same location to announce his candidacy for governor in the Democratic primary on January 25, 1968. Although an unsuccessful bid for the office, it gave Briscoe the experience and knowledge to run for governor in 1972. He won that election.

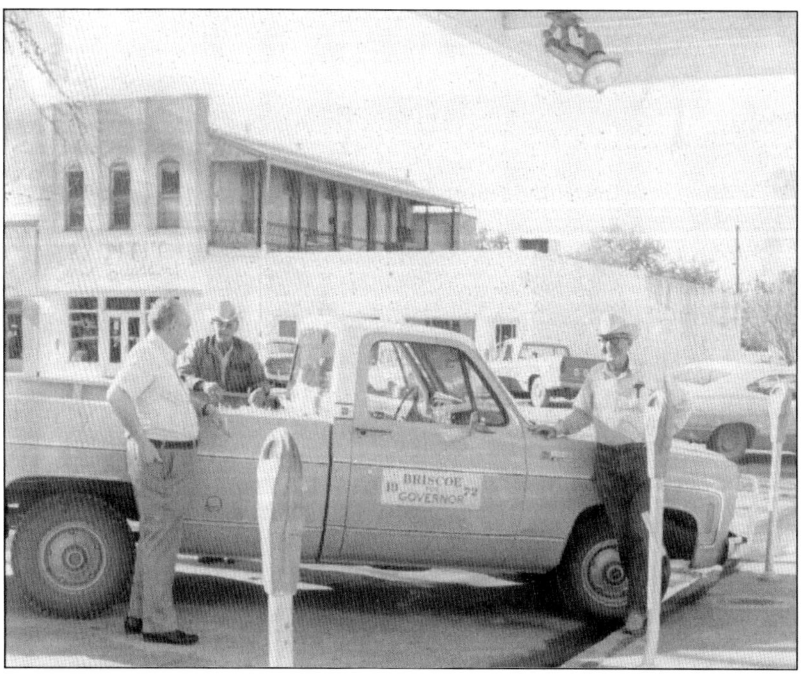

Local support for the homegrown boy Dolph Briscoe was strong as he made his push for the governor's office in 1972. Photographed in front of the *Uvalde Leader News* office are Harry Hornby Jr., Harry Watkins, and Charley Griffin Jr.

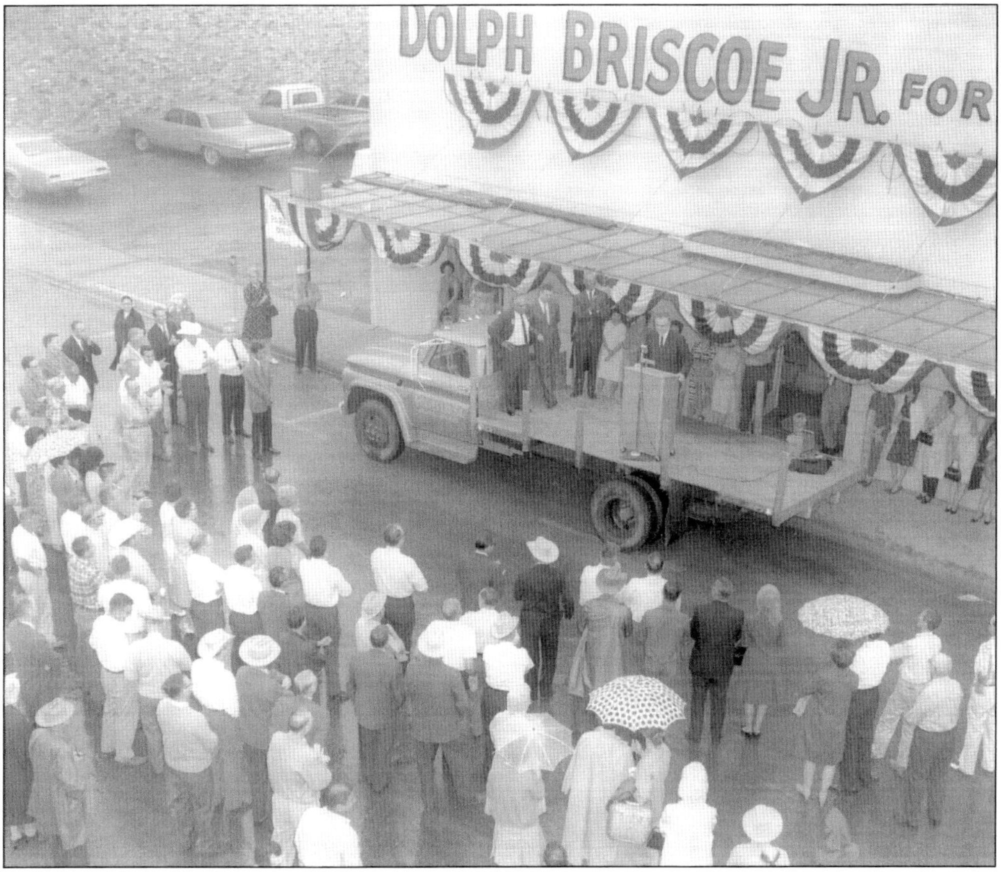

Dolph Briscoe campaigned hard for governor in 1972. Running on a platform that called for less government and no new taxes, Briscoe took a moderately conservative campaign approach that was also anti-Austin establishment. With his beloved wife Janey at his side, he hit the campaign trail. They campaigned jointly and separately and Janey Briscoe proved to be a tireless worker and never lost her enthusiasm for the cause. It was a hard-fought battle but in the end, Briscoe became the 40th governor of Texas. The Uvalde headquarters of the Briscoe campaign was in the old Uvalde Wool and Mohair warehouse.

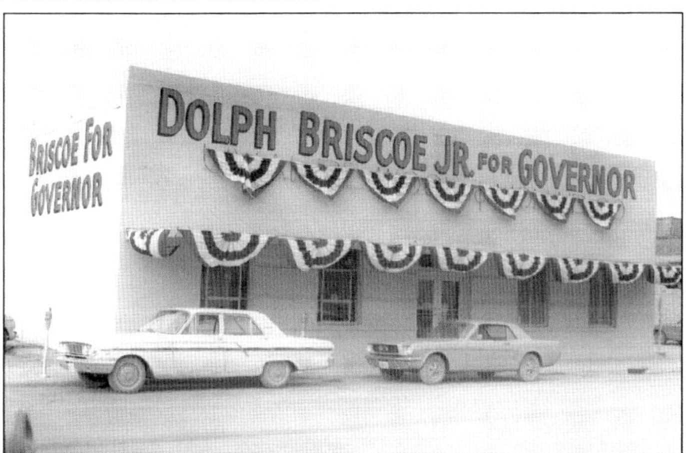

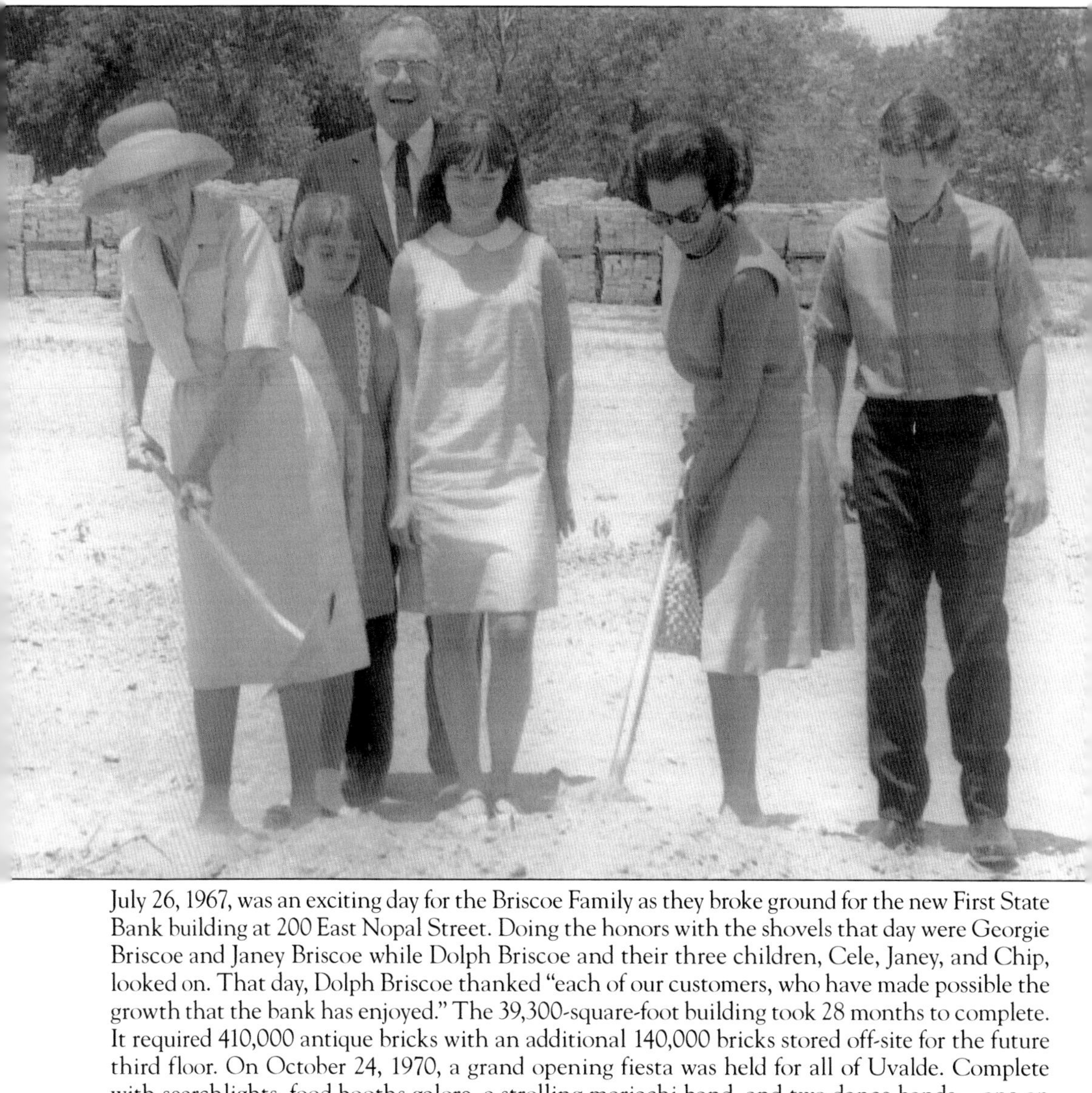

July 26, 1967, was an exciting day for the Briscoe Family as they broke ground for the new First State Bank building at 200 East Nopal Street. Doing the honors with the shovels that day were Georgie Briscoe and Janey Briscoe while Dolph Briscoe and their three children, Cele, Janey, and Chip, looked on. That day, Dolph Briscoe thanked "each of our customers, who have made possible the growth that the bank has enjoyed." The 39,300-square-foot building took 28 months to complete. It required 410,000 antique bricks with an additional 140,000 bricks stored off-site for the future third floor. On October 24, 1970, a grand opening fiesta was held for all of Uvalde. Complete with searchlights, food booths galore, a strolling mariachi band, and two dance bands—one on each side of the building—over 8,000 people attended the best party Uvalde has ever had.

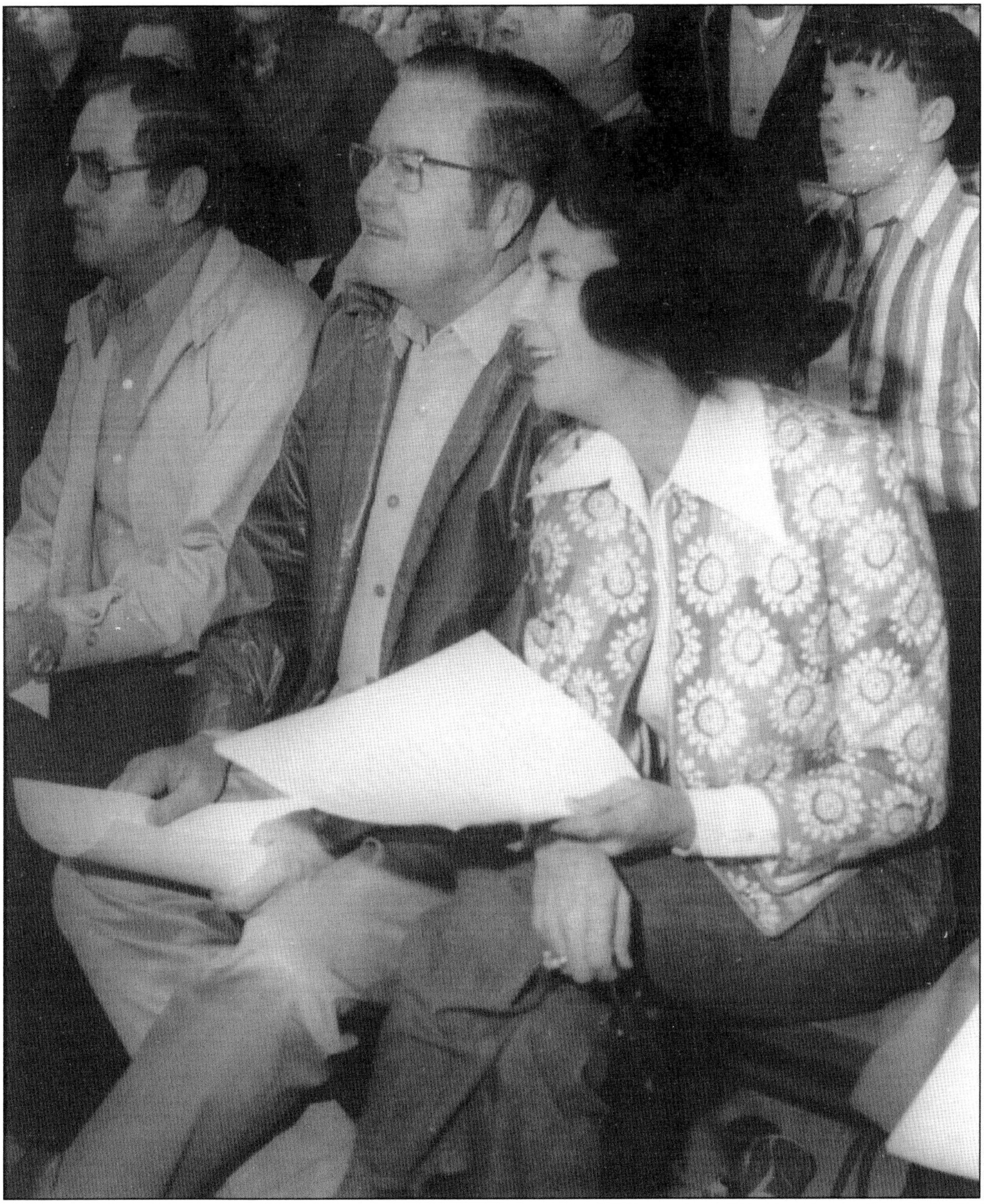

Dolph and Janey Briscoe led very active lives. From their early days as newlyweds on the ranch on the Dry Rio Frio when they battled screwworms and lived without electricity, to life in the governor's mansion, they were always a team. Uvalde was home and they were fully engaged in the community and worked hard to make it a better place for all. Community service work was just as important as any business venture they undertook. After leaving the governor's mansion, Janey served six years as a regent of the University of Texas. Later, she raised $5.1 million for a children's wing at the University of Texas, San Antonio Health Science Center. One of her most fulfilling projects, the children's wing now carries her name. Janey Briscoe passed away from heart disease in 2000. She and Dolph Briscoe shared 58 wonderful years of marriage. Dolph Briscoe passed away on June 27, 2010. They were both buried at the family cemetery at the ranch on the Dry Rio Frio.

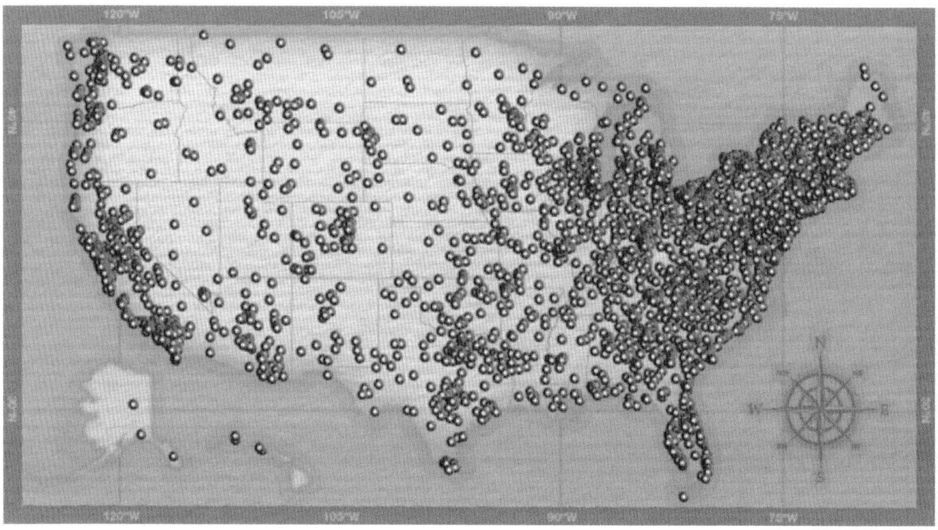